The book was inspired by my son Kristian after he graduated with a degree in Scottish Medieval History at Stirling University.

The early historical narrative was gleaned from several academic works with the intention of creating the background from which the Highland Games evolved in an endeavour to tell a continuous story that links past heroes to present day champions.

Contributions were made by:

Jack Davidson QC – historical research

Harry Doyle – historical research

Charlotte Edmunds – graphics

Linda Edmunds - editing

Historical information was gathered from several works, including the following:-

The Highland Fling by Jack Davidson
Donald Dinnie by David Webster
The Lords of the Isles by Ronald Williams
Fire & Sword by J Michael Hill
The Highland Warrior by David Stevenson
Somerled by Kathleen MacPhee
The History of the Rebellion in Scotland in 1745 by John Home
The Highland Clearances by John Prebble
Rob Roy MacGregor by W.H Murray
Behind Enemy Lines by Sir Tommy MacPherson

CONTENTS

PREFACE

Extract from *Scotland on Sunday* (31 08 2014)

The promotion of Highland games overseas accelerated during the 1960s, 70s, and 80s as Webster took groups of heavies on tours of America, Canada, Scandinavia and Japan. Also important during the same period was Douglas Edmunds, a heavy athlete, who has promoted the sport and culture worldwide. Edmunds is a giant of the games literally and figuratively, twice world caber champion. The World Highland Games Heavy event Championships are staged by Edmunds and his family, organised from their home in Carmunnock, a sort of ranch for heavies in which, at any given moment, one can stop by and find Russia's strongest man singing Lead belly songs in the front garden.

Edmunds known on the scene as The Godfather and, as he is rather unwell at the moment, spends his time at Dunfermline seated at the side of the field, a Don Corleone-ish presence, black-clad and crag-faced, receiving tribute from the international athletes who approach for respectful handshakes and the chance of a few words.

"I've been involved in the Highland Games since I was 17 and I'm now 70," he says. "I've been involved in more Highland games, either as an organiser or as an athlete, than anyone else in history. One of the things I've always tried to do is bring the games into prominence. It annoys the hell out of me that the Scottish Government and others don't recognise their economic and cultural importance. Everybody and their granny's wee society seem to get funding, but not the games. There's this idea that they are always going to be there, but they are not. The Games are in decline and without foreign athletes they'd be in big trouble.

Edmunds believes that as well as creating an exotic, crowd-friendly spectacle, the international heavies raise the standard, forcing domestic athletes to train hard if they are to have a hope of winning. He is strongly opposed to the system of having two tiers of prizes – one exclusively for the Scots. "To me, that's just looking after your own midden-heap. It's a pathetic attempt to keep your wee pot of money to yourself and not on in the interests of the games at all."

A NATION IS BORN

Emperor Titus was impatient at the lack of progress made by the Roman general, Agricola, in his quest to subjugate Caledonia. Following the defeat of Queen Boudicca in the South the Romans expected to dominate the entire island. Instead the fierce tribes of the North resisted the Roman advance therefore imperilling the notion of Roman invincibility. The defiant warriors were called Picti - referring to the practice of painting their entire bodies prior to battle. Some fought naked, committing acts of savagery accompanied by the dreadful screeching battle horns called Carnyx. Rumours of cannibalism abounded and an association with evil spirits prevailed, due to the abductions and executions that occurred during night raids when evil spirits were believed to come out of the darkness. The Romans were frustrated because they were unable to bring the Picts into a conventional pitched battle with the Picts preferring guerrilla tactics that were so effective in destroying morale.

Under pressure, Agricola formulated a plan to attack the Pictish heartland in what is now the North East of Scotland. He would concentrate attacks on their granaries following the harvest. This would elicit a massive response to protect vital winter sustenance. In the year 83 AD battle hardened troops were quickly marched to the North from the settlement at York and elite legions sent by galley up the north eastern coast. The Roman force numbered about 20,000 men, encountering about 30,000 Picts who had assembled on a hill called Mons Graupius. The Picts were in a horseshoe formation intending to surround the Roman advance by flanking the frontal attack. The tactic was frustrated by the Roman cavalry that had been placed on the wings which easily overcame the light Pictish chariots. In the fierce fighting that followed the disciplined Roman formations crushed the tribesmen at the bottom of the hill, killing their leader Calgacus and about 10,000 of his men. The remaining 20,000, seeing the disaster before them, withdrew and disappeared into the woods to fight another day.

Agricola had won a battle but had awakened a demon. The defeat brought the disparate tribes together and alliances were formed with the wild red-haired men from the West that the Romans referred to as the Scotti. They came together to destroy the common enemy. In the year 88 AD the Roman stronghold at Ardoch was surrounded. The encampment was protected by high wooden palisades and deep trenches, designed as killing grounds for defending archers. Initially the Romans felt secure in their stout, wooden barracks with thatched roofs and heavily stocked granaries. The wily Picts did not attack the formidable defences but instead deluged the fort with fireballs cast from a distance by whirling the balls at speed before releasing a barrage like modern mortar bombs. The dry wood and the copious amount of hay in the interior of the stockade was quickly set alight and soon became a blazing inferno, trapping the inhabitants between the walls of the perimeter. The terrified multitude were engulfed in flames or were put out of their misery with a hail of arrows – those that escaped were later killed in the surrounding forest.

Today the fort at Ardoch can be plainly seen with the deep trenches still evident, recent excavations have revealed charred wood indicating the intense heat that prevailed during the incident.

It was not until the year 108 AD that another serious attempt was made to subdue the Picts. The 9th Legion was despatched to the Kingdom of Fife in an attempt to establish Roman power in the region. Proudly bearing their standard and bristling with intent they set on their way and were never heard of again. Not even a sandal or a footprint was found. Six thousand men had disappeared into thin air and word spread that it was the work of evil spirits. Such rumours were probably engendered by the Picts themselves. Remnants of stories have only emerged in recent years regarding the mystery of the "**Lost Legion**." After being harried and reduced by Pictish guerrilla tactics it is likely that the legion would have sought refuge at the Roman Fort in Cramond where funeral lion statues were recently discovered.

Stories abound about the enormous cavern system near Cousland. A recent exploration by Scottish Water found an amazing spectacle, an underground lake with a perpetual blue yellow fireball of burning gas, indicating that the air was poisoned by methane gas. The ground above was also susceptible to subsidence and occasionally fissures would open. Cousland was also of interest due to a rumour that the Templar Knights had buried a vast treasure following their European demise. The power of the order diminished in 1307 when they were persecuted by Philip of France who coveted their great wealth. After they were disbanded by the Pope they hid their treasure in many secret locations. A letter also exists in the Edinburgh archives (from Mary Queen of Scots) stating she would never disclose the secret she had learned at Rosslyn Castle. Being so close to the Templar fortress the area became a magnet for treasure hunters. A suppressed story tells of an intrepid young man being lowered through a fissure to the bottom of the cavern. He did not find any treasure but shouted back that he had found a Roman standard, skeletons of dead horses and human remains wearing Roman armour. When his friends pulled him to the surface he was dead, having succumbed to the deadly gas below. Following the incident Scottish Water secured the area and prohibited access.

It appears likely that the pursuing Picts deliberately hounded the beleaguered Romans into the apparent safety of the cave system. The Picts believed that the place abounded with evil spirits and thus the death of Calgacus would be avenged. The disappearance of the 9th Legion inspired an atmosphere of mystery and terror which contributed to the Roman withdrawal and the construction of Hadrian's Wall which now approximates to the modern border between England and Scotland.

After the Romans the realm of Dalriada evolved, populated by the Scotti and their Irish kinfolk. It was an idyllic world dominated by the sea where wind powered galleys and birlins brought trade to a thriving Celtic world that encompassed the northern sea board of Wales, the Isle of Man, Northern Ireland and Western Scotland. The main cultural influence came from Ireland with its ancient games, music and religion. Some say the modern Highland Games have their beginnings in ancient Ireland where the Tailteann Games entertained the people of Dalriada. There is a legend that King Lugh introduced the games to honour his mother Tailte in the 7th century BC. The games included martial arts such as wrestling, spear throwing, archery, slinging, running, horse racing, feats of strength and almost any competition that related to the skills of a warrior. These were great social occasions with music and dancing. Some would have included the ***Teltown*** marriage which lasted for a year and a day and could be ended by having the couple stand back to back, one facing north and the other south and simply walk away from each other. The games spread throughout the region, their size dependant on the prestige of the local King and the music from harp and pipes became a feature of the Gaelic world.

The Irish religion of Christianity thrived and came to Western Scotland in 563 when St Columba, an Irish nobleman, arrived on Iona. Christianity eventually spread to the neighbouring Picts who were constantly at war with Dalriada. St Columba courageously travelled up the Great Glen to the palace of Bridei, the most powerful Pictish King, where he was commanded to engage in a magical duel with a druid magician. His victory greatly impressed the King and it was said that he had the power to cow the fearsome Kelpie that lived in Loch Ness.

Christianity was also introduced into the southern Britannic Kingdom of Strathclyde by St. Ninian who established a base in Whithorn from where missionaries like St Mungo made incursions into pagan Pictland. St Mungo (also known as St Kentigern) settled in Glas Cu in 543, later known as Glasgow which translates as ***dear green place.*** He established his church on the banks of the Molendinar Burn where the modern cathedral now stands. The subsequent gatherings of pilgrims led to Glas Cu becoming an important settlement.

The Picts had a stronghold in Glen Lyon, a long narrow valley that was guarded by tall conical towers at each entrance. Remnants of the stone structures can still be seen in Abernethy and features a doorway high above the ground to foil intruders. After the Romans, the main enemy of the Picts were the Angles from Northumbria who defeated a local warrior tribe called the Gododdin and took control of the Lothians. In 685 the triumphant Angles moved north and engaged the main Pictish army at Dunnichen, near Forfar. Seeing that he was vastly outnumbered, the Pictish chief lured the confident Angles into hilly, broken terrain which limited their ability to attack en mass. He then split his army in two and sent the weaker half to confront the enemy while keeping the stronger force concealed behind Dunnichen Hill. After a short skirmish the weak forces retreated back over the hill and the exultant Angles broke ranks to chase them down. The scattered Angles were then ambushed by the well organised Picts and virtually wiped out. Their King, Egfrid and his retinue were all killed and the power of Northumbria was broken forever.

Gregor with Pictish Stone

Picts honoured their warriors who in turn were obliged to maintain a constant state of battle readiness while the non-elite were responsible for domestic chores. A man's status depended on his physical strength which was assessed on his ability to lift the ***Pictish Stone***. This stone can still be found in Glen Lyon which is also known as the "glen of stones". It is an egg shaped piece of granite weighing about 140kg that had to be lifted chest high and placed on a platform. The smooth glass-like surface brings to mind the many hands that would have embraced the stone over thousands of years. The Picts did not have a written language but they left a legacy of carved stones which serve as a monument to their culture. A carved stone depicting the events at Dunnichen can still be found in Aberlemno churchyard.

Bridei's victory over the Angles marked the beginning of Pict dominance under one ruler. After his death in 693 the Dalriadan Scots became the greatest enemy due to the increasing influence of Irish missionaries on Pictish culture. Nechtan MacDerile ruled from 706 to 724 and expelled the Columbian monks to the west of the country before he also became a monk and resigned his kingship. Nechtan was succeeded by Oengus MacFergus who was a violent, ambitious man. He began by executing the King of Atholl, having him ceremoniously drowned. He then captured Dunadd, the centre of Scottish Dalriada. He also tried to conquer the Britons of Strathclyde but his hopes foundered on the impenetrable fort of Dumbarton Rock. After Oengus died, the Scots threw off Pictish rule but the idea of a united kingdom had been born. Intermarriage between the royal families had made the rulers almost interchangeable. A shared religion also helped to bring the Picts and Scots together but it was the arrival of a terrifying common enemy that finally led to the united kingdom of Scotland.

It began with Nordic pirates raiding coastal settlements and churches and grew to become a full-scale Viking invasion. In 839 a united army of Picts and Scots was destroyed. With the Picts on the East in the direct line of attack and the Dalriadan Scots cut off from their Irish cousins it was soon realised that no group could survive in isolation. Kenneth MacAlpin the King of Dalriada took advantage of the situation and brought the sacred Stone of Destiny from Dunadd to the Pictish royal centre at Scone and was anointed the first King of Scotland in 848.

THE TERROR

The relative tranquillity of Dalriada was brought to an end by the arrival of the Norwegian Vikings who had long been uneasy neighbours of the Picts in the Orkney and Shetland Islands. In 795 they arrived in Iona and desecrated the Abbey that had become the spiritual centre for both Dalriada and Pictland. Churches and monasteries were easy prey and any notion of sacrilege was far from their minds. Their ferocity and courage came from a conviction that death in battle assured them a place in ***Valhalla.*** Vikings from Denmark also raided Northumberland, sacked the religious centre of Lindisfarne and chased many of the indigenous population into Scotland.

In 840 a Viking chief called Thorgills ravaged the eastern shore of Ireland, then sailed up the Shannon as far as Lough Ree and plundered the monasteries at Clonmacnois and Clonfert. Dublin was fortified and became their centre of operations. Thorgills sent a large fleet of some sixty-five longships to Leinster where they engaged the Dalriadic army killing the King of Dalriada. The Dalriads were also driven out of Islay and the Hebrides. Thorgills' violence came to an end when he was captured in 845 by the Irish and drowned in Lough Owel. However, the rich treasures that could be plundered from the various religious centres caused the remaining Vikings to fight each other fiercely and when the Danes arrived in Dublin they hacked their Norwegian kin to extinction.

An example of the irascible nature of the Vikings is demonstrated by the tale of Onund and Vigbiod. The former had lost a leg in a previous battle but still had the zest for a fight. When he heard that his enemy, Vigbiod, had sailed with eight ships to an island named Bute he set off to find them with five longboats. When Onund approached he was taunted by Vigbiod and asked how he could fight with a wooden leg. Onund then sailed his ship around a cliff and when out of sight, landed some of his men and bade them carry many large stones to the edge of the cliff. When battle was joined Onund let his ship drift under the cliff. Thinking his enemy was trying to escape, Vigbiod closed in, whereupon the men at the top of the cliff rained down the great stones, maiming and killing many of Vigbiod's crew. Onund had his leg wedged with a log under his knee and stood firm to await his enemy. Vigbiod came forward hewing and slashing and sliced off a portion of Onund's shield. He then struck the log that Onund had under his knee and lodged his sword in the wood. As he struggled to pull it free Onund cut off his arm and proceeded to finish the job.

The Danes were driven out of Dublin by a Norwegian war chief called Olaf who began to establish a mixed race in Dublin by encouraging his warriors to integrate with the local population. He also married Kenneth MacAlpin's daughter which helped broker a permanent settlement. The mixing of Gaelic and Viking blood was the beginning of a new warrior breed. Furthermore in 870 Harald Thickhair decided to subjugate the whole of Norway into one kingdom after winning a great sea battle off Stavanger. A large number of dispossessed chiefs and their followers were expelled or fled for their lives. This led to the Viking raids becoming a basis for mass colonisation. The Vikings and their families came as settlers and integrated with the Gaels of Dalriada, others went to Iceland where there was ***an abundance of stranded whales and plenty of salmon***.

Harald also sent a fleet to Scotland to clear out any residual opposition to his authority and allowed local chieftains to emerge so long as the accepted him as their overlord.
The Vikings then dominated the affairs of Dalriada for the next hundred years and through intermarriage with the local population, clans, such as the Morrisons and the MacLeods formed.

It was not until Brian Boru became the King of Cashel in 979 that the disparate tribes of the interior united to oppose Viking rule. Not surprisingly the King of Leinster who had Viking blood in his veins sided with the Norsemen of Dublin. Both sides met in a narrow pass called Glenmama in the Wicklow Mountains. The Viking forces were virtually wiped out and the king of Leinster ignominiously captured having been found hiding up a tree. Brian then occupied Dublin and was crowned the High King of Erin. He brought a period of peace when monasteries reopened and churches were built. He married the dowager Queen, Gormflaith, the widow of the Viking King of Dublin. History reports she was a beautiful woman and accustomed to satisfying her whims. She longed for the Viking ways and eventually sent her son to Orkney to persuade Sigurd the Strong to invade Dublin offering herself as the dynastic prize.

Sigurd allied with Brodir of Man and arrived off Dublin with a huge fleet in 1014. When they disembarked the Viking force stood about a mile and a half wide. Arrayed against them were about twenty thousand Irish. Brian Boru was now an old man and passed the leadership to his son Murchad, who was famous for being ambidextrous, fighting with a sword in each hand.

Before the battle of Clontarf began the excitement swelled at the prospect of a preliminary challenge between two warriors from opposing sides. Plait the son of a Viking chief called out Domnal the High Steward of Alban. He came forth from his battalion and shouted –

"Where is Domnal?"

"Here, thou reptile"

- was the reply.

The duel started with both endeavouring to slaughter the other. When they fell each was clutching the other's hair with their swords impaled in each of their hearts. Before the bodies could be moved they were ignominiously stamped into the earth when the opposing sides rushed over them to engage in the ensuing battle.

A Viking invader portrayed by Hafthor Julius Bjornsson – height 6ft 10ins and weighing more than 400lbs.

For a long time the battle raged until the Leinster line finally broke, throwing the Vikings into disarray. Sigurd the Strong chose to stand and fight by his Raven Banner. Eventually he was confronted by Murchad brandishing his two swords. With his right hand he smashed Sigurd's helmet then clove his neck with the other, leaving him to die under a melee of fleeing soldiers. Murchad moved on to confront Eric the son of the King of Lochlann and according to a scribe -

The inlay of Murchad's sword had melted with the excessive heat of striking and the burning sword had cleft his hand. He cast the sword from him and laid hold of the top of the foreigner's head and pulled over his coat of mail. They fought and Murchad put the foreigner down by force of wrestling. He then took the foreigner's sword and thrust it through his ribs. The foreigner drew his knife and gave Murchad such a cut that his entrails fell to the ground before him. Then shivering and fainting he tried to descend on Murchad but he had not the power to move. So they fell by each other.

After the battle the fleeing Brodir of Man came across Brian Boru kneeling in prayer to thank God for his great victory. Recognising the old man he decapitated him with a battle axe but was then was caught by the pursuing Irish. Outraged by the loss of their King Brodir probably endured the traditional Viking custom of the ***Blood Eagle.*** This involved peeling the skin from the back, then breaking the ribs and pulling out the still attached lungs, displaying them like the wings of an eagle to ensure a slow and hideous death.

The Vikings who had settled in England were also heavily defeated at Stamford Bridge near York by King Harold Godwineson. The battle is remembered due to the heroic defence of the crossing by a giant Norwegian axeman who killed more than forty Englishmen before being cut down. When the Vikings were finally driven back to their ships their last great raid on English soil ended in disaster. Celebration of a great victory was curtailed when news was received that William of Normandy had landed an invasion force near Hastings. Harold had to muster his depleted army and march south to confront a new enemy. It is said that William only became the Conqueror in 1066 because the English army had been exhausted by the Vikings.

Following the weakening of Viking power it fell to ***Magnus Barelegs***, the new King of Norway, to establish a firm control over the Kingdom of Man and the Isles. He made an agreement with Edgar, the King of Scotland in 1098, in which he would possess all the lands in the West provided that he could go between them and the main land with a ship's rudder in place. Magnus had his men pull his ship across the isthmus near Crinan using ***roller logs*** while he sat holding the rudder and claimed possession of the fertile land of Kintyre. Edgar was able to secure the east and south of the country without being distracted by hostile neighbours.

The Viking retention of the west of Scotland and the influence of the Norman Conquerors had a profound effect on the culture and solidarity of the entire country. Scotland had evolved into a two nation state with the Viking Gaels in the North West and a conglomerate of Picts, Angles, Saxons and French Normans in the rest of the country, separated by a different language and culture.

Edgar's father was King Malcolm III, otherwise known as Canmore (meaning big head) which may have referred to his physical stature. He had become increasingly influenced by English culture and language, especially after his marriage to Princess Margaret, the daughter of Edgar Atheling, the Anglo Saxon claimant to the English Throne after Harold had been killed at Hastings. Many English nobles were driven north by William the Conqueror's purges and confiscations. They were given sanctuary in Scotland and it is said that the King loved to entertain his English guests with the antics of his warriors who would participate in games devised by Malcolm himself. They would include wrestling, stone lifting, throwing spears, maces and hammers. A stone carving on the wall at the back of the royal residence at Balmoral clearly depicts Malcolm sitting among his warriors. Many considered him to be the father of the modern Highland Games.

Queen Margaret was a sophisticated religious woman who did much to civilise her war-like husband and increase the anglicisation of the Scottish court. Malcolm was killed in battle at Alnwick in 1093 and his beloved queen died shortly afterwards. Both bodies were eventually brought together and buried by the altar at Dunfermline Abbey. It is said that when Margaret's body was disinterred the area was pervaded with the scent of fresh flowers and an overwhelming force ensured that she was buried alongside her husband. Margaret was subsequently canonised by the Pope and their resting place is considered a shrine to the Highland Games aficionados.

David I, the youngest son of Malcolm, had spent a great deal of his minority at the English court and had married the Conqueror's niece which bestowed him the Earldom of Huntingdon. He therefore granted favours to a large number of his Norman friends and allowed them to settle in Scotland. Many originated the great families of Ayrshire and Southern Scotland. They include the family of FitzAllan, the ancestors of the Stewarts of Dundonald, the Campbellos who became the Campbells of Symington, De Brus of Carrick and the Douglases of Galloway. In the North they established their influence by building a cathedral at Elgin.

While the Normanisation of the mainland gathered pace the former Gaelic Lords of Dalriada were encouraged to reclaim some of their old estates in the West. So when Gillebride and his son Somerled with Viking blood in their veins came from Ireland and landed in Argyll around 1130 they were not welcomed and had to take refuge in a cave on Morvern. It was a time when Viking pirates were still creating havoc and had recently killed the chief of the local Clan MacInnes. When another band of pillagers arrived the clan gathered to find a new war captain. Aware of his pedigree and impressed with his strength of limb and character they invited Somerled to be their leader. After receiving a pledge of loyalty he led his new warriors to the Viking camp and with a clever strategy pretended to surround it with a large force. Although the Vikings were greater in number they fled to their boats and in disarray they were attacked and slaughtered. From that day Somerled began to establish his leadership and was eventually crowned ruler of Argyll under the overlordship of the King of Norway. It is likely that Somerled would have embraced the ancient Druid ceremony at the summit of Dunadd where ancient Kings were anointed after stepping into the sacred footprint which can still be found in the present day.

The remaining Viking stronghold was the Isle of Man, presided over by Olaf the Red, who also claimed jurisdiction over the northern Isles. When Olaf set out to quell a revolt on

Skye he asked Somerled to assist in the expedition. Somerled agreed on condition that Olaf would sanction his marriage to his daughter, Ragnhilda. Their union set the blood line for future generations of Highland Chiefs who considered the Lowland Scots as foreigners.

Realising that control of the sea was essential for the maintenance of power in the region Somerled embarked on a programme of building a fleet of ships that were technically superior to the Viking longships. Although smaller they were much more manoeuvrable due to the attachment of a tiller rather than an oar on the right-hand side of the boat.

When Olaf was assassinated by one of his chieftains he was succeeded by his son Godred who proceeded to extract a savage revenge. The local chiefs asked Somerled to intervene and that they would support his claim to the Northern Isles. Hearing of the conspiracy Godred assembled his fleet and met Somerled off the coast of Islay. In January 1156 a great sea battle raged throughout the night called the battle of the Epiphany. By morning both sides were badly damaged and no side could claim victory. A treaty was agreed whereby Godred held the islands north of Ardnamurchan and Somerled gained all the islands to the south except Man itself. However two years later Somerled invaded Man and took over the entire region.

It was inevitable that the avaricious Normans would see rich opportunities in Somerled's expanding dominions. They had already grasped the rich regions of Wales and established an estate in Northern Ireland. An invasion was launched to gain control of the western mainland and was repulsed with great losses. Afterwards Somerled visited the King of Norway to confirm his right to hold the Isles and Malcolm the 4th, faced with the possibility of intervention by the Vikings, confined his actions to securing the rest of the country. Galloway was overwhelmed in 1161 and a kinsman of Somerled was captured and taken to Edinburgh where he died shortly afterwards. Moray was then attacked and it became clear that Walter Fitz-Allan the Steward of Scotland and main advisor to the King had an interest in procuring Arran and Bute. He persuaded the King that he should plan another invasion to annex mainland Argyll and complete his ambition of consolidating the Scottish mainland.

The ancient Celtic Earls called the Rai were increasingly concerned by the Norman - inspired hegemony and something had to be done to protect their interests. Somerled decided to make a pre-emptive attack and sailed up the Clyde with one hundred and sixty ships to confront Fitz-Allan's army which was camped in Renfrew. Somerled was then sixty-four years old and had expected the Earls to supply horsemen to support his sailors against the Norman cavalry. When the Earls failed to appear Somerled remained undaunted and leading from the front, attacked the enemy. A chronicler from the mainland side gave the following description of subsequent events -.

"And in the first clef of battle the baleful leader fell. Wounded by a spear, slain by a sword, Somerled died. And raging waves swallowed his son and many of the wounded and thousand fugitives; because when the fierce leader was struck down, the wicked took

to flight and very many were slaughtered, both on sea and land – Thus the enemies' ranks were denuded and repelled; and the whole kingdom with loud voices praised Saint Kentigeren."

King Malcolm showed his respect for the fallen hero by having his body recovered from the battle ground and sent to Iona for burial.

Somerled left three sons who gained the peace by conceding Arran and Bute to Fitz-Allan. Their father's estates were divided between them. Ranald the eldest inherited the title of Lord of Argyll and Kintyre which included Islay and all the islands south of Ardnamurchan. The Isle of Man reverted to a Norse king called Ragnvald which indicated the continuing influence of the Vikings. Dougall inherited Lorne, Jura, Coll, and Mull. Angus, the youngest, received the northern territories of Moidart, Morar, Knoydart and Arisaig. However Angus and his sons were later killed by the Norsemen of Skye and Dougall took over most of his possessions. Dougall became the progenitor of Clan MacDougall of Lorne that was to have an important role in future events.

Ranald left two sons, Donald and Ruari, from his marriage to Fiona the daughter of the Earl of Moray. While Ruari took control over his uncle's lands in Moidart and the northern islands, Donald established himself in Islay and his son Angus Mor became the first MacDonald in history.

Malcolm was succeeded by Alexander II who had been troubled with Gaelic pretenders to his throne, some receiving assistance from the Somerled family. In response Alexander sent his navy on an expedition to extend his western frontier, expelling Ruari from Bute and Cowal in favour of the Stewart family and installing a Strathclyde knight called Colin Campbell in Loch Awe. After failing to seduce the MacDougalls away from their allegiance with the Vikings he attempted to renegotiate the settlement that had been made with Magnus Barelegs. This was rejected by King Hakon of Norway and Alexander responded by assembling a fleet of ships near Oban but shortly after arriving in Kerrera Alexander died and the threat dissipated.

There was peace for about ten years until the young Alexander III was persuaded to further his father's ambition to take the Isles. He offered to buy them from Hakon and threatened to take them by force if necessary. When this was also rejected he encouraged the earl of Ross to raid Skye which was still part of the Norse kingdom of Man. This had the desired result of provoking Hakon who summoned his vassals to Norway for a council of war.

The Viking fleet left Norway in July accompanied by the MacRuaris. The fleet anchored off Kerrera and was joined by the ships from the Isle of Man and the MacRuairi galleys. Dugall MacRuairi took advantage of the situation and raided Rothesay Castle while Hakon sailed on to Lamlash Bay. Meanwhile Alexander had assembled his troops directly across the estuary at Ayr while the Dominican monks of Arran tried to broker a peace treaty. As the negotiations lengthened into the autumn Hakon sent Dugall MacRuairi to forage up

Loch Long for supplies. When they reached Arrochar they hauled their galleys overland to Loch Lomond using the traditional log rolling technique and raided the surrounding area.

Hakon grew impatient at what seemed to be delaying tactics and moved his fleet nearer the shore off Cumbrae. On the first day of October 1263 a great storm blew up which drove many of Hakon's ships onto the shore at Largs. The local militia attacked the stranded Vikings but were repulsed when about a thousand Norsemen disembarked to help with the salvage. Lookouts were then placed on the escarpment to give the alarm when the main Scottish army arrived. However there was insufficient time to complete the rescue and the beached Vikings were either killed or driven into the sea. After the initial slaughter enough reinforcements landed and eventually drove the Scots back up the escarpment. This allowed the surviving Vikings to wade back out to the waiting boats. By the next day the Scots retreated and allowed the Norsemen to retrieve their dead and burn their stranded ships.

Hakon died as he retreated homewards and his successor Magnus of Norway sold the Isles to Alexander. In 1266 a treaty was signed at Perth giving amnesty to the chieftains that had supported Hakon and finally brought the Western Isles under the Scottish Crown. The Viking era had ended but they had left a permanent legacy with their bloodlines contributing to the formation of a fierce warrior race called The Highlanders.

VIKING GAMES

Being a proud Scotsman and a descendant of Clan Morrison I took an interest in the Viking festival that takes place in Largs every year during the month of August. Bearing in mind that if the Battle of Largs had been won by the Vikings the North and West of Scotland may well have become part of Scandinavia and the Norman dominated south would have been absorbed by England with no Highlanders to fight for the cause.

Today the momentous event is celebrated with the staging of a Viking Festival which includes the creation of a Viking Village, Norwegian music and dancing and the burning of a Long Boat. To me this was not sufficient commemoration and needed something more red blooded commensurate with the nature of the real Vikings. As a race they valued physical strength and prowess in battle.

My first visit to the Viking realm of Iceland was with the Scottish Athletic team in 1964. At that time Reykjavik was no more than a large fishing port with an all pervading smell of whale oil. The women were particularly beautiful and I deemed myself lucky to catch the eye of a winsome Valkyrie at a night club. She was the wife of a fisherman and under the protection of his mates who balefully stared as we swayed to the music. I was unaware of the drama that was unfolding when a team mate and Glasgow policeman called John Scott intercepted an Icelander brandishing a knife with the intention of ending my amorous advances. Mayhem then broke out and it was time to make a quick exit realising the Icelanders were a proud and close knit people.

After watching the young Jon Pall Sigmarsson's antics at The World's Strongest Man competition held in New Zealand in 1983 I invited him to the Carmunnock Games the following year and a lifelong friendship was forged (see **Giants and Legends**). My house became known as the Viking headquarters and many Icelandic athletes have enjoyed coming to the Highland Games over the years.

During the 1980's I set out to stage a series of Viking games with real Vikings challenging the best of Britannia in contests that would have been familiar to the adversaries that took part in the actual battle. I had long been an admirer of the Icelanders who had produced so many champions despite the small population of their homeland. I was also aware that many Scottish women had been carried away by the Viking raiders for breeding purposes when they set up new colonies outside Norway. On the other hand male captives were sold as slaves or merely killed for pleasure. In fact the Icelandic Museum of Viking Heritage in Akranes records that more than seventy five percent of Icelandic women can trace their bloodline back to Gaeldom. Having been advised by the chairman of the Icelandic Glyma association about old Viking traditions and not wishing to be prosecuted for staging dangerous events, I contrived to come up with a programme that would still portray the spirit of a warrior race.

The venue for the Largs Games was the Kelburn Castle Estate on the site of the original 13th century castle that would have overlooked the battle from the escarpment above the beach where the landing took place. Our host was the Earl of Glasgow whose ancestors had fought against the Vikings. When I introduced Jon Pall to the Earl I did not realise his Viking background appreciated only strength with scant regard for privilege. He turned to me and said with a mischievous grin -

"Ah Douglas I thought you were Lord of Glasgow"

Prior to the games a Viking longship was drawn along the esplanade with the World's Strongest Man waving to astonished onlookers from the prow of the ship. A small boy sat behind blowing a horn destined to become one of Scotland's greatest athletes. In its wake marched the Viking warriors wearing horned helmets with their honed muscles glistening in the sun. They were a formidable group of men.

The Vikings parade along the Largs esplanade with Jon Pall Sigmarsson waving to the crowd as a young Gregor gets ready to blow his war horn.

The games opened with a grand confrontation between the descendants of ancient warriors that had fought each other for more than three hundred years in the past. During the course of the coming battle the pipes and drums reverted to being instruments of war - the pipes to exhort the warriors into action and the drums to signal the order of combat. Each of the teams stood abreast and faced each other across a divide. Sixteen from Iceland faced sixteen of the best in Britain. Following a signal the bagpipes played a rousing tune and the two groups slowly moved towards each other while maintaining their lines. When they had reached a five metre face off the pipes stopped and the opponents stood still, malevolently glaring into each other's eyes. The Vikings stood stripped to the waist while the kilts of the opposition swayed in the wind. Suddenly there was a roll of drums which was the signal to engage. The big men grabbed each other and with frantic action tried to throw their opponents to the ground. When the drumming ceased they disengaged and to the sound of the bagpipes playing a slow lament, the survivors slowly retreated and the vanquished were removed.

At the end of the first encounter Jon Pall Sigmarsson, winner of four World's Strongest Man titles, had defeated the mighty Geoff Capes who had won the same title twice. Only four Brits had survived and although badly shaken they were still defiant. Among the vanquished were renowned Scottish strongmen such as Chris Black, Brian Bell, Davy Sharp and Scotland's reigning strongest man Ian Murray who with his long curly red hair was known as the Highlander.

Four of the remaining Vikings were selected to take on those still standing. The latter were Kevin Connelly, Peter Tregloan, Peter Trelfall and Robert McNamara. Kevin was a rugby player known as Big Rocky, Peter was the British Power Lifting Champion and the other two were British wrestling champions. The order of battle was repeated while the rest of the Vikings stood in reserve.

After the second round three Brits survived with only McNamara beaten by a wild man called Garda Villamsson. The next encounter placed Kevin Connelly against Magnus Ver Magnusson, Peter Tregloan against Jon Pall Sigmarsson and Joe Trelfall against Garda Villamsson.

Kevin Connelly had no answer to the power of Magnus who was then the European Power Lifting Champion. The fight between Sigmarsson and Tregloan was an awesome affair with the Viking eventually winning. During the heat of battle the referee received something in his eye which turned out to be a squirt of pus, ejected when Jon Pall squeezed his opponent so hard that the spots on his back burst with explosive force. The Brits were able to salvage some pride when Trelfall, who as the then current British Backhold Champion, beat Garda with consummate skill.

The final confrontation pit Joe Trelfall against Jon Pall and even with all his skill Joe succumbed to the Viking's overwhelming power.

At the end we had to put on a special challenge involving the best of three falls between Villamsson and Trelfall to satisfy the animosity between them. After two falls they were even but Garda's savagery was no match for skill and after a protracted struggle the Brits were able to acclaim a hero.

The Viking ranks had been bolstered by two interesting characters named Gudbrander Sigurosson and Guomunder Omar. The former was 6ft 5ins and the latter was called Steve McQueen for his uncanny resemblance to the Hollywood hero. Both were officers in the Icelandic Special Forces and had just spent some weeks buried in snow in the Icelandic wilderness as part of their training. They were subsequently chosen to stand guard during the momentous discussions at the Reykjavik Summer House between Gorbachev and Regan which ended the cold war. The overall leader of the Vikings was a hulk of a man called Hjalti Arnason also known as Ursus the Bear.

The initial battle was followed by individual and team games that were designed to reflect the warrior culture of the Vikings.

Stone lifting is a part of Viking folklore. The most famous icon being the piece of black granite called the ***Husafell Stone*** which rests in a church in the village of Borgafind in the Reykholt area of rural Iceland. It weighs approximately 200kgs and is only released under the supervision of a guardian. It was once used as the gate for a sheep-pen and the challenge was to carry it around the enclosure. The legend relates that none could beat the shepherd's daughter. This chimes with the answer given by Jon Pal Sigmarsson when asked who the strongest person in Iceland was. His easy answer was the enormous women that skinned the fish by the harbour.

Lifting the Fisherman's Stones is also an Icelandic tradition whereby the strongest fisherman can lay claim to the biggest share of the catch. The original stones can still be found on an Icelandic beach.

One of the individual events was throwing ***Thor's Hammer*** simulating the Viking war hammer. In Norse mythology Thor was the Viking God of War, the son of Odin, fierce, red haired and red bearded. He wielded the mountain crushing hammer called ***Mjolnir*** which, when thrown, never missed its target and always returned to his hand. Our event consisted of throwing a 15kg short hammer overhead for distance and accuracy.

Iceland is called the Land of Ice and Fire because of the constant geothermal activity creating an environment that reflects the fiery temperament of its warriors. One of their pastimes was a tug-o-war across a fire pit using a sheep skin which they pulled with one hand. It was not the Viking way to let go and the loser would have to jump through the flames to retain his pride. We devised an event which we called the ***Ring of Fire*** whereby two opponents tried to push each other out of a flaming circle by thrusting at each end of a pole. Safety concerns prevented the event occurring at Largs but it was spectacularly employed at Garmich in Germany a few years later.

A simulation of the ***Viking Boat Pull*** was carried out using large tree trunks which were rolled over small runner logs. This enabled large loads to be conveyed over a considerable distance by a concerted team effort simulating the ruse carried out by **Magnus Barelegs** when he claimed the land of Kintyre. The competition involved two teams of five men with three of them pulling the load as two others fed and recovered the runners while acting to prevent the logs skewing off their rollers. A more effective scenario would have been to provide for a sixth man to sit astride the log to bark out instructions like the captain of a ship.

The desecration of coastal life was brought to an end by Somerled and we are reminded of the rape and pillaging represented by the ***Loading Race***. Two sets of young ladies were corralled in a holding area while the Vikings and Brits raced to carry them away. The strongest gained an advantage by lifting two at a time.

Another event was a foot race with a difference reminding us of the story about Somerled pursuing the Viking pirates as they tried to escape with their booty. One team is given a start with the aim of carrying a designated burden over a sanctuary line before being caught by the chasing team. A mere tap by a pursuer was not enough as the quarry had to be stopped in his tracks, preferable by being tackled. The roles were reversed in a second round and points awarded according to the number of ***Plunderers*** who managed to ***Escape***.

Another popular event involved the rhythmic beating of a drum to coordinate the ***Battering Ram Race.*** Two opposing teams of at least six men endeavoured to batter a hole through a stout stockade. Both teams competed alongside each other, racing to create a hole big enough to allow all their warriors to pass through. On one memorable occasion at the Viking Challenge during the Carmunnock Games in 1990, victory was denied to an international team when the giant American, O. D. Wilson got stuck in the hole.

The finale was called the ***Death March*** because afterwards the competitors were exhausted and unable to continue. Two bands of warriors marched alongside each other, in single file with the leader carrying a 300lb load. When he collapsed the next in line took up the burden and the team with the last man standing declared the winner.

After the games in Largs the Vikings insisted on staying at the Newlands Hotel in the Shawlands area of Glasgow where women were plentiful and friendly.

Iceland's most popular daily newspaper published a report on the games. The following extracts were roughly translated by Heidar Geirmundson suggesting a reason for the adoption of the thistle as Scotland's national emblem.

Extract from "Morgubladid, Sunnjdagur" 27 09 1987

This year, the people of Largs on the west coast of Scotland honour that 700 years have passed since the last battle against the Viking took place, but that battle was fought in Largs where the townfolk won. Legend states that when the townfolk heard the Vikings were coming they covered their beaches in thistles. When the Viking walked to shore (barefoot according to stories) loud and angry screams could be heard from far away and

heroic efforts were not present. If the thistles were the deciding factor in the battle is not known but the battle ended with the Vikings being kicked out and did not bother the Scotsmen any more.
A great monument was raised, remembering those who were lost in this historic battle and stands on the beach reaching high into the sky and referred to as the needle.

HEISI GEIRMUNDSSON

The presence of the Icelandic Vikings is all thanks to the collaboration between Jon Pall Sigmarsson and Douglas Edmunds. The former does not need introduction but Douglas is

Jon Pall's agent overseas and has held countless strongman and highland games for many years.

The Scotsmen did not think it was necessary to cover the beaches in thistles this time. The descendants of the Vikings got a lot warmer welcome than their ancestors but we are pretty sure that the ancient Vikings did not have to stand in line to show a passport when they travelled between countries.

In addition to watching the traditional Highland Games they had the pleasure of watching the biggest assembly of bagpipers in the world which brings bands from numerous countries and Scotland to the Cowal Games. At the end of the competition the bands walked through the town playing and it took hours, the Vikings were sure that the bagpipe sounds would echo through their heads for eternity.

The Viking games in Largs started with a parade through the town with all the competitors following a Viking Longboat with Jon Pall Sigmarsson present at the front in all his glory.

The weather was at its best on the day of competition, but the competition was held on the property of the Duke of Glasgow right outside of Largs, on a freshly mowed land under a magnificent hill.

The competition started with a fight between the Viking and the Scots. Sixteen Vikings and sixteen Highlanders walked towards each other with bagpipes and drums playing. When the groups met in the middle they fought until the bagpipes stopped. They tallied the score and ten Vikings were left standing but only five Scotsmen. The second round was a complete annihilation because all the Scotsmen lost.

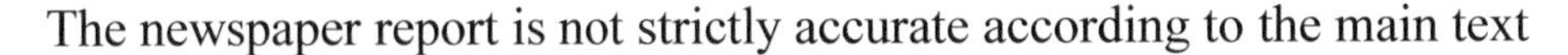
The newspaper report is not strictly accurate according to the main text

WRESTLING

FREEDOM

Following the defeat of the Vikings the country experienced a short period of peace. However the Norman King of England coveted the Scottish throne and many of the magnates were infused by Norman blood and the security of the country was tenuous. By 1286, King Alexander III (who had no heir as his three sons had died before him) was fearful of a civil war and he forced his nobles to agree to the succession of his infant grand daughter, Margaret of Norway. He was a vigorous, middle-aged man, had remarried a young French woman and was still hopeful of producing a legitimate heir. After feasting in Edinburgh he insisted on riding home to his young wife during a stormy winter night with his journey taking him over the treacherous waters of the Forth estuary and on through the darkness to Kinghorn. In his haste he lost the company of his companions and was found the next day at the bottom of a cliff with a broken neck.

The young princess Margaret did not survive the arduous journey from Norway and died in the Orkneys bringing the business of succession into turmoil. The Guardians of Scotland which included Bishop Wishart of Glasgow, the High Stewart and John Comyn of Buchan favoured John Balliol whereas the majority of the Earls preferred Robert de Brus. Failing to agree they made the terrible mistake of referring the final decision to Edward I of England who had just conquered Wales and saw an opportunity of adding Scotland to his domain. John Balliol was eventually chosen but had to swear subservience and accept Edward as his overlord. Balliol's perceived weakness caused a furore throughout Scotland and to add insult to injury the legally important Great Seal was taken to England

Balliol was ridiculed and called the ***Toom Tabard*** (meaning empty coat) for humiliating the nation. The Scots finally showed their defiance by refusing to support Edward's war with France and instead made a separate treaty. Edward considered this an act of treason and prepared to mount an invasion. Adding fuel to the fire the influential John Comyn raided Cumberland and laid siege to Carlisle Castle which was ironically defended by Robert de Brus. This enraged Edward who was renowned for having a fiery temper and he rushed to take his revenge by attacking Berwick. The town was burnt, no quarter was given and babies were torn from their mothers and put to the sword. The atrocities were among the worst in English history. Edinburgh then surrendered to Edward's army and John Balliol was imprisoned and forced to abdicate. Scotland was virtually enslaved and deprived of the sacred relics of nationhood including the Black Rood with its fragment of the true cross and the Stone of Destiny. Most of the Scots nobles were forced to give an oath of fealty and attached their seals to the notorious ***Ragman Roll***. All the major towns were put under the control of an English sheriff who imposed crippling taxes and were garrisoned to ensure compliance. The emasculated nation simmered with resentment and protest was inevitable. There was an early report that a William le Waleys (Wallace) got into trouble with the authorities in a Perth tavern. Sometime later he slew the Sheriff of Lanark in revenge for some perfidious act. Here was a man whose volatile character is typical of today's Scottish stereotype and any affront to his pride had dire consequences. Some say he was in charge of a group of lawless brigands. He was certainly a big man, estimated to be about 6ft 5ins, judged from the size of a replica of his sword which is on display at the Wallace Monument on Abbey Craig by Stirling. His deeds were acclaimed among the hard pressed people and were seized on by Bishop Wishart, Sir Andrew Moray and others who were planning to ferment a revolt. However most of the southern nobles had Norman sympathies and would not risk their titles for a commoner.

Wallace raised a people's army drawing support from lowland peasants, outlaws and the dispossessed who had vengeance in their hearts. Undaunted they marched on Stirling where they were joined by a defiant Earl of Moray and his Gaelic clansmen. By September 1297 the Scots had camped on Abbey Hill where they had a good view of the plain below and the thick woods hid their numbers. The arrogant Norman knights amassed their heavy cavalry at the other side of the river eager to get at the ragged foot soldiers that Wallace had sent before them. Both sides were separated by a narrow bridge and one can imagine the Scots taunting and deriding their proud enemy in typical fashion by beating their targes and baring their arses to entice them across the bridge.

Hugh de Cressingham, the hated collector of taxes led the charge and when sufficient had crossed Wallace released his main force from their cover. The bridge was blocked and the stranded vanguard driven onto a loop of land by the river's edge. Some of the knights were unable to manoeuvre in the swampy ground and were pulled from their hamstrung horses and either speared or hacked to death. Others backed into the river Forth and drowned due to the weight of their armour. On the other side of the river the rest of the English army, under John de Warenne the Earl of Sussex, could only watch while their colleagues were slaughtered to the last man. It is said that in the aftermath Cressingham's body was flayed and cut into pieces and widely distributed as tokens of victory.

Wallace pursued the disconsolate Normans back to England, raided Cumbria and tried to take Carlisle Castle which was once again successfully defended by Robert De Brus. During the next few months Wallace raided Scone and came to the assistance of Neil Campbell of Loch Awe when he was attacked by a barbarous Irishman called Macphadian who had been commissioned by Edward as part of a pact with the MacDougalls who were trying to gain control of the Western Highlands. A fight took place at the Pass of Brander after which Macphadian jumped into the river Awe and swam to the other side. He was followed by Duncan de Lorne who cornered him in a cave. He then cut off Macphadian's head and placed it on a rock above the battlefield in defiance of Edward's intrusion.

In 1298 Edward made a treaty with France which released his army to march north and deal with the rebellion. His army consisted of about fifteen thousand men including two thousand cavalry and the rest were infantry and bowmen. Many were mercenaries drawn from the continental wars and the experienced archers also included crossbow men. Wallace realising he could not confront such a host, retreated before them and restricted their supplies. Bad weather also prevented Edward's fleet from reaching Edinburgh with food and money. His army came close to starvation and the Welsh mercenaries rioted which resulted in many being killed. Wallace's strategy almost succeeded as the English army came close to disintegration. At a critical moment the Scottish army was reported to be encamped at Callendar Park near Falkirk and being only thirteen miles distant, the English rallied and rushed to engage them.

Wallace was vastly outnumbered having about seven thousand troops. His spearmen formed into four schiltrons, bowmen filled the gaps and a small band of infantry under John Comyn formed the rearguard. The English Cavalry attacked the array, overcoming the archers who stood firm before falling under the galloping hoofs but the infantry took flight. Only the schiltrons with their long spikes were able to disrupt the horsemen. Edward then withdrew the cavalry and let his archers shower the formations with arrows. When the Scottish cavalry belatedly arrived they saw the battle being lost as the schiltrons began to crumble. The Grandees, with only a lukewarm support for Wallace, did not wish to risk their estates for a lost cause and turned away. With the schiltrons broken the English charged again and began slaughtering the remnants of the people's army.

Wallace was wounded but managed to escape into the trees of Torwood. He evaded capture for the next seven years and spent a considerable time abroad trying to win support for Scottish freedom. When he was eventually captured on 5 August 1305 he had letters of safe passage from King Hakon of Norway, Philip of France and John Balliol.

When Wallace was charged with treason he replied -

"I could never be a traitor to Edward for I was never his subject"

He was taken to the Tower of London, stripped naked and dragged through the streets at the heels of a horse. He was then hanged but released while still alive, castrated, and eviscerated before his bowels were burnt before him. His agony ended when they finally cut off his head. The quartered limbs were displayed at Newcastle, Berwick, Stirling and Perth and his head stuck on a spike on London Bridge.

Edward sought to bring his enemies to heel by terrorising them into submission instead he created a national hero that would forever rally the Scottish nation.

Robert de Brus had been loyal to Edward and when he died his vigorous young son called Robert the Bruce, sought Edward's support for his claim to the Scottish Crown. Robert had already gained favour by helping to retake Stirling Castle and had sworn a holy oath of fealty to Edward but it became obvious that Edward wanted to have the crown for himself. With his ambition frustrated Robert began to consort with the King of France. John Comyn, a nephew of Balliol and enemy of Bruce saw the opportunity of getting rid of Bruce by informing Edward about this dangerous liaison. With danger looming Bruce had to act decisively and arranged to meet Comyn at the Church of the Minorite Friars in Dumfries. Both men were unable to reconcile their differences and a violent quarrel broke out in which Bruce drew his knife and stabbed Comyn to death. Bruce fled to the sanctuary of Bishop Wishart of Glasgow and confessed to the sacrilegious murder. When Edward was informed he flew into a rage and petitioned the Pope to have him excommunicated. Having no option, Bruce declared himself King of Scots on Palm Sunday 1306. Support was lukewarm with only two of the seven Earls attending the coronation; they were Atholl and Lennox accompanied by Bishop Wishart.

King Edward's Warden in Scotland caught up with Bruce's small band at Methven Wood. Fortunately one of his companions was Sir Neil Campbell and they took flight to his estate in the Western Highlands. At the behest of Edward, the MacDougalls of Lorne saw this as an opportunity to avenge Comyn and get rid of their unwanted neighbour. On the way to Campbell's Castle at Innis Channel, Lame John MacDougall ambushed Bruce and his small band of followers at Tyndrum. A fierce battle took place but Bruce managed to escape due to his fighting skills. Seeing his quarry escaping, Lame John summoned the Marthokey brothers, deemed ***the hardiest in the land***, and ordered them to pursue and kill Bruce. Taking a third man they managed to trap Bruce between the brae and the loch but they had underestimated the calibre of the man and he killed all three of them. During the fight Bruce's plaid was torn off and his brooch was found clasped in the hand of one of the corpses. Today it can be seen among the heirlooms of Clan MacDougall of Lorne.

Bruce fled south to Loch Lomond where he was given shelter by the Laird of Lennox. From there he was taken to the Mull of Kintyre where he received the protection of the MacDonalds and then taken by the MacRuairi galleys to the safety of Rathlin Island.

Bruce returned with a band of Irish in 1307 and managed to regain his lands in Arran but two of his brothers landed in Loch Ryan and were captured and hanged. Undaunted he entered the Galloway hills and gradually gathered his supporters – the most important being Sir James Douglas otherwise known as the ***Black Douglas***. They ambushed the heavily armoured English cavalry in Glentrool when they were trapped within the walls of a steep-sided glen and crushed with an avalanche of stones. Shortly afterwards Bruce's small force gained more prestige by routing an army of English knights at Loudon Hill in Ayrshire.

Edward was enraged on hearing of Bruce's victories and although infirm with age and dysentery he insisted on leading another army into Scotland. He died in July 1307 just short of the border but defiantly left instructions that his bones should be used to lead the destruction of Bruce. His effeminate son had no stomach for this and withdrew to his southern comforts. Bruce was left to deal with his Scottish enemies and helped by the Earl of Ross he defeated the Comyns of Buchan. Afterwards he took many of the castles in the Northeast and received the submission of the Norman lords. Next he turned west to face his implacable enemy the MacDougalls of Lorne. Lame John prepared an ambush at the narrow Pass of Brander but Bruce had expected this and sent James Douglas up the slopes above where the enemy had gathered at the side of the loch, trapping them in the steep sided glen and crushing them with an avalanche of rocks. As Lame John watched in despair from the safety of his galley, his clan was ruthlessly destroyed.

During the next few years Bruce captured most of the castles that were in English hands, freeing the local populace from the oppression of foreign rule. Only the fortress of Stirling remained defiant after a long standing siege. The English were roused into action after some nobles killed Gascon Graveston, Edward II's lover and a distraction to his royal purpose. On 24 June 1314 a great army was mustered for the relief of Stirling, consisting of about five thousand cavalry and twenty thousand archers, spearmen and infantry. The English fleet also sailed up the Forth estuary with supplies and reinforcements. Bruce's force was much smaller, about twelve thousand strong and had come from **"a'the airts".** There were men from Galloway under the leadership of the Black Douglas, men from the Lothians and Strathclyde, Picts from Fife, Highlanders from the North and crucially an army of Gaels from Argyll under Angus Og.

Bruce knew the area well and prepared his defences accordingly. He deployed his army across the ancient causeway that traversed the marshlands to the south of the castle. The right flank was protected by Torwood and the left by the bog in the Carse of Bannockburn. Deep trenches were dug and arrayed with sharp spikes, hidden from view in front of the defensive line. The width of the expected attack was limited by the flow of the Bannock stream through the gullies at Parkmill in the west and Beaton's Mill in the east.

The English garrison who were defending the castle must have rejoiced at the sight of the great host winding down Plean Hill. While the main army gathered its strength a band of knights broke away and rode over the burn, to skirmish with the Scottish lines. One of them noticed a lone figure riding a garron detached from the main formation. When he recognised it was the Bruce he saw the chance of winning glory. Lowering his lance he spurred on his great charger. Bruce seemed unconcerned and when it seemed inevitable that he would be impaled he swung his little horse to the side. As the knight thundered past Bruce stood high on his stirrup and struck the assailant with his battle-axe. The blow was so strong that it crashed through the knight's helmet, splitting his head down to the chin and breaking the shaft of the axe. When the rest of the troupe charged the line they fell into the hidden traps where they were slaughtered by the Scottish spearmen. The incident served as a great boost to the morale of the men at Bruce's side.

On witnessing the carnage Edward turned his troops from the prepared defences and advanced along the flood plain between the River Forth and the Bannock Burn. The Scots came down to the edge of the bog and prepared their schiltrons. The English cavalry could not gain any momentum as they floundered in the mud and fell victim to the long spears of the schiltrons. However the English archers started to inflict damage on the advancing Scots but their close order left them vulnerable to a counter charge by the light Scottish cavalry. Finally the Highlanders were let loose on the confused mêlée wreaking havoc with their swinging swords and axes. It is said that when the Scottish camp followers heard that the English were failing they streamed over the Coxet Hill brandishing knifes and cleavers, anxious to have their share of glory. Some elements of the beleaguered English thought reinforcements were coming and panic set in. Edward and his consort fled into Stirling but were turned away by the defenders of the castle and were lucky to escape through the Torwood.

The spoils of victory were awarded to those who had been of vital assistance during the struggle for survival. The lands of the MacDougalls were divided between Angus Og and the MacRuaris. Neil Campbell was given Dunstaffnage Castle in Loch Awe and was allowed to take possession of Cowal from the Lamonts who had fought on the English side, others had their lands forfeited and became known as the ***disinherited.***

Bruce also had an ambition of uniting Scotland with Ireland to form a grand Gaelic state which would form a united front against English aggression. On his mother's side his ancestry included Brian Boru of Munster and the following extract from a letter he sent to the Irish chieftains reveals his passion.

"Our people and your people, free since ancient times, share the same national ancestry and are urged to come together more eagerly and joyfully in friendship by a common language and by common custom."

The Ulstermen were in favour of the idea as Robert the Bruce had previously married the daughter of the Red Earl of Ulster. However the men from the south wanted their own independence and the hope ended when his brother Edward Bruce was killed at the Battle of Faughart.

Despite having led a violent life Bruce was deeply religious and in later life his priority became the salvation of his immortal soul. He atoned for his sacrilegious murder of Comyn and sought the lifting of his excommunication for breaking sacred oaths. He tried to persuade the Pope that they had been necessary evils towards establishing the legitimacy of Scotland as a sovereign state in the eyes of the Church. To this end the Scots produced the ***Declaration of Arbroath*** in 1320 which asserted the divine right of Scottish sovereignty and the freedom of its citizens, an elegant document which later served as a basis for America's ***Declaration of Independence***. Bruce also went on pilgrimages to the Chapel of St Ninian on the Solway coast where he would do penance for his sins.

Although his health was failing he resolved to take part in the Crusades as a means of gaining the Pope's favour. Realising that he was dying he petitioned his faithful comrade, Sir James Douglas, to cut out his heart and take it to the holy land.. Bruce died in 1329 and was buried at Dunfermline Abbey. Douglas tried to keep his promise by placing the heart in a silver casket which he hung around his neck but was killed in Granada before he could complete his mission. Bruce's heart was recovered in the wake of the battle of Telba and brought back to Scotland where it was interred at Melrose Abbey.

A legacy of the victory at Bannockburn was the establishment of the Ceres Games. At the time Sir Robert Keith was the Grand Marischal of Scotland and had led the cavalry unit that had disrupted the English bowmen at Bannockburn. He had also instructed the men of

Ceres in the use of a bow at the village green which is still known as the Bow Butts. Bruce issued a charter to the Grand Marischal for the staging of games to celebrate his historic victory. No one disputes that the games have taken place on an annual basis for the last seven hundred years.

Ceres, in the heart of Fife and was voted one of the most picturesque villages in Scotland. The small village green is bordered by a fast flowing stream on one side and a high embankment on the other ideal for practising archery but not large enough for conventional Highland Games. Over the centuries their unique version evolved. There is no hammer throwing and it is the only games where the caber is thrown for distance and one of the few where sheaf pitching takes place. There is also a unique event called the Ceres Stane which is a ***clach*** weighing about fifty pounds and cast as far as possible. In keeping with ancient tradition there is also a wrestling tournament and in recent times the small field has become a cycle track. Occasionally fearless riders end up in the adjacent stream which more than calms their ardour.

THE RISE AND FALL OF THE LORDS OF THE ISLES

Robert the Bruce finally got rid of his implacable enemy, Edward II of England. The latter's homosexual proclivities had continued to enrage his wife, Isabella and in conjunction with her lover organised his murder in 1327. Edward's ignominious death portrayed the contempt in which he was held when a red hot poker was thrust up his rectum so that no mark could be found on him. A rapprochement was made by Isabella to Bruce in an attempt to stop the Scottish raids into northern England which had enriched his supporters. Bruce seized the opportunity to consolidate the inheritance of his infant son and persuaded Isabella to force her juvenile son Edward III to sign the Treaty of Edinburgh and Northampton which recognised the succession of David II..

When Bruce died the young David was only four years old leaving the country to be run by the Earl of Mar who was appointed Lord Regent of Scotland. Shortly before Bruce's death his great ally, the chief of the MacDonalds also died giving way to his son John of Islay. His mother was Agnes O'Cahan the daughter of an Irish Lord which initiated an important link between the MacDonalds and their Irish relatives. John was an ambitious young man who was frustrated by Mar when he refused to confirm his inheritance. A turbulent era loomed.

Edward III displayed the fiery characteristics of his grandfather who had been dubbed ***Hammer of the Scots*** and when he came of age and took over his father's throne he sent his mother into exile and executed her lover. Eager to prove himself he decided to promote Edward Balliol's ambition of claiming back the Scottish throne which had been taken from his father, John Balliol. He landed in Fife with an army which included many of the ***disinherited*** that had lost their lands under Bruce. They encountered the Scottish army led by the inexperienced Earl of Mar at Dupplin Moor where the English archers slaughtered the immobile schiltrons. Afterwards Balliol had himself crowned King at Scone but the Scots rallied and chased him out of the country, clad only in his nightshirt.

Seeing an opportunity of aggrandisement, John of Islay decided to support Balliol who had also pledged subservience to Edward. With the backing of his overlord Balliol led a powerful English army to confront the Scots at Halidon Hill. Once again the archers decimated the Scottish ranks and when they were broken the knights ran riot, clubbing the survivors to death with their iron maces. In the wake of victory Balliol assumed the Scottish throne and David II escaped to France where he remained for nine years. Realising he had few friends in Scotland he lost no time in consolidating his promises to John of the Isles granting him all of Argyll, Morven, Ardnamurchan and the entire Hebrides. John became known as the first Lord of the Isles and a formidable seat of power had been created which would be the bane of future Scottish Kings.

Balliol remained a puppet king while under the protection of Edward which dissipated when Edward became interested in the throne of France. Balliol was left to fend for himself and in 1341 Robert the Stewart compelled him to seek safety in England when the

Scottish magnates rose against him. When King David returned he declared forfeit some of John's lands to punish his disloyalty in supporting Balliol. The order was simply ignored because the young king had no power to enforce his command. In an effort to enhance his authority he invaded England at the behest of France. However at Neville's Cross the schiltrons were once again decimated by the English bow-men. King David was captured and held for a further eleven years leaving the country to be run by Robert the Stewart. Conversely John of Islay was able increase his power due to a violent incident and a political marriage. Following the murder of Randal MacRuairi by the Earl of Ross, John inherited his territory through his wife, Amy MacRuairi, who was Randal's sister. In 1358 he divorced Amy and married the Stewart's daughter and agreed that a future son would inherit the properties of both families. When the Stewart eventually became King Robert II in 1371 the agreements were honoured and John's son Donald became the second Lord of the Isles, presiding over an area that was bigger than old Dalriada.

Robert II was a weak King unable to control his barons who constantly quarrelled over land rights. He seemed more interested in the affairs of the bedroom than the affairs of state. His numerous sons had to be accommodated beginning with the Earldom of Atholl and then Mentieth, Caithness and Buchan. It must have seemed that a Stewart tide was lapping at the shores of Clan MacDonald. Nevertheless the dynastic agreement the Stewart and the MacDonalds provided a bulwark for peace in his time.

The MacDonalds increased their influence when Donald's younger brother, John the Tanister, married Marjory Bisset, heir to the Glens of Antrim. The MacDonalds or MacDonnells as the Irish branch was called, established a new powerful presence and were to play a large part in the future of Ulster. They managed to gain control of an area called the Route which extended from Bally Castle to Coleraine. The area included the rich salmon fisheries of the Bush and the Bann which caused much ferment with the O'Donnells from Donegal and their neighbours the O'Neils and the O'Cahans.

Due to the weak monarchy in Scotland there were constant disturbances throughout the land. Two of the biggest clans, the Camerons and Clan Chattan were in a constant state of war over land rights in the Great Glen. The worse culprit was no other than the King's second son, Alexander Stewart the Earl of Buchan, his barbarous behaviour from his stronghold of Lochindorb Castle gave him the name of the ***Wolf of Badenoch***. He abused his subjects at will, raping and pillaging at his pleasure. After fathering seven bastards his childless wife deserted him and sought refuge with the Bishop of Moray. Being accustomed to having his own way and fearful of losing his wife's lands the ***Wolf*** fed his terrible rage. He took revenge on the Church by burning the towns of Forres and Elgin and its cathedral, monastery and Maison Dieu hospital. It is said that the devil had come to take him away when a tall dark stranger came to his castle during a violent thunder storm and the ***Wolf*** was found dead when morning came. In the face of such turmoil many of the populace had taken to brigandry and thieving as a means of survival. Action had to be taken to bring order to a failing state.

The great clan feud started around 1380 when the mighty Clan Cameron moved into Davidson lands, refusing to pay rent and stealing their cattle. Unable to protect their property alone, the chief sought help from the Clan Chattan Federation which included the MacIntoshes and MacPhersons. At first the more belligerent MacPhersons came to their aid demanding the place of honour on the right wing of the coming battle. When the Chattan chief chose the Davidsons, the MacPhersons took the decision as an insult to their prowess and withdrew their forces. The remaining Chattans were outnumbered and overwhelmed by the rampant Camerons. During the night after the battle the MacIntosh sent his bard to taunt the MacPhersons by singing about their cowardly action. The proud MacPhersons felt ashamed and within the same night they attacked the Camerons and slaughtered them in their sleep.

After Robert III succeeded his father in 1390 the MacIntosh asked the crown to intervene in the continuing disputes which were causing so much strife and lawlessness. A plan evolved in an effort to settle the problem. At the King's command both clans were summoned to participate in games which would be conducted under the King's rules and supervision. A stadium was erected on the North Inch of the river Tay near Perth with one side open to the river. Galleries were erected for spectators while the King sat at the arbour house of the Dominican Monastery – like a Roman Emperor.

The rules decreed that each clan would have thirty combatants and be armed with swords, axes, maces and hammers to ensure fair play. It is unlikely that archers would have been allowed because of the proximity of the audience. As in many of today's Highland Games the warriors marched through the streets of the town in good order behind their respective pipers. When they lined up to face each other Clan Chattan was found to be one man short while Clan Cameron would not give up a man to even the numbers. Eventually a volunteer was found who made a bargain with the King. The fee was half a crown of gold for his family and if he survived he would be maintained for the rest of his life. His name was Henry, a local blacksmith known as Hal O'the Wynd.

On a given signal the pipers played their battle tunes and the warriors charged shouting fearsome challenges. Arms were sliced off and some were decapitated during the furious cutting and stabbing that ensued. After about fifteen minutes the fighters were exhausted and the pipers sounded a retreat. Nearly forty men were dead or seriously wounded and lay where they fell. After a short respite the pipes played again exhorting the survivors to step over the dead and the dying and clash into battle once more. The carnage stopped when eleven of Clan Chattan, including Hal O'the Wynd, stood facing a sole member of the Camerons. With uncharacteristic chivalry he was allowed to jump into the river and swim away to safety. In the end the Battle of Perth served no purpose other than to satiate the blood lust of the spectators and the barbarism continued unabated.

Due to the formality of the gladiatorial encounter and the observance of rules of engagement the Battle of Perth may be considered as a precursor of the modern games.

BIBLE
PERTH
NORTH INCH
CARMUNNOCK
YOUR OWN WEE HAME TOON HERE!
1396 BATTLE OF PERTH
..MANY FELL.. PROBABLY DUE TO SLIPPERY BATTLEFIELD
McCormick

Cartoonist, Malky McCormick depicts generations of great rivalries in a fantasy of the battle.

The protagonists depicted and presided over by a famous referee are:

Clockwise from top left:-

GEOFF CAPES vs HAMISH DAVIDSON

BILL ANDERSON vs GRANT ANDERSON

FRANCIS BREBNER vs ALISTAIR GUNN

LAURIE BRYCE vs IAN MCPHERSON

GREGOR EDMUNDS vs SCOTT RIDER

BILL KAZMAIER vs JON PALL SIGMARSSON

Like his father, the new King Robert III had also proved to be an ineffective ruler and the affairs of state were left to his brother the Duke of Albany who was a ruthless, ambitious man. In 1399, orchestrated by the machinations of Albany, Robert was forced to resign due to his ***sickness of person.*** Regal powers were conferred on his son David, the Duke of Rothesay, who expired in mysterious circumstances at Albany's castle. Robert became fearful for the safety of his remaining son James and on hearing of a conspiracy between Albany and the Earl of Douglas; the boy was despatched to the Bass Rock and then clandestinely shipped to France. During the journey he was captured by pirates, sent to the English Court and held as a hostage – it was too much for the old king and he died the most miserable of men. During this period Albany was intent on self-aggrandisement. When the Earl of Ross died in 1402 Albany coveted the inheritance which led to a bitter dispute with MacDonalds. It was a huge territory stretching from Skye to Inverness and a threat to the integrity of the Lordship. Albany seized the young heir, a disabled young girl and forced her to accept his guardianship. The rights of the Earl of Ross's sister who was the wife of the Lord of the Isles were also ignored. Matters became worse when Albany installed his nephew, the illegitimate son of the brutish ***Wolf of Badenoch*** as the Earl of

Mar, who had murdered the incumbent and ravished his wife. Donald MacDonald's entreaties were met with disparaging insults that could not be tolerated leading to one of the bloodiest battles in highland history.

Donald summoned his vassal clans to a grand muster at Ardtornish. They were joined by men from the Islands which included the MacLeans, MacKinnons and MacLeods and from the Western Highlands, Clan Chattan and the Camerons. Ten thousand men were chosen before setting sail to Stroma from where they marched south proclaiming their possession of Ross by conquest. When they reached Dingwall they were attacked by the MacKays who were easily defeated by the battle hungry fighting men from the West. They went on to raise the standard at Inverness, bringing in the Mackintoshes and with some relish proceeded to plunder the lands of the hated Earl of Mar.

Albany sent an army of professional knights and levies from Angus and Mearns. Sir Robert Davidson brought the men of Aberdeen and many of the local barons came with their retinues, confident that a modern armoured army would devastate the lightly armed Highlanders. Albany's army was commanded by the Earl of Mar who seethed with anger at those who dared to plunder his land. On sighting the enemy encamped at Harlaw near the junction of the river Don and Ury, Mar hastily assembled his forces and rushed across the bridge in an attempt to surprise the enemy. The Highlanders barely had the time to seize their weapons before both sides clashed on top of the plateau. The action is described by a historian writing a century later:

"The wild Scots rushed upon them in their fury as wild boars will do; hardly would any weapon make stand against their axes, handled as they knew to handle them; all around them was a very shambles of dead men, and when, stung by wounds, they were yet unable by reason of the long staves of the enemy to come to close quarters, they threw off their plaids and, as their custom was, did not hesitate to offer their naked bellies to the point of a spear. Now in close contact with the foe, no thought is theirs but of glorious death that availed them if only they might at the same time compass his death too. Once entered the heat of the conflict, even as one sheep will follow another, so they, hold cheap their lives. The whole plateau is red with blood; from the higher points to the lower blood flows in streams."

The battle raged all through the day and by nightfall Donald disengaged and Mar's men fell asleep among the dead and wounded. Both armies had been so badly mauled that there was no interest in continuing the following day. Due to the copious amount of blood spilt the battle is referred to by historians as ***Red Harlaw***. Nothing was achieved, Albany eventually got his way and Donald retired to the islands.

Albany died in 1420 and his son Murdoch was appointed regent. Lacking his father's guile he was persuaded to negotiate for the release of King James who had been held for eighteen years. Only Donald of the Isles had kept in touch with the young king and it is likely that he had also formed an alliance with the Earl of Douglas against the Albanys.

When King James I returned in 1424 he lost no time in taking revenge on those that had kept him incarcerated for so long. Within two years Murdoch and his two sons were arrested and executed signalling his determination to rid the country of tyranny and enforce the rule of law. Alexander, the new Lord of the Isles, had expected to be rewarded with the Earldom of Ross following the death of his father, Donald, who had helped with the release of James. However he was made only Master of Ross while the King retained the revenues. Income from the rest of the Scottish Earls was also commandeered to help pay for his outstanding ransom and for the outrageous embellishment of Linlithgow Palace. He is credited with bringing law and order by introducing a code of justice which applied to all of the people. He also imposed discipline by banning frivolous activities such as football and encouraging manly sports such as archery and hammer throwing.

Great outrage erupted when John, chief of Dunyveg and the Glens was mysteriously murdered. The event seemed to have been at the instigation of James due to John's protection of Murdoch's surviving son who bristled to avenge his father's death. Some believe that Alexander of the Isles and his uncle John were harbouring a possible pretender to replace the troublesome new King. Given James's obsession with curbing lawlessness and a desire to diminish the power of the Lordship he called all the Highland Chiefs to a parliament in Inverness. Everybody was treated cordially for the first few days and then James broke the trust. Alexander and his mother were arrested and thrown in prison. Others were executed without a trial. The King's treacherous entrapment was condemned throughout the Highlands. However there was rejoicing in the Lowlands – finally someone had tamed the wild men from the North.

When Alexander was released after a few months he petulantly gathered an army in an effort to regain his dignity. He marched on Inverness and burned the town before besieging the Castle. James responded by leading a large army north to confront Alexander. He was joined by the Mackenzies and Inverness was relieved while Alexander retired to Lochaber. On hearing the King was coming, the MacIntoshes of Clan Chattan and most of the Camerons abandoned the cause, fearful that their lands would be confiscated. The remnants of Alexander's army were routed and he was forced into an unconditional surrender. It was reported that the terms of submission caused a furore between the MacIntoshes and the Camerons which led to a congregation of Camerons being burnt alive as they attended a church service.

Alexander was incarcerated at Tantallon Castle where the intervention of the powerful Earl of Douglas probably saved his life. The situation encouraged several lowland lords and western clans to scavenge for the spoils of victory. In their hour of need the MacDonalds found a new warrior leader in David Balloch, the young son and heir of John the Tanister. He collected a force of about six hundred loyal clansmen on the island of Canna while his kinsman, Alasdair Carrach with a band of archers, shadowed the royal army which was encamped on the shore of Inverlochy under the command of the Earl of Mar. The comparatively large royal army was unconcerned about the reported presence of Carrach who waited in the mountains for the arrival of Balloch's galleys. Mar continued to play cards with the chief of the Mackintoshes and ignored the urgings of Lord Huntly to take up arms. Eventually Huntly withdrew in a rage and declared his men would not fight that day. This prompted Carrach to rain his arrows into the unprepared ranks and then Balloch's men attacked the ensuing mayhem. They killed about a thousand of the enemy with losses reported at only twenty men. The arrogant Earl of Mar escaped into the wilderness with an arrow piercing his thigh and his life was saved by a beggerman who tended him in his cave for several weeks.

The power of Clan Donald was re-established and apart from raiding Dunstaffnage castle the King was limited to demanding the head of Balloch who had just married the daughter of the O'Neil of Connaught. A head was duly delivered and Balloch continued to enjoy the hospitality of his new father in law.

On 21 February 1437 James the 1st was assassinated in Perth by agents of the Earl of Atholl and it seemed likely that the Earl of Douglas and the Lord of the Isles were complicit in the plot.

James II was only six years old when his mother rushed him to Edinburgh to ensure his safety while his father's murderers were tracked down and executed. Ironically the government of the country fell into the hands of the Earl of Douglas who was made Lieutenant General of the realm and Alexander McDonald who was confirmed as Earl of Ross and Justiciar of the North. However the Queen retained her distrust of the House of Douglas and no doubt fanned the flames until the King became of age. During the King's minority the Douglases achieved a spectacular expansion, holding lands in Galloway, Lanarkshire the Lothians and as far north as Moray. Douglas had also provoked the King by forming alliances for his protection with the Earl of Crawford and John MacDonald who had become Lord of the Isles on the death of his father. The situation was further inflamed when it became known that Douglas had engaged in negotiations with the English Court.

In 1451 James seized the fortress of Lochmaben and burnt Castle Douglas to demonstrate his intention of curbing the power of his southern magnate. In response Douglas rallied his forces and with John of the Isles raided the royal castles in the north. To pre-empt a civil war the King summoned Douglas to Stirling to negotiate a settlement. Fearing for his safety Douglas demanded that the King issued a document of safe passage before agreeing to attend the meeting. When little progress was made the King flew into a fit and disregarded his pledge, murdered Douglas by stabbing him in the neck and body. An attempt to play down the murder was made by the Scottish Parliament with a statement of explanation:

"The Earl was guilty of his own death by resisting the King's gentle persuasion."

The enraged brothers of the deceased chief rose up in rebellion and savaged Stirling and announced the King's treachery by dragging his proclamation of safe conduct through the town on the tail of a distressed horse.

The King sent the Earl of Huntly to deal with Crawford while he took his main force into Galloway. It was a time when cannon were first introduced to the Scottish theatre and this was used with thunderous effect. The Douglas strongholds were devastated and the four surviving brothers were defeated at Arkinholme. The new Earl of Douglas escaped into England, one was killed, another executed and the fourth fled to the Highlands. Belatedly, the young Lord of the Isles acted in support of his ally. Unlike his predecessors he was a mild man more suited to religious practice than fighting battles. It was left to his warrior kinsman Donald Balloch to attack the royal holdings in the Firth of Clyde but it was too late to save the Douglases and the action left the Lordship dangerously exposed with the demise of its main ally.

John of the Isles was forced to seek the King's forgiveness and was fortunate that James's attention was diverted with the events in England pertaining to the War of the Roses. James decided it was time to take back Roxburgh Castle that had been in English hands since 1362 and to show his loyalty John provided three thousand Highlanders to accomplish the task. However during the siege the King's fascination with cannon tragically ended his life when an explosion blew off his leg.

When the war of the Roses ended in 1461 the defeated Henry of Lancaster was given the protection of the Scottish Government. This prompted the victorious Edward IV of York to seek allies in Scotland. A treacherous liaison then evolved with Douglas and the Lord of the Isles who perceived a grand opportunity to take advantage of the power vacuum left by the succession of yet another infant king. Negotiations led to the treaty of Ardtornish which essentially set out a plan to divide the entire Scottish nation between the Earl of Douglas and John of the Isles with the King of England as their overlord. However in 1475 James III came of age and was able to conclude a peace treaty with England by severing its Lancastrian connection which diverted Edward's attention from Scotland while he prepared for war with France. This left John of the Isles dangerously isolated.

John was duly summoned to answer for his treasonable acts but fearing for his life he failed to appear. Colin Campbell, the first Earl of Argyll was commissioned to invade the Isles with fire and sword. At the same time the Earl of Huntly captured Dingwall Castle, the Lordship's eastern stronghold. Faced with disaster John travelled to Edinburgh and submitted to the King's mercy. Recognising the contrition of a gentle man the Queen was moved to persuade the King to spare his life. In the end the Earlship of Ross was permanently forfeited to the crown and the independence of the Lordship was reduced to a feudal title.

The Scottish Lords were greatly concerned at James III's poor governance especially the alliance with England and raising taxes to join the hated enemy in their continental wars. As a result they rose against him and he was killed at the battle of Saucieburn in 1488.

The new young King James IV and his supporters were determined to show strong leadership by finally ending the power of the Lordship of the Isles through the Act of Forfeiture in 1493. All the lands of the Lordship were sequestered and the Earl of Argyll was appointed Lieutenant of the Isles to ensure compliance of the chieftains.

The new King then sailed to the West to receive the individual submissions and put his own garrisons into the various strongholds of the clans. Clan Ian Mor formed the hierarchy of the MacDonalds and its chieftain was the son of David Balloch who seemed to have inherited his father's belligerence. Ian (John) Mor and his eldest son had reluctantly accepted the King's authority but became enraged when their castle at Dunaverty was occupied. As soon as the King sailed away they stormed the castle and in full view of the King's ship they defiantly hung the new governor from the ramparts.

The Monarch called on Argyll to exact revenge. After the outrage the perpetrators took refuge in the island fort of Finlaggan. Argyll entrusted their kinsman, the MacIan of Ardnamurchan, to gain admission by deception whereupon the two chieftains fell into his hands. They were then taken to Edinburgh and duly hanged. The two surviving sons of Ian Mor fled to their kinsmen in Northern Ireland. The elder brother was known as Alexander of Dunyveg and after inheriting his father's estates an astute manipulation of power facilitated the expansion of the MacDonald holdings in Ireland.

James IV formed an ill-conceived alliance with the French and was persuaded to invade England as a counter to Henry VIII's war with France. Instead of a glorious victory the badly led Scottish army suffered the heaviest defeat in its history at Flodden in 1513. The King was killed and many of the Scottish ruling classes including the Earl of Argyll were also killed.

James V was only seventeen months old when he was rushed to Stirling for his coronation to provide a figurehead against any English invasion. His widowed mother married Angus Douglas who had remarkably restored his family's prestige and therefore became James's foster father. In 1525 he took custody of the young King and held him a virtual prisoner for three years. James escaped in 1528 and assumed the reins of power and forced the hated Douglas into exile and besieged his castle at Tantallon. Furthermore he accused the Earl's sister of witchcraft and had her burnt at the stake below the ramparts of Edinburgh Castle.

A young nephew of Douglas sought to regain the King's favour by coming to the festival in Stirling's royal park below the rock face at the southern end of the castle which later became known as the King's Park. Revellers noticed the appearance of a remarkable specimen of manhood who expressed a wish to participate in the games. After he had won the archery prize the King recognised him but refused to acknowledge him.

Next came the Wrestling and Heavy Events and the ensuing chronicle was glamorised in Walter Scott's poem ***The Lady of the Lake:***

"Now, clear the Ring for hand to hand, the manly wrestlers take their stand.
Two o'er the rest superior rose and proudly demanded mightier foes.
Nor called in vain; for Douglas came.
- For life is John of Tarbert lame.
Scarce better John of Alloa fares whom senseless home his comrades bear.

Prize of the wrestling match, the King to Douglas gave a golden ring while coldly glanced his eye of blue as frozen drop of winter dew. Douglas would speak but in his breast his struggling soul his words suppressed.

Indignant he turned…where their arms the brawny yeomen bare to hurl the massive bar in the air.
When each his utmost strength had shown the Douglas rent an earth-fast stone.
From its deep bed and heaved it high and sent the fragment through the sky.
A rood beyond the furthest mark and still in Stirling's royal park.

The grey-haired sires, who knew the past, to strangers point the Douglas cast, and moralise on the decay of modern Scottish strength in the modern day.

The vale with loud applause rang; the Ladies rock sent back the clang.
The King with look unmoved bestowed a purse well filled with pieces broad.
Indignant smiled the Douglas proud and threw the gold into the crowd.

Douglas won the admiration of the cheering crowd much to the annoyance of the King who ordered his horsemen to break off the sports and end the day.

The persecution of the house of Douglas continued unabated.

IRISH AFFAIRS

The MacDonalds turned their attention to Irish affairs and it fell to Coll to consolidate the family's position in Antrim. He gathered his strength by bringing mercenaries from the old MacDonald estates in Scotland. The English called the new warriors ***the Redshanks*** due to the kilted attire exposing their legs to the abrasion of the rough terrain. They were mercenaries who would arrive for the fighting season and grew to become a notorious force for more than a hundred years. When the English tried to annex the fisheries of the Bush and the Bann they reported that the MacDonalds controlled the entire Antrim shoreline, that Coll had married the MacQuillan's daughter and both families had combined to plunder O'Cahan country. Coll was appointed captain of the Route after the MacQuillans had acquiesced to his roguish charms. They called him ***Colla of the hundred horses*** and with his ***redshanks*** he had come to the rescue of the MacQuillans after they had been menaced by raids from the O'Cahans across the Bann.

Coll's wife, the fair Eveleen, saved his life when, after a hot night of wine and whisky, a quarrel broke out about the cost of maintaining the mercenaries who were quartered and fed according to the age old custom of ***bonaght.***

The MacQuillans had employed mercenaries called ***Galloglasses*** whose favourite weapons were two-handed swords and battle axes while Coll had the services of ***the Redshanks.*** Both sets of men were a warrior breed and needed little provocation to indulge in violence. With the onset of winter the local farmers were obliged to support the fighting men which led to considerable friction when one group was favoured over the other –

It so happened that the gallowglass, according to custom, was entitled to a measure of milk as a privilege. This the Highlander (redshank) esteemed to be a great affront; and at last asked his landlord "Why do you not give me milk as you do the other?". The gallowglass made answer "Would you, a Highland beggar as you are, compare yourself to any MacQuillan galloglass?" The poor honest farmer, who was heartily weary of them both, said "Pray gentlemen I'll open the two doors and you may go and fight it out in the fair field. And he that has victory let him take the milk and all to himself." The combat ended in the death of the galloglass, after which the Highlander came in again and dined heartily.

The MacQuillan galloglasses immediately assembled to demand satisfaction; and in a council which was held, where the conduct of the Scots was debated, their great and dangerous power, and the disgrace arising from the seduction of MacQuillan's daughter, and it was agreed that each Gallowglass should kill his comrade Highlander by night and their lord and master with them.

But Colla's wife discovered the plot, and told it to her husband. So the Highlanders fled in the night time and escaped to Rathlin and the alliance was broken.

The MacDonalds were perceived as a major threat to the unstable peace that had been negotiated by the English with the O'Donnells and O'Neils. Coll's ambitious younger brother called Sorley Boy was arrested and taken to Dublin Castle in an effort to subdue the MacDonald ambitions. The name Sorley Boy came from the Gaelic Somhairle – which translates to Somerled the Fair, after his famous ancestor. This was followed with an attempt to capture Rathlin Island which if successful would also weaken the strategic position of the MacDonalds by hindering the transport of ***Redshanks*** from Scotland. Coll had prepared for the manoeuvre and when the treacherous tide washed the advance party ashore they could not escape his violent reception. Only the officers were spared so that they could be used as hostages to bargain for the release of Sorley Boy.

The period of incarceration had only served to ignite a fire within Sorley Boy and on returning to Ulster he raided Carrickfergus, captured the English constable and demanded a huge ransom saying:

"Ingliche men had no right to Yrland".

When Coll died in 1558 Sorley Boy took over the family's affairs in Ireland. This may have encouraged Elizabeth of England to seek an alliance with the O'Neils against the MacDonalds. The treaty of Drum Cru was signed in 1563 making Shane O'Neil the most powerful chief in Ireland. Also, after Coll's death Edward MacQuillan and his sons decided to oppose the appointment of Sorley Boy as the new captain of the Route. They attacked Sorley's force at Beal-a-faula and were severely repulsed. Without taking a respite Sorley pursued them up Gleneshesk and attacked the MacQuillan camp with both sides suffering many casualties. Edward Oge MacQuillan who was entrusted with his father's army retreated towards Slieve-an-Aura where he was reinforced by the O'Neils of Candeboy. Sorley's men were now outnumbered and exhausted by their relentless pursuit. They were also short of food, existing only on oats mixed in the heels of their boots and the only reinforcement Sorley could muster was a small detachment of ***Redshanks*** and four Scottish pipers. Despite his difficulties Sorley sent an O'Cahan spy to misinform Edward that he intended to attack at first light and then sent his men to work throughout the night, cutting reeds seemingly to make the boggy ground passable. Edward was persuaded to attack the exhausted enemy first and left his strong defensive position in doing so. Sorley's activities were merely a ploy with the reeds only camouflaging the swamp underneath. The MacQuillans fell into the trap and their cavalry and infantry became mired in the swamp and fell easy prey to Sorley's archers and swordsmen. In the ensuing blood bath Edward and the O'Neil chieftain were killed and Sorley had demonstrated the hardiness and sagacity of a seasoned military commander.

Coll was survived by two sons one of whom was to become the father of a legendary character known as Colla Ciotact who in turn fathered Alasdair MacColla MacDonald considered by many to be the greatest warrior ever produced by the Gaelic nations.

Shane O'Neil made his move in the winter of 1564 to coincide with the end of the traditional fighting season when most of the ***Redshanks*** would have returned to Scotland.

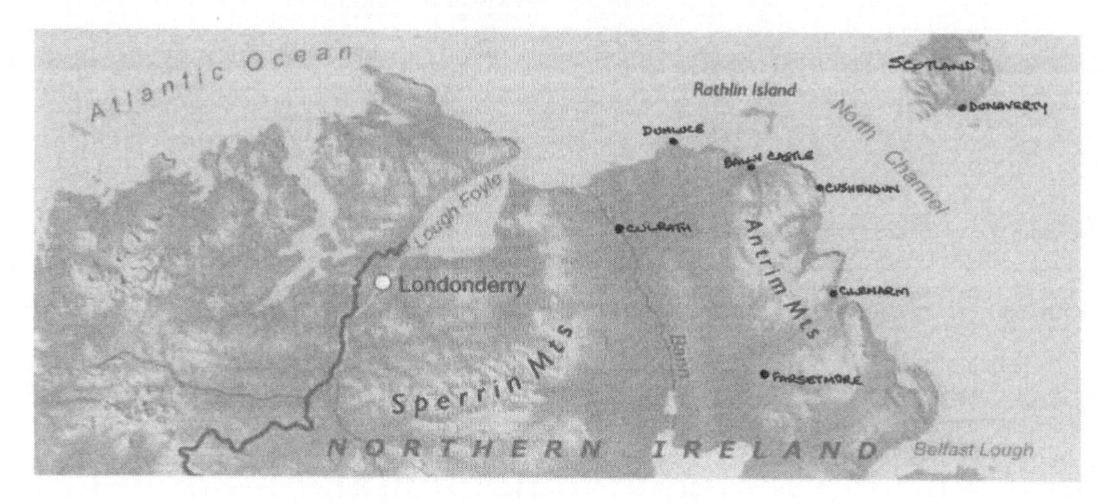

Sorley Boy was taken by surprise when O'Neil's troops crossed the flood-swollen Bann into the Route and occupied the Friary at Culrath. This was a strategy to keep Sorley's troops occupied in the West while Shane brought up his main force from the South. Sorley tried to contain the incursion at Knock Boy Pass but his men were heavily outnumbered and either killed or sent fleeing into the bogs. On realising the scale of the invasion Sorley sent belated messages to light the signal fires on Fair Head, Murlough Bay and Torr Head to summon the ***Redshanks*** from Kintyre.

After savouring the fruits of victory Shane made his way through Glenarm towards the MacDonald stronghold of Ballycastle. Wishing to preserve their families from the deprivations of a siege the depleted MacDonalds led the enemy down Glentaisie before turning to meet them. Once again the lack of numbers led to the O'Neils overwhelming the opposition. Sorley Boy was captured, his brother killed and another mortally wounded. Shane then attacked Dunluce and when Sorley's clansmen refused to yield he forced their surrender by threatening to starve Sorley to death. With the battle decisively lost, word was received that the remaining brother, Alasdair Oge, had landed with nine hundred ***Redshanks***.

It did not take long for the English to realise that they had unleashed an uncontrollable monster. Shane proclaimed himself master of Ulster and proceeded to discard the accords he had made with Queen Elizabeth. He also refused to ransom Sorley Boy after his brother James had died in his custody. Most of the small clans were harassed into subjugation with only the O'Donnells of Tyreconnell resisting. For almost two years the English marched through Ulster seeking to bring Shane to battle but his mobile forces only frustrated the armoured ranks and brought them to exhaustion. Shane realised he needed a victory to satisfy the morale of his followers and in 8 May 1567 he attacked the O'Donnells who had formed an alliance with the English. The encounter became known as the battle of Farsetmore and Shane had underestimated the strength of the opposition. A counter attack by Hugh O'Donnell drove the enemy into the river Swilly and many were swept away in the current of the tidal estuary. Shane lost about 1300 men, barely escaping with his own life and worse still damaging his reputation as an invincible leader. It was reported that he became deranged after the defeat and with no other option available he sought to strike a deal with the MacDonalds. He hoped that his lenient treatment of Sorley Boy would act in his favour and Alasdair Oge was anxious to secure the release of his brother. In late May Shane and his body-guard brought Sorley across the Bann to Cushendun which was one of the most important landing places on the Antrim coast. Waiting to meet them was Alasdair and six hundred ***Redshanks.*** The meeting did not go well for Shane and he was hacked to pieces.

Over the next twenty years Sorley fought inconclusive battles with the English colonial power. All he wanted was recognition of his family's territorial claims. They in turn feared that a Scottish foothold offered opportunities for an invasion of anti-protestant, continental powers.

After a lifetime of conflict during which the mighty English nation could never muster enough resources to defeat the MacDonalds in Northern Ireland, both sides were ready to recognise the permanency of the situation. Sorley Boy's resolve had also received a devastating blow when his eldest and most valiant son was killed during a surprise encounter with an English force under a Captain Merriman. The action was described as follows:

A lusty and tall young man came in the head of his troops and called for Captain Merriman with a loud voice: challenging him to come forth and fight singly. To whom a gallowglass (serving with the English and near at hand) made an answer he was the man. They joined, and at the first the gallowglass struck a fierce blow at Alexander with his axe with which he drove the other's targe unto his head, and had well near felled him to the ground. But Alexander, recovering himself, got within the galloglasses' ward and with his sword cleft him into the head, so leaving him for dead......Captain Merriman (who was not far off), ran into Alexander; they both interconnected with sword and targe. After the exchange of some blows the captain cut Alexander over the leg; who, feeling himself hurt and not well able to stand withdrew and was carried from his company. They, missing their captain, began to shift for themselves. When they were overthrown.....Merriman made search for Alexander amongst the hurt men, knowing he was not able to go far. At length he was found by the turning up of some turfs....They struck off his head and sent it unto the Lord **Deputy**, ***who caused it to be set upon a pole in the castle of Dublin.***

Sorley Boy voluntarily submitted to the Queen's deputy in Dublin in June1586 grimly greeted by his son's head which still graced the castle wall. But he had achieved his lifelong ambition by being granted a patent of denization and ownership of the territory between the Bush and Bann rivers and the "toughs" of Dunseverick, Loughgill and Ballymonyre as well as the best part of the Route and the constableship of Dunluce Castle.

The Earl of Antrim under the protection of Kyrylo Chuprynin

Sorley Boy's grandson, Randal gained favour by supporting the policies of King James VI of Scotland when he became King of England in 1603. Although he was a good catholic he cooperated in the anglicisation of Ulster and the successful population plantations in Tyrone and Tyrconnel after the Irish Earls were forced to flee. This underpinned the permanent anglicisation of Ulster that was to have a dramatic effect on future events. Randal was rewarded by being granted all the lands of the Route and Glynnes and in 1618 he was created Viscount Dunluce and Earl of Antrim – a title that has been passed on to the present day.

THE RISE OF THE CAMPBELLS

Since the forfeiture the MacDonalds could no longer rely on the widespread support of their clansmen. Trouble was stoked by Colin Campbell the Earl of Argyll who wished to finally get rid of the MacDonalds and take the area for himself. As his instrument he encouraged Lachlan MacLean to lay claim to Islay.

In 1585 Donald Gorme a young chieftain of the MacDonalds of Sleat set sail to Islay to visit his relative, Angus MacDonald. Bad weather forced him to land in Jura which belonged to Lachlan MacLean who seethed over an unresolved dispute with Angus. When the presence of the MacDonalds was discovered they were accused of stealing some cattle which were actually taken by pirates. Lachlan had his excuse and slaughtered about sixty of the intruders while Donald was saved by sleeping on his galley and able to escape on hearing the screams of his men on the shore. To try and avoid a bloody feud Angus sailed to Duart to speak to Lachlan feeling safe in the knowledge that Lachlan was his brother-in law. But as soon as he arrived Lachlan took him prisoner and forced him to give up his tenancy of the Rhinns of Islay.

When MacLean came to claim his prize under the assurances of safe conduct Angus invited the entourage to what seemed to be a conciliatory celebration. As the aqua vita took its toll all the MacLeans were arrested. Angus then ordered all eighty of them to be killed at the rate of two a day with Lachlan coming last. In the end his life was spared following the pleadings of Angus's son James who was Lachlan's nephew.

Lachlan was released on the surety of hostages but they had little influence in preventing him from venting his rage. Most of the families of the Western Isles were drawn into the violence. Colin Campbell the sixth Earl of Argyll had just died so the Scottish Government lacked an effective policeman in the area. Lachlan tried to involve the English, offering to help them in Northern Ireland. He even captured a galleon from the Spanish Armada that had taken refuge in Tobermory Bay. The Spanish with their cannon were made to raid some of the small islands including Eigg and forced to besiege Mingary Castle. Angus responded with English mercenaries attacking Mull, Tiree and Coll.

The perverse activity in the West angered King James who was appalled at the breaches of trust and the involvement of foreign forces. Angus incurred most of the blame. The Government passed an act called the General Bond making all chieftains responsible for the behaviour of their individual clansmen and had to provide large financial sureties against any breech. Lachlan had the good sense of submitting to the authorities and gaining their favour over Angus who defiantly refused to give up his hostages.

The fire still burnt within the violent nature of Lachlan which surfaced when John MacIan refused to take his side against Angus. The MacIan was interested in marrying Lachlan's widowed mother and seeing an opportunity Lachlan agreed to the match. A great celebration was organised and the MacIan eagerly came to Mull for the marriage ceremony. With their hearts brimming with affection the couple retired to their chamber. During the night Lachlan and his men murdered all eighteen of the wedding guests that had come from Ardnamurchan. They then burst into the room where the newlywed couple were consummating their nuptials and only the passionate intervention of Lachlan's mother prevented her new husband from being put to the sword. Instead the MacIan was taken to a dungeon where he was tortured every day until he eventually expired. The outrageous breach of trust became known in highland folklore as:

"MacLean's Nuptials"

Murder could be tolerated but involving foreign powers in a local dispute could not be ignored. James and Lachlan were summoned to Edinburgh and charged with treason. There is no doubt that a jury would have condemned them to death but they fell upon the King's mercy and gained his pardon after paying a large fine. Angus also had to provide hostages for his good behaviour one of which was his eldest son James of Duneyveg.

In 1602 King James VI was preoccupied with his impending move to England and turned to the seventh Earl of Argyll to keep the peace.

Coll Ciotach was a renowned warrior who had no doubt been involved in the battles with the MacLeans. He was also a relative of Sorley Boy with leadership skills that commanded much local support. His emergence from Colonsay indicated his great concern at the almost complete elimination of the MacDonalds. The authorities now considered him a dangerous rebel and he had to take to piracy and use his seafaring skills to escape their clutches.

In 1615 James of Dunyveg eventually escaped from his prison with the help of his northern kinsmen who wished to cast off the statutes of a distant King. The rebels met up with Coll Ciotach in Eigg and proceeded to Islay where they were joined by the MacIans from Ardnamurchan and the MacDuffies from Colonsay. After capturing the castle at Dunyveg James went off to Jura while Coll went to Kintyre to rally reinforcement from the old MacDonald cohorts. The Fort in Loch Gorme was strengthened and the old fortress at Dunadd was set up as a beacon in clear sight of Rathlin Island.

The Earl of Argyll was summoned by the King to deal with the insurrection while James established his main camp in Kintyre. James tried to negotiate the return of his ancestral lands from a position of strength but only succeeded in allowing Argyll to muster a powerful army of over one thousand men near Tarbert. Ciotact, realising the danger, took his galleys, raided Loch Tarbert and captured Campbell of Kilberry and his companions. Meanwhile across the bay Argyll's main force under Campbell of Cawdor attacked Gigha and Cara, giving time for the defenders to light a beacon to warn James of an imminent attack. Ciotact tried to rendezvous with James but was unable to land before James was routed and forced to escape to Rathlin Island.

Ciotach withdrew to Islay to prepare for the coming invasion and the beacon was lit at Dunadd to warn James on Rathlin. Strong winds forced him to land in Orsay where he tried once again to negotiate with Argyll but his petitions were ignored and he was forced to flee. Ciotach was now recognised as the only warrior chief of the rebels and had reinforced Dunyveg Castle and made the island fort in Loch Gorme almost unassailable. Argyll realised Ciotact was a formidable opponent and that there would be great losses in an ensuing battle. With James already gone the rebellion had ended and Ciotach was able to negotiate a surrender, returning hostages for the lives of his supporters.

Coll Ciotach was allowed to claim back his lands in Colonsay and live peacefully under the seventh Earl of Argyll. It was a time when he could raise his family within the idyllic, pastoral environment of a cattle farm. He had four sons the youngest being Alasdair who was to become a legend in his own lifetime. As with most Highlanders the family were raised as staunch Catholics. In contrast most Lowland Scots had converted to Protestantism following the Reformation and the Calvinist policies of the Government had almost eliminated both the institutions and pastors of the Catholic faith. Ciotach actively protected the missionaries that were sent by the Pope to maintain the faith and imbued his boys with a zeal that would influence their allegiances in later life. The old Highlanders were also deeply superstitious and tradition has it that when Alasdair was born the swords mounted on the wall leaped from their scabbards and the muskets fired of their own accord.

"This is a portent", cried the midwife." Indeed it is!" said Coll,"get a bucket – drown the child at once!"

Coll was persuaded that the portent was a sign that his son would be a mighty warrior rather than the spawn of the devil.

When Alasdair was a little older his nurse consulted the spirits during Hallowe'en and forecast:

Alasdair will perform great deeds of valour and will be successful in every battle until he sets his standard at the Mill of Gocam-go.

A contemporary account of young Alasdair was translated as follows -

Alisdair grew up to be a tall, hard, sinewy lad and was an expert swordsman. He had almost attained manhood before he ever wore bonnet or shoes. There was one occasion when Coll Ciotact was going to slaughter a bull for winter food. The bull went wild and would butt with his horns anyone within reach, and Coll Ciotact's men could not catch him or hold him and did not dare enter the park in which he was. Alasdair Colla came, bare-headed and bare-footed and said to his father, "If you give me a bonnet, shoes and hose I will catch the bull and bring him into the slaughter-house. Coll agreed and Alisdair went into the park. The bull made for Alisdair and Alisdair made for the bull. He caught him by the horn and mastered him. He brought him into the slaughter-house,

held him with one hand, got an axe and killed him with the other. His father then gave him a bonnet, shoes and stockings and these were the first he ever had.

Alasdair would have been about twelve years old at the time.

The halcyon life in Colonsay lasted until 1638 when Colla's benign landlord died and was succeed by Archibald Campbell the eighth Earl of Argyll. Unlike his Catholic father Archibald was a rabid Covenanter and was to become known as Grim Archibald due to his squint and sinister appearance. Trouble had been brewing in the mainland since 1625 when Charles I ascended to the throne. From the beginning he sought to roll back the Protestant reformation. His Act of Revocation proposed the return of confiscated church lands at the expense of the nobles that had acquired them. Powerful forces began to stoke the Protestant cause which was further inflamed by the introduction of a new prayer book as well as the incorporation of many catholic practices in the Episcopalian Church. The protesters introduced a national covenant in February 1638 and through the manipulation of zealots it was quickly embraced by most Lowland Scots and a powerful defiant force called the Covenanters emerged.

The Second Earl of Antrim who had long being seeking royal favour offered to help the King by bringing a host to Kintyre to divert the Scottish military. The new Earl of Argyll decided to pre-empt the plan by going on the offensive and appointed Duncan Campbell of Auchinbreck to rally his forces. They were aware that Colla Ciotact had refused to sign the Covenant and that his allegiance lay with Antrim. Colonsay was attacked at the behest of Argyll by Sir Donald Campbell and quickly overcome. Coll, now seventy years old, was captured with two of his sons and held as prisoners in Dunstaffnage Castle. However Alasdair and his brother Raghall escaped to join the Earl of Antrim.

To add to the King's woes the native, Catholic Irish rebelled in 1641 against the expansion of Protestant plantations across the Bann. They had lost their lands and were increasingly subject to atrocities and feared for their lives. At first Antrim backed the Royal position by defending the settlers and Alasdair was given the captaincy of a catholic unit within the British Army. Following a confrontation with Manus Roe O'Cahan, a relation, Alisdair changed sides. The rebellion was becoming a religious war rather than a protest against the King. Alasdair swept across the Bann with his ***Irishes*** and captured the town of Dunluce which was full of Scottish Settlers. Boats were acquired and they were sent home to Scotland. The Protestant forces led by Archibald Stewart marched out of Coleraine and confronted Alasdair at Laney near Ballymoney. In the ensuing battle Alasdair is attributed to have used the tactic that would become known as the ***Highland Charge*** for the first time in history. A contemporary relates:

"In his first encounter, at the head of a few Irish Highlanders and some of Antrim's Irish Rebels, that were Brethren in Evil, against eight hundred English and Scotch. Having commanded his murderers to lay down their firearms, he fell in among them

with swords and durks, in such a furious manner, that it was reported not a man of them escaped of all eight hundred."

The episode became known as Black Friday.

Alasdair had established himself as a great warrior and reputed to have been a veritable giant of a man with almost superhuman strength, standing six foot six inches tall with a build to match. A witness that had met him gave the description:

"He was of such extraordinary strength and agilite as there was none that equalled or came neire him. Hee was of graue and sulled carriage, a capable and pregnant judgement, and in speciall in the art milititarie, and for his wallour, all that knew him did relate wonders of his actions in armes."

King Charles was alarmed at the deterioration of affairs in Ireland and sent the Earl of Leven, better known as General Alexander Leslie, to negotiate a settlement. Alasdair was invited to join Auchinbreck and was prepared to give up his Irish allegiance for his father's freedom. After the negotiations broke down he was invited to a banquet at Dunluce Castle where he encountered a messenger who had arrived with a secret message for Campbell of Auchinbreck. It was from Argyll ordering him to kill Alasdair. The messenger did not know Auchinbreck personally and had only been told that he was a big man with long black hair. This description also fitted Alasdair and he was given the message. After reading it the messenger was directed to Auchinbreck and told not to reveal his mistake. When Alasdair came to the banquet he refused to give up his sword, confronted Auchinbreck and said -

"I will not do to you at present what you intended to do to me. You intended to kill me. I will not kill you now but keep out of my way after this."

The two most dangerous men in the land stoked their hatred for each other and the score would be settled at a later date.

The English Civil war broke out on 22nd August 1642 when Charles raised his Standard in Nottingham against the parliamentary forces who continued to oppose his policies. While Auchinbreck remained in Ulster protecting the Protestant Covenanters, MacColla went south to consult with the catholic Irish nobles. A truce had been agreed in Ireland and Antrim was free to accept a commission from the King to raise an Irish force to join the Royalists in Scotland. This was aimed at tying down the covenanter army to prevent them reinforcing the English parliamentarians. The venture was also seen as a golden opportunity to win back his ancestral lands and resurrect the fortunes of the MacDonalds. The council at the Confederation of Kilkenny gathered to select the Major- General of the Irish army and the proceedings were described as follows:

When the nobles of Ireland gathered to appoint the man to lead their army into Scotland, there were two noble Irish heroes who expected to have that honour, through having many of their friends at the assembly. Properly, by long tradition, the honour should go to the strongest-arm in Ireland.

"Here it is", claimed Alasdair, drawing his sword and in defiance of all who would oppose him. "Where is the next strongest?" queried the Council. "It is here!" replied Alasdair, passing the sword to his left hand. No man would dare oppose him, and he came to be their commander.

The story helps to explain the name of Ciotach given to Alasdair's father which some believe to mean left-handed. Others have the opinion that Alisdair was ambidextrous which could help explain his prowess by being able to fight with a sword in each hand.

MACDONALD'S REVENGE

Alasdair MacColla finally embarked to Scotland in June 1644 with four ships carrying about sixteen hundred men and by his side the faithful Manus O'Cahan. They sailed from the southern Irish port of Waterford, braving the hazards of encountering the English parliament's naval patrols. Fortune favoured them as Liverpool had just fallen to the Royalists allowing Alasdair's fleet to pass through undetected. To the north of Rathlin they intercepted a merchant ship and on board they found a group of eminent protestant ministers who were returning from Ireland after advocating the Covenant to thousands of protestant planters. Among them were Dr John Weir and the Rev. Hamilton who loathed Catholicism and expected to be badly treated or even killed. But Alasdair intervened to protect them. He wanted prisoners that could be exchanged for his father and brothers and retained only eight of them and liberated the others. Alasdair's conduct was in stark contrast to the behaviour of the English naval commander, Captain Swanley which was more typical of the sectarian hatred that prevailed. He was responsible for the worst atrocity committed in the name of the English parliament. About two months prior to Alasdair's voyage he captured a ship carrying troops sent from Dublin to fight for the King. After separating the English from the Irish he had the latter tied in pairs, back-to-back and thrown overboard. About seventy men and two women vainly struggled for their lives to the raucous amusement of the murderous crew. The event was gleefully reported as follows:

"The Irish because they were good swimmers, he caused to use their natural art, and try whether they could tread the seas as lightly as their Irish boggs and quagmires, and binding them back to back, cast them overboard to swimme or drown, and to wash them to death, from the blood of the Protestants that was upon them."

On reaching the Scottish mainland some men under the leadership of O'Cahan were landed and sent to take Kinlochhaline Castle. Mingary Castle was then assaulted by land and sea and surrendered the next day on giving quarter to the garrison.

One of Alasdair's frigates left to pursue a prize and was chased back by Captain Swanley. Shortly afterwards Argyll came with five war ships and summoned the castle to submit and render its prisoners or have no quarter. Two of Alasdair's ships were taken and a third wrecked on the rocks. Argyll then went away, promising to return with Ciotact in exchange for the ministers and Sir Donald Campbell was left to form a blockade. Realising there was no escape by sea Alasdair secured the castle with a strong garrison and left with his army under cover of darkness.

The original plan was to invade the West to complement the royalist forces under John Graham, the Marquis of Montrose in the South and the Earl of Huntly in the East. But both insurrections had been defeated by strong covenanter forces. Undaunted Alasdair forged on, hoping to gather support from the old MacDonald allies as he marched into Lochaber.

However most of the chiefs took the view that it was a temporary Irish incursion and that their support would simply incur dire consequences. He moved on to Kintail hoping that the Mackenzies would provide reinforcements. However word had spread that two powerful armies were assembling against them. In the West Argyll had brought back Alistair's bitter enemy, Auchinbreck, from Ireland to organise a Campbell offensive. In the East a powerful covenanter force had assembled at Stratherrick to block any advance on Inverness. Alasdair responded by crossing the Corrieyairack Pass into Badenoch and instead of employing a policy of diplomatic persuasion, the fiery cross was sent out commanding all men to follow the King or face fire and sword. This was enough to rouse the loyalties of some Macintoshes, McPhersons and Farquharsons, providing about eight hundred men. Others like Dougal McPherson resisted and had his house burnt and property raided.

They marched on to Atholl where there were royalist sympathies but on arrival they found a hostile garrison who, like others, saw Alasdair as a foreign invader. He was left to reflect on the possible failure of his mission and according to a witness -

"He stood a little part from his men and in deepe contemplation and profound silence, lifts up his eyes to heavin, and with a short mental prayer, and invocates the aid of his Diuine Majesty."

It was then he heard the pipes and there was a fuss about the camp. Before him stood a highland gentleman who introduced himself as the Marquis of Montrose. The men of Atholl also rejoiced and as Stewarts they pledged themselves to the royalist cause. The King had appointed Montrose Lieutenant General of Scotland and he was just the man to bestow the credibility that Alasdair needed.

Montrose was anxious to establish his military credentials and persuaded Alasdair to march south to engage the lowland army. The latter's priorities lay in the Northwest with his passion to defeat Argyll and win the release of his father but first he needed to build his strength for the forthcoming conflicts. Their first objective was the covenanter stronghold in Perth and they march down through the Sma' Glen to join Lord Kilpont and James Stewart of Ardvorlich who between them had brought around five hundred men from the Stirling area. They approached Perth from the West and the two armies met at Tippermuir. The Covenanters numbered about six thousand, roughly twice as many as the Royalists. The essential difference lay in the calibre of the men. The Irish were tough, experienced mercenaries who had survived bloody conflicts in Ulster and the Highlanders had honed their fighting skills in a society where strength and fighting ability was essential to achieve manhood. The other side mainly consisted of farmers and townsmen who had been hastily levied into service by inexperienced leaders. The Covenanters were better equipped with muskets, some cannon and cavalry. Alasdair's men relied mainly on their dirks and swords.

Alasdair's ***Irishes*** *took* pride of place in the centre while the flanks were commanded by Montrose and Kilpont. The battle started with a unit of cavalry trying to provoke the Royalists into discharging their muskets and breaking ranks but they stood firm. The ***Irishes*** then launched a ferocious attack. First they fired their one and only musket volley before rapidly closing with the enemy, denying them the opportunity of using their superior fire power. As the ***Irishes*** set about carving up their hapless foes the cavalry were assailed by highland bowmen who had a much faster rate of fire than the beleaguered musket men. The covenanter lines soon broke and thousands of terrified men were slaughtered as they ran. One Irish officer proclaimed that it was possible to walk from the battlefield into Perth over the bodies of the slain without touching the ground -

"It was as if the hounds of hell were drawn up before our ports bathed in blood and demanding more with hideous cries."

In the aftermath of the battle Alasdair and Montrose triumphantly entered the town and were feted by the Burgers. As they were trying to win popular support the ***Irishes*** were commanded to remain in the countryside. They were content to plunder the well-equipped bodies of the fallen leaving many naked on the field. News was received that another covenanter army was gathering in Stirling and although an order was made to plunder the land of James Stewart it was countermanded by Argyll who threatened to execute anyone found guilty of robbery. This may explain the murder of Lord Kilpont by Stewart while they walked along the river. Kilpont was heard to say -

"He would not meddle in that business."

After which Stewart stabbed him with a dagger and fled. He had been seeking his friend's support for the assassination of Montrose to ingratiate himself with the Covenanters.

After Kilpont's death his men left to take his body home for burial and along with the departure of some men from Atholl, Montrose was left with about 1500 men.

With a depleted force Montrose bypassed the strongly fortified town of Dundee and marched towards Aberdeen. He had hoped to gain support from the Royalists of the shire such as the Gordons and although none came they did not stand against him. The covenanter force defending the city included the Forbes, Frasers and Crichtons, mustering about three thousand men alongside a large troop of cavalry led by Sir William Forbes of Craigievar. When the armies lines up to face each other Montrose sent a drummer boy offering terms in the King's name and threatening to give no quarter if the burgh did not surrender. He received his answer when the boy was shot as he returned to the line.

The battle started with the same ineffectual foray by a unit of cavalry as seen at Tibbermore, again trying to lure the enemy into discharging their muskets. Seeing the futility of this tactic, Forbes attacked with his cavalry, aimed at the centre with the intention of breaking the formation. Under Alasdair's leadership the Irishmen merely opened their ranks at the last minute, allowing the horsemen to pass through unmolested. The ranks then closed behind them and the troop was surrounded and massacred. Forbes was ignominiously captured. The fighting on the flanks was fierce and although outnumbered, the Royalists held firm, using the weapons gained from the spoils of war at Tippermuir. Alasdair then ordered his ***Irishes*** to lay down their muskets and charge with ***sword and durk***. However the men from Aberdeen did not break easily but when the remnants of the cavalry galloped off they were left to their fate. Eventually they broke off and ran only to be pursued and cut down in their hundreds.

"Thair wes littil slauchter in the fight, bot horribill wes the slaauchter in the flight"

The indomitable spirit of the ***Irishes*** is encapsulated by the report that an Irishman trailing his leg, so shattered at the thigh by a cannon-ball that it hung by a mere shred of skin, hailed his comrades with a loud cheery voice.

"Ha, comrades such is the luck of war, neither you nor I should be sorry for it. Do your work manfully. As for me, sure my Lord Marquis will make me a trouper, now I am no good on foot."

With these words he coolly drew his knife and without flinching cut away the skin with his own hand and gave the leg to a comrade to bury.

On winning a hard fought victory the Irish and their comrades were not restricted to the outskirts of the town. This time they burst in -

"Hewing and cutting down all maner of man thay could overtak within the toune – killing, robbing, and plundering of the toune at thair plesour - hvilling, crying, weiping, mvring, throw all the streittis."

On seeing a well-dressed man they would make him undress so not to damage his clothes before killing him. Women were raped in the town and others taken and made to become camp followers.

After the battle Montrose retreated to Atholl arriving in October 1644 and Alasdair left with his men with the intention of relieving Mingary Castle before winter set in. Montrose then made his way to Badenoch and on to Huntly trying to avoid confrontation with the enemy until Alasdair returned.

Alasdair MacColla's reputation had been much enhanced by his impressive victories and he started to win the support of sympathetic chieftains. As he made his way to the West he encountered Smooth John MacNab who also had the reputation of being a great warrior. Some years before the McNeishes ambushed a food consignment belonging to the MacNabs which included the vital winter supply of whisky. The incident took place at the west end of Loch Earn. Afterwards the McNeishes retired to their keep on an island near St

Fillans and felt safe in the knowledge that they possessed the only boat on the Loch. When the servants brought back the news to their chief, Finlay McNab, the old man was incensed and called in his four sons. Exhorting them into action he poured out his wrath and proclaimed -

"The night is the night, if the lads were the lads"

They did not need much persuasion which led to a famous event that is now commemorated on the chief's coat of arms. Smooth John MacNab (the name is a misnomer) was a large young man with a big head. He immediately left with his brothers and sailed from their castle in Eilan Ran down Loch Tay. On reaching a suitable location at the bottom of a mountain they lifted and carried their boat over the high pass of Glen Tarken and down to the shore of Loch Earn. Under cover of darkness they then rowed to Neish Island and quietly destroyed the boat belonging to the McNeishes to cut off any escape.

The McNeishes were bawdily celebrating with the stolen whisky when they heard a loud hammering at the door. Old McNeish asked who was there and what did they want. In answer came the question -

"Who would you least desire?"

"Iain Min" (Smooth John) was the terrified reply.

"He it is and a rough man you will find him tonight!"

The McNabs burst down the door and set about the seven men who were aglow with the whisky. All their heads were cut off and put into a sack Afterwards the MacNabs rowed back and started up the mountain carrying their boat and plunder. About half way they were exhausted and decided to leave the heavy boat and carry on with the whisky and trophies. Remnants of the abandoned boat could still be found well into the twentieth century

When the brothers neared Eilan Ran they were challenged by a look out who received the answer ***"Gun Eagal!"*** meaning ***Dread Nought,*** which later became the clan motto. Their step mother asked what was in the sack that John carried over his shoulder. He opened it and rolled out the severed heads -

"***Boules for the bairns***", he replied.

Turning to his father he said -

"The night was the night and the lads were the lads!"

During the blockade at Mingary conditions had deteriorated due to lack of food and poor hygiene. Most of the captives were released in exchange for supplies and aqua vita. Only the Presbyterian ministers continued to be held but just before Alasdair appeared John Weir died of fever whereupon his prayer never to see Alasdair again was answered. With Alasdair's enhanced reputation as a warrior Sir Donald Campbell judiciously withdrew and the siege was lifted. John MacDonald the captain of Clan Ranald was among the first to greet the conquering hero, bringing about five hundred men and forty cows to feed the starving garrison. Alasdair had hoped to trade the ministers for the release of his father but despite the urging of the church elders Argyll had spitefully transferred them away from Dunstaffnage down to the impregnable fort of Dumbarton Castle.

Having secured Mingary, Alasdair journeyed to meet Montrose at Atholl and was joined by the Stewarts of Appin, the Men of Keppoch, the MacDonalds of Glencoe and some of the Camerons. The Catholic priests that travelled with the army rejoiced in the support for Catholicism among the clansmen but were disappointed with the response of the Camerons. This they put down to them being ***less civilised and less susceptible to piety***. Montrose on the other hand had lost many of his followers and desperately needed Alasdair's reinforcements. It was becoming increasingly clear that Alasdair commanded more loyalty than Montrose and was a more charismatic leader in battle. Winter was now closing in and the normal campaigning season coming to an end. Argyll had moved back to Inveraray believing himself to be safe behind the impenetrable snow-covered mountains. However an army had to be fed and Alasdair persuaded Montrose that raiding the rich land of Argyll would provide winter sustenance for his men. Furthermore the MacNabs had offered to lead them through the secret passes. Smooth John and his men sought the opportunity of taking revenge on the Campbells who had taken over their ancestral lands after they were defeated by Bruce at the Pass of Brander. Since that time the Campbells had been their overlords. With Alasdair's help they were able to overpower the garrison on Loch Dochart which was the last obstacle on their way to the West.

When Argyll heard the royalists were within a few miles of his castle at Inveraray he commandeered a fishing boat and fled down Loch Fyne to rally the covenanter army that was wintering in Stirling. Montrose realised that due to a lack of boats he could easily be trapped in the Argyll peninsula so he allowed most of his men to go home with their plunder before mustering at Kilcumin. Meanwhile the vengeful Campbell army under the brutish Sir Duncan Campbell of Auchinbreck was assembling on the shore of Inverlochy.
With the news that another covenanter army had arrived near Inverness; Montrose was concerned that he would be attacked from both sides. With typical daring Alasdair decided to lead his men over the mountains, taking a circuitous route in an attempt to surprise Auchinbreck. This involved a two day march through deep snow with many of his men bare-legged in freezing temperatures. They went by way of Glen Tarff and crossed the pass of Allt Na Larach rising to about two thousand feet over the mountain then down to Glen Roy and over the river Spean. But the element of surprise was lost when they were discovered by a Campbell scouting patrol. Alisdair had about fifteen hundred men and they were about to face a force of three thousand.

It was on Sunday 2nd of February, the day of the Catholic feast of the Purification and when Alasdair's men lined up for battle they fell on their knees and prayed to the Virgin Mary. It was also time for the timorous Earl of Argyll to withdraw to the safety of his galley. According to a contemporary account -

"Upon Sunday, the second of February, being Candlemas day, about the sun rising, both the armies draw up in battle. By Auchinbreck, as general for that day, the two regiments that Argyll had brought from Stirling were placed in the right and left wings; their van was a strong battalion of highlanders, with guns, bows and axes. In the rear or main battle, were all prime men, and the greatest strength of the army, with two pieces of ordinance.

The Marquis of Montrose divides his army in four battles, the major, Alasdair MacDonald, had the leading of the right wing; Colonel O'Cahan had the leading of the left wing, both those were Irish forces; the Stewarts of Appin, with those of Athol, Glencoe and Lochaber, had the van. MacDonald, the captain of Clanranald, and Glengarry had the rear brought up by Colonel James MacDonald. The Marquis had a reserve of Irish and other highlanders. It fell to O'Cahan, with the left wing, to charge Argyll's right wing; he was commanded by the major (MacColla) not to give fire till he gave it in their breasts, and this course in the right wing he rightly observes also; and then patiently receiving their shot, without giving fire, till they fired into their beards, both wings made a cruel havock of the enemies: leaping amongst them with their swords and targes, they quickly put them to disorder, and disperses them over the field. Their van, perceiving themselves naked, and their wings broken and dispersed they did hardly withstand the shock of Montrose's van, who charged them, and following their charge in a close body, with such strength and fury as they were forced to give back upon their rear; who instead of opening their ranks to receive them, and give the enemies a new charge, they quit their standing, breaks their order, and flies confusedly towards the castle wherein they had places fifty soldiers. Sir Thomas Ogilvie, with a troop of horse, affronts two hundred of them that made for the castle, and forces them to flee with the rest up the side of the lake."

The Campbells in the centre won the admiration of Montrose with their furious charge which forced Alasdair's right flank to buckle. This was countered by the Camerons who rushed into the fray from the braes of Corpach. Both Campbell wings were broken by the Irish and then Montrose ordered his Highlanders in the centre to charge with devastating effect.

In the front line, among the carnage, Alasdair MacColla fought like a Viking berserker. It is alleged that instead of armour he wore six cowhides for protection against the scything blades. He must have stood out like a colossus swinging his two-handed sword with terrible effect. Some say he beheaded twenty-two opponents in the heat of battle. His main objective was the hated Auchinbreck who was also a mighty warrior. There is no evidence that they were able to confront each other but a witness describes what happened when Auchinbreck was captured and brought before Alasdair. He was offered a choice of death by hanging or decapitation. The general defiantly replied:

"Two evils and no choice!"

Whereupon –

"The gallant Sir Duncan of Auchinbreck was slain by Major General Alester MacColl, who, by one blow of a two-handed claymore, swept off his head and helmet together."

While the Earl of Argyll sailed out of harm's way his men were pursued for up to eight miles. None would have escaped if Alasdair's men had not been exhausted by the furious fighting after their long trek and lack of victuals. Fourteen Campbell barons and twenty men of quality were taken prisoner and some seventeen hundred of their men lay dead on the battlefield.

The mantle of Campbell invincibility had been broken and there was exultation among many of the western clans that had been subjugated by their overlordship. Perhaps they could regain their old freedoms and practice their catholic faith without covenanter interference. Alasdair was enthusiastically followed by the Camerons, McNabs, the Stewarts of Appin and the McGregors. Even Sir Lachlan MacLean of Mull arrived with eleven hundred men. He was a hero to his own and a feared ogre to his enemies. People fled and recalcitrant children despatched on a rumour the ***bogie man*** was coming.

Among the wealth of important prisoners taken was Sir Donald Campbell the owner of Mingary Castle and one of Argyll's most important henchmen. With the Rev. Hamilton still surviving in captivity the Covenanters in Edinburgh were now able to force Argyll to negotiate with Alasdair for the release of his father and brothers and they were finally traded in May 1645.

Montrose was aware that for him to be ultimately successful in the cause of the King he would have to defeat the forces in the south of the country and draw them away from England. He set about recruiting the eastern clans but in contrast to Alasdair's efforts he received only lukewarm support from the Mackenzies, Lovats and Grants. Even the Earl of Huntly refused to join but his two swashbuckling sons, Lord Gordon and his brother Lewis, came along with about two hundred cavalry, an important asset in a lowland campaign. Montrose moved on to Turriff where he was met by a delegation from Aberdeen who begged for mercy on behalf of the town's citizens, bearing in mind what had happened during the last occupation. As he was on a recruiting drive, aiming to win over the local population, he promised that the wild ***Irishes*** would not come near the city. Montrose was unaware that the Burghers had also sent a message to Lieutenant General Baillie, the commander of the Lowland Army and a force under General Hurry was nearing the city. Expecting a cordial reception Montrose allowed his officers to participate in the pleasures of the town. During the night Hurry's men surprised the revellers killing and capturing all the royalists they could find. One of Montrose's closest friends, David Farquharson, confronted the raiders and when he gave his name they immediately shot him down. He was described as -

"Ane of the noblest capitans amongis all the hielanderis of Scotland."

Crucially most of the cavalry horses including the animals obtained from Huntly were rounded up and driven away. Panic gripped the town after Hurry retreated and word was spread that Alasdair MacColla MacDonald was coming with one thousand Irish. It was mostly a bluff and only the houses of prominent Covenanters were raided but Alasdair was able to obtain considerable compensation for the losses. With Hurry's men in the north and Baillie in the south, Montrose united his men with the intention of eliminating Hurry before tackling Baillie.

Hurry was a resourceful soldier having gained much experience in the English Civil war. Having learned that Montrose had encamped at Auldearn he decided to march through the night in a blinding rainstorm to take him by surprise. As dawn broke on 9th of May 1645 some musketeers were given permission to test their wet guns towards the sea so that the noise would be muffled. However one of Alasdair's scouts heard them which allowed Alasdair to set up a forward defensive line to give Montrose an opportunity of rousing his troops. This left the big man dangerously exposed to the rampant charge of an overwhelming number of professional warriors. Knowing that he needed to win time he decided to move forward into the rushing enemy -

"He was ever in the front, with his strength, his curage, and dexteritte let his enemies' see, even with terror, wonderful feats of armes for his fellows to imitate, his strong arme cutting whatsoever and whosoever did him resist. He brak two swords; and when they had fastened a number of pikes in his targe, wherewith they could have born three or four ordinarie men to the ground, they could not make him to shrink, or bow so much as an knee to the ground; but with a blow of his sword and the strength of his vallarous arme cute all the pikes asunder that stuck in his targe, whill non durst approach within the lenth of his weapon."

The Gordon cavalry arrived just in time to save Alasdair's fighting Irish from being overwhelmed by the attacking horde. Lord Gordon attacked one flank while his brother attacked the other. Seeing this Alasdair is said to have shouted -

"Those ar indeed the vallient Gordones and worthie of that name which fame hath carried abroad of them."

In the thick of battle Alasdair MacColla was ably supported by brave companions. When he was forced back many were killed around him as they strove to protect his retreat to the yards and dykes of the town. After Alasdair broke his sword during the furious battle, Davidson of Ardnacroish gave up his weapon so that Alasdair could continue the fight. In doing so, sacrificed his life for his beloved chieftain. One of the last to retreat was Ranald MacKinnon who was shot by a bowman as he discharged his pistol. The arrow pierced both cheeks and remained sticking out of his head. He threw down the pistol and tried to draw his sword which remained stuck in its scabbard. As he lowered his targe he was pierced by a pike through the neck and chest. When he turned to seek cover one of the pike men rushed to finish the job and was met by Alasdair who killed him with a single blow. Ranald was able to recover from his wounds and fight once again. Another report tells of a blacksmith called Robertson from Atholl who fought with a cooking pot on his head. Alasdair asked him how many men he had killed and the reply was nineteen. Alasdair exclaimed -

"By Mary I have killed only twenty one and I wish every one of my men was a tradesman like you."

When Montrose's main infantry arrived to reinforce Alasdair's line the exhausted Covenanters broke. Hurry and Elgin were forced to flee for their lives while their infantry were granted no quarter and three thousand corpses were left on the field.

In the aftermath of the battle Alasdair continued westwards, anxious to see his father and brothers again. On his way he plundered and pacified the Frasers, Lovats and Mackenzies who had sided with the Covenanters.

Montrose went to the aid of the Gordons who had proved to be the mainstay of his personal support. Learning of Alasdair MacColla's absence, Baillie marched against the Gordons but had not reckoned on the presence of Manus O'Cahan. The battle of Alford took place on 2nd of July 1645 and was Montrose's only victory in the absence of Alasdair MacColla.

Now that the Highlands had been effectively conquered it was time to rally in support of the King. The war in England had not gone well for Charles and his main army had just been destroyed by Cromwell's army at Naseby on 7th of June 1645 Alasdair MacColla had also been sent West on a recruiting drive and once again the western clans came in support of their triumphant hero. Montrose formally promised Patrick Roy MacGregor and John MacNab that their ancient lands would be restored and despite the death of the gallant Lord Gordon at Alford the Gordons remained committed to the cause. The covenanter Government was also in disarray as the bubonic plague gripped Edinburgh forcing the regime to move to Stirling.

With five thousand men under his command Montrose marched towards Stirling to confront the Scottish Lowland Army which was camped at Kilsyth. Although Baillie was nominally in charge of the seven thousand strong Lowland Army, he had lost credibility with the covenanter committee which included Argyll. When Baillie positioned his formation to face Montrose an argument broke out among the nobles as to their disposition. With some disgust Baillie started to move his units to suit the demands of the committee. This caused considerable confusion among the ranks as they jostled for position. On the other side, Montrose's formations were ready for action. Alasdair had placed the fierce MacLeans in forward positions and at the centre of the van were his Highlanders and Irish Warriors. Montrose placed his infantry behind MacColla's men and his cavalry was led by Alistair Gordon on the flanks.

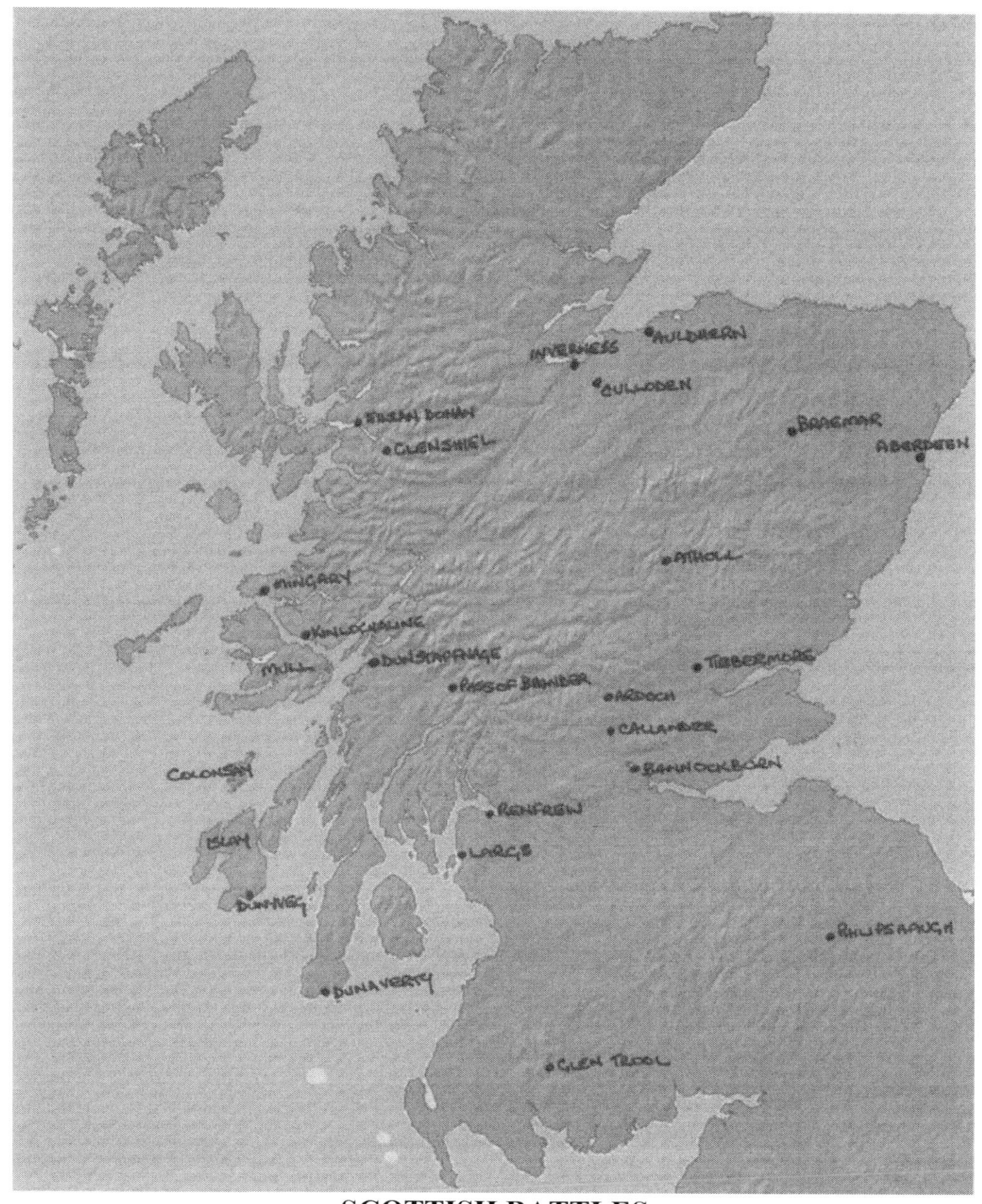

SCOTTISH BATTLES

It was a hot day on 15th of August 1645 and being the Feast of the Assumption, the devout Alasdair placed his fate on divine intervention. He ordered his men to discard their armour and plaids and to fight in their white shirts with the long tails tied between their legs. This made them more agile and gave a means of identity in the coming melee. In contrast to many of their opponents the Gaels were hard men, extremely fit and the survivors of a bitter campaign. They also considered themselves of high descent compared to the Lowlanders who were led by ***petty barons and churls.*** On seeing the confusion before him, Alasdair ordered a highland charge which immediately overwhelmed the Covenanters. At the same time the Gordons managed to flank and route the covenanter right wing. The battle was soon won and in the aftermath –

"Bodies like clothes a- bleaching are stretched on hill-sides, ignoble of aspect **were left for women to weep for.** ***Of the covenanter nobles, who were present in large numbers at this battle, some saved themselves by a timely flight, and, thanks to their good horses, reached the strong castle of Stirling. Others slipped away to the Firth of Forth, and got aboard some vessels at anchor near the shore. Among these was Argyll, who for the third time, took boat and escaped. Even then he did not think himself safe till they had weighed anchor and stood away far out to sea."***

The Covenanters lost at least four thousand men and some say as many as six thousand. After six consecutive victories there was no opposition left - Montrose had won Scotland for the King.

THE LOST CAUSE

The triumphant Montrose was appointed Lord Governor of Scotland by King Charles I. He was the political leader of the victorious army but there is no doubt that his success was due to the unflinching efforts of Alasdair MacColla MacDonald. Montrose had fought for his King but MacColla had fought for his religion and the restoration of the MacDonalds.

Following the victory at Kilsyth, Alasdair took about six hundred of his men through Ayr shire where there was a rumour of some resistance from the Earls of Cassilis and Eglinton. But all resistance melted away when word spread that the mighty Alasdair MacColla was coming. Instead the Countess of Louden embraced him and entertained him sumptuously, no doubt infatuated with her handsome, heroic guest.

Montrose camped at Bothwell Castle and on 18th of August summoned the Scottish Parliament to meet in Glasgow on 20th of October. Rather than have to victual his army for a prolonged period and to prevent them from pillaging the city he allowed the Gordons to go home with many of the Highlanders. This included Alasdair MacColla who left with a troop of a hundred and twenty men, leaving most of his personal Irish troops under the command of Manus O'Cahan. It was agreed that the departing troops would return ***"within forty days in greater strength and numbers."***

In the absence of Alasdair MacColla, on September 4th, Montrose left Bothwell with a reduced force to meet with the Marquis of Douglas who commanded about one thousand cavalry. They had intended to join up with the King but events had gone badly in the South. Charles had been militarily defeated in England and the agreed support from the Irish Confederation had been withdrawn after he reneged on a promise to return Ireland to the catholic faith. As Montrose encamped at Philiphaugh, near Selkirk, the covenanter army that had been fighting for Cromwell under the experienced leadership of General David Leslie was free to come back to Scotland. Montrose knew that Leslie had crossed the border with a formidable force and without the vigilance and sagacity of Alasdair MacColla he had not mustered his troops accordingly. While taking breakfast in Selkirk, some four miles away, he was informed that Leslie was upon him. He raced back with the rump of cavalry that had not deserted but he was too late to save his infantry. Vastly outnumbered by an army of four thousand, the seven hundred Irish resisted bravely but were surrounded and virtually eliminated. Only Manus O'Cahan and two other officers were spared for later execution. Afterwards in a hideous revenge for the years of ravaging throughout the realm their wives and camp followers were rounded up and massacred -

"There were three hundred women that, being natives of Ireland, were the married wives of the Irish. There were many big with child, yet none of them spared, all were cut in pieces, with such savage and inhuman cruelty, as neither Turk nor Scythian was ever heard to have done the like. For they ript up the bellies of the women with their swords; till the fruit of their wombs, some in embryo, some perfectly formed, some crawling for

life, and some ready for birth, fell down on the ground, weltering in the gory blood of their mangled mothers. Oh! impiety; oh! horrible cruelty."

At the command of the covenanting chiefs some were thrown from a high bridge to drown in the river below. When some struggled to the side they were bludgeoned and hurled back into the waters.

On hearing what had happened at Philiphaugh, Alasdair marched through Cowal into Argyll and Lorne, gathering men from the MacLachlans, McNeils and MacDougalls and soon he had two thousand men under his command. In the Western Highlands the Campbells were attacked by the Camerons, Clanranald and MacDonalds of Glencoe and in December Lachlan MacLean joined forces at Kilmore. The combined army then set about purging the Campbell name. Some sought survival within their stout castles others became refugees. Without the necessary cannon to attack the strongholds Alasdair tried to starve them into submission. The only substantial resistance made by the Campbells was at Lagganmore in Glen Euchar. After a vicious fight the surviving Campbells were driven into a barn which was blocked and set on fire. Alasdair was prepared to commit atrocities to bring the Campbells into submission and was vengeful after what had happened at Philiphaugh. One of their leaders, Campbell of Bragleen, managed to escape being burnt alive by bursting through the burning door with a peat basket over his head. The spirit of the man appealed to Alasdair's chivalry. Bragleen asked to be given a chance of survival by fighting his way out of a circle of men. With little chance of success he was given a sword and surrounded. Suddenly he threw the sword high in the air causing his assailants to glance upwards less it land on them. With their attention diverted he managed to escape through their ranks. Alasdair was impressed and Bragleen was allowed to escape.

In the aftermath of Philiphaugh, Montrose fled north and tried in vain to rally a new army. But in April circumstances conspired against him when Charles decided to avoid being captured by Cromwell's victorious Parliamentarians by escaping from Oxford and surrendering to the Scottish Covenanter Army in Newcastle. The King then issued a royal decree instructing his forces to lay down their arms and disband their armies. Huntly complied immediately and with no means of protection Montrose escaped via Norway to the court of the Prince of Wales in St Germain.

The King would have found refuge in Scotland if he had acceded to demands for him to sign the Covenant. He steadfastly stuck to his religious principles, then in treacherous fashion and fearful that the presence of the King would cause a further revolt in Scotland the Covenanters decided to sell him to the English. A price of £200,000 was agreed and to the taunts of the local people shouting ***Judas! Judas!*** King Charles I was traded on 30th of January 1647.

The war had been lost and many of the royalist supporters left MacColla with his band of loyal Highlanders and surviving Irish to continue the fight, numbering about eight hundred men.

Some of the ***Judas*** funds were used to form Leslie's ***New Model Army*** which consisted of hard-bitten, professional soldiers that had survived the English War. Supplied with the latest equipment, including cannon, Leslie was commissioned to mop up the remaining resistance.

Ciotach, with Alasdair's full authority had symbolically installed himself in Dunyveg as the new chief of Clan MacDonald. Hopes were high when Antrim obtained agreement from the Irish Confederation in Kilkenny to send a new army to Scotland numbering five thousand men. The plan was disrupted when it became known that Cromwell intended to send a large army with the intention of overthrowing the Confederation and conquering all of Ireland. Alasdair MacColla's services were now needed in Ireland as well as Scotland.

On learning Leslie had landed in Inveraray accompanied by the Earl of Argyll with his ***New Model Army***, Alasdair decided it was time to save his loyal companions and ordered a tactical retreat. He decided to ship his men back to Ireland from Largie for temporary refuge while he sought reinforcements. On the night before departure he set his standard on a hill near the port and found it blowing the wrong way, he then learned the place was called ***Gocam-go*** which reminded him of the forecast made by his nurse after she consulted the spirits during Hallowe'en when he was a child.

"The heart of a hero, that never turned away from an enemy, now became as the heart of a child."

With no room left in the boats about three hundred men were left to track south to Dunaverty to be picked up later. With Argyll thirsting for blood Leslie lost no time in moving forward and was able to trap the remaining men in the castle.

Dunaverty was a small castle placed on a high cliff above the sea at the southern tip of the Kintyre peninsula. It was built mainly as a look-out point and signalling station where a bonfire could easily be seen from the Irish coast. Accommodating three hundred men must have been extremely uncomfortable but they were able to resist the efforts of Leslie's three thousand troops, repulsing repeated assaults and inflicting heavy casualties. The defenders were well provisioned with food and ammunition and might well have survived until Alasdair's promised return. However after some days it was found that the castle was supplied with water through a pipe from an outside source. When the garrison was deprived of water they were forced to surrender. Having done so they suffered a further five days without water. Leslie was minded to spare his captives but was urged to permit their slaughter by a chaplain called John Naves, who had been appointed by the covenanter General Assembly. Some were put to the sword; others were tied in pairs and thrown off the cliff into the sea. Evidence of the atrocity was found in 1812 when a violent storm broke up a sandbank, revealing a pile of bones.

Leslie laid siege to Dunyveg and after a few days of resistance old Coll Ciotach, without regard to his personal safety came out to parley. His proposals were rejected and he was allowed to return to the castle. This was followed by a letter to his old friend, the captain of Dunstaffnage who had been his keeper during the long years of imprisonment, asking for whisky under the pretext of coming out for further negotiations. Ciotach was now seventy-six years old and perhaps the need for aquavit outweighed his personal concerns. Leslie decided that his honour was being impugned and realised the old man was merely employing delaying tactics. When he came out again without an armed escort he had him arrested. After a few days of hard fighting a negotiated surrender was reached. This time there was none of the ritual slaughter as Leslie was anxious to conclude the affair.

Ciotach was to be taken to Edinburgh; however Argyll diverted him to Dunstaffnage so that he could take his personal revenge and on 21st of September he was hanged using the mast from his own galley as a gibbet.

When Alasdair MacColla landed in Ireland with about eight hundred men he quickly realised there was very little chance of retuning to Scotland with reinforcements. With the end of the civil war in England the protestant Parliamentarians turned their attention to conquering Ireland. The war was now about territory and religion. The Parliamentarians hated the catholic religion and were determined to protect the Protestant Plantations. The Irish Confederation was intent on recovering the lands occupied by the planters and re-establishing Catholicism. The Irish had three main armies. Ulster was commanded by Owen Roe O'Neil who had won a great victory against the Scottish Covenanters at Benburb in 16th June 1646, preventing them returning to Scotland to aid the Campbells during Alisdair MacColla's vengeful rampage. The Leinster army was led by General Thomas Preston and the Munster Army by Lord Taaffe. Alasdair preferred to join O'Neil which would have put him close to Kintyre and his Scottish interests but the confederate authority was fearful of uniting two such powerful warriors, mindful of the tempestuous nature of O'Neil. Instead Alasdair was appointed Lieutenant General under Taaffe along with half of the force he had brought from Scotland, the rest, led by Angus MacDonald of Glengarry, were attached to the Leinster Army. MacColla was also made governor of Clonmel where he would have socialised with the local Irish chiefs.

Preston and Glengarry moved to attack the Parliamentarians occupying Dublin while Taaffe marched to encounter Murrough O'Brian who had been ennobled as Lord Inchiquin. The latter had based his army in the Cork area to protect the local protestant Planters and had zealously subdued the local Irish, receiving a dreadful reputation and became known as -

"Murrough of the burnings!"

The Leinster Army was routed by the English at Dungan Hill but the ***Redshanks*** under Glengarry stood their ground almost to the last man -

"Whoe neurer yett experimented the arte of flight, of thire number…one hundred was the most that escaped that furie."

Taaffe deployed his troops on the hill of Knocknanuss while Inchiquin camped on another hill about a mile away. The Irish had about seven thousand men including twelve hundred cavalry whereas Inchiquin's force was about five thousand. Taaffe had been a political appointment and fearing that Inchiquin would not come due to his superior numbers naively issued a challenge to put two thousand men into the field to fight the same number.

"More for recreation that with a suspition that it might breake your army"

Inchiquin was made of harder stuff and started manoeuvring his cavalry to confuse Taaffe as to his intentions. The Irish army was split into two wings each separated from the other by an obscuring hill. Alasdair commanded the right wing with his Highlanders and ***Redshanks***. The majority of the troops remained with Taaffe on the left wing and the cavalry was split between both groups moving between both wings.

The battle started in the afternoon of 12th November 1647 with Inchiquin pounding Alasdair's infantry with cannon. His men grew restless and were released into their customary highland charge. Inchiquin left his infantry to deal with MacColla's men and switched his cavalry towards Taaffe's position whose initial attack had been driven off by the musket men. Taaffe's men were caught in disarray and routed. Taaffe even cut down some of his own men in a hapless attempt to stop them fleeing from the field. On the other side of the hill Alasdair MacColla was hacking his opponents to pieces in his customary manner. Alasdair then detached himself while his men rushed on to plunder their vanquished foe. Accompanied by a small unit he moved to investigate the events on the other side of the hill. He was then surprised and overwhelmed by a strong force of cavalry sent by Inchiquin to rescue his beleaguered men. A convincing version of the subsequent action is as follows -

"Then began the mortalitie on either side, the event doubtfull until at length, the heroycke and valiant reddshanke, never yeldinge but rather gaining grounde, were all for the most part slaughtered, theire warlike chieftaine behavinge himself like another Jonathan, that none durst aneere (come near) him, no such feates was seene by our progenitors acted by an ordinarie man whoe could not be either killed, vanquished or taken prisoner."

With no concern for his own welfare Alasdair MacColla decided for the first time in his life to yield in order to prevent all of his men being killed. One account maintains that quarter was granted by a coronet of horse called O'Grady who then restrained Alasdair and his men with rope fixings. A Major Purdon then appeared and expressed his fury that such a dangerous enemy had been spared. In cold blood he shot Alasdair through the head, thereafter living in infamy as the man who had treacherously murdered the greatest warrior in Gaelic history.

Alasdair's funeral was organised by Donough O'Callaghan, a member of the Confederation Supreme Council. Significantly he was treated as a member of the O'Callaghan family and buried in the family plot. Today one can still follow the route taken by the cortege along the rural road beside the ruined chapel. A pibroch called ***Allistrum's March*** was played at the funeral and for two hundred years it was sang throughout Munster. Alasdair's body was later disinterred and up until the beginning of the twentieth century his remains were displayed in a glass case so that generations could pay their respects. The unusually large bones confirm that he was indeed a big man in stature as well as spirit.

Alasdair MacColla died on 13th of November 1647 at the young age of twenty seven years. He had been victorious in twenty six battles and never defeated in combat, always leading from the front and an inspiration to his men. He fought primarily for his religion and homeland with the royalist cause only of political expediency. Many historians attribute Montrose's leadership to be the main factor in the success of the Scottish campaign. This is clearly not the case as the downfall of Montrose was largely due to the absence of Alasdair MacColla. He was more able to win the support of the Highlanders and maintain the loyalty of his men. Here was a man that would take communion and attend mass before reeking bloody havoc on the enemy, a leader of men who were willing to sacrifice their lives on his behalf.

There is no doubt that Alasdair MacColla is also one of Scotland's greatest heroes and as yet remains unlauded. Alasdair's wife and two sons were able to settle in Antrim but persistent folklore suggests that he might have left another legacy. It is said that Alasdair fathered a son with O'Callaghan's daughter.

According to the Castle Magner Historical Society -

"The Cromwellian transplantations wrought a scattering of the O'Callaghan Lioas Clan but the tenantry were largely left in place. After the Restoration, Ellen, wife of the transplanted Chief recovered two thousand acres of ancestral lands around Clonmeen. Her youngest son Patrick who returned with her was reputed to be the child of Sir Alasdair MacColla Ciotact McDonald – the Scots commander at Knocknanuss. Patrick's name was a feature of his descendant families; it did not appear in the multiplicity of other O'Callaghan lines. The long round-shouldered Herculean McAlasdrum back is also said to indicate his strain."

Absolute proof of the lineage was destroyed when Cromwell's troops burnt many of the parish records. The claim receives some corroboration due to the fact that after MacColla's death at Knocknanuss his body was retrieved by the O'Callaghan chief and interred in the family grave in Clonmeen.

THE END GAME

Charles the 1st was executed by the severing of his head on 30th of January 1649, leaving his son Charles II heir to the throne. The people of Scotland were outraged at the atrocity and even more so by the English occupation. Both the moderate Covenanters and the Highlanders were polarised into resisting the greater evil. The Mackenzies, who were moderate Covenanters, seized Inverness Castle from the invaders and then joined the Robertsons and Stewarts of Atholl who were Royalists. The Gordons and Ogilvies also supported the rising but there was no overall leader and they were scattered after their first encounter with Cromwell's troops. Montrose saw an opportunity and with misplaced gallantry he left the royal court in France and landed in Kirkwall the following year with an expeditionary force, hoping to restore the monarchy. Without Alasdair MacColla's credibility only a few rallied to his standard. On 27th of April his army was routed in Carbisdale farm and his horse shot out from under him but he managed to escape. Half-starved he gave himself up to MacLeod of Assynt hoping for cordial treatment but he was merely handed over to Leslie and taken to Edinburgh. As soon as he arrived he was met by a hangman and condemned without the paraphernalia of a public trial. To the discomfort of the hardliner Covenanters he was much lamented when driven through the high street towards the gibbet.

Characteristically he gave his executioner a tip saying -

"Fellow, ther is drink monie for dryving the cairt!"

Montrose was hanged on a scaffold that was thirty foot high and his limbs distributed for display at the Edinburgh Tolbooth and the gates of Stirling, Glasgow, Perth and Aberdeen.

Following extensive negotiations the Covenanters gave way in to public pressure and invited Charles II back to Scotland in defiance of the regicides south of the border. He anchored in the Moray Firth in midsummer 1650. Unlike his father he was willing to sign the Covenant and on his journey to Edinburgh was feted and cheered wherever he went, bonfires were lit and bells were rung. Although the Scots were willing to share their King they resisted any control from the English Parliament. This enraged Cromwell who committed his army to a full scale invasion which served to unite the disparate groups in Scotland to the royalist cause – all except the duplicitous Argyll who had been elevated to a Marquis. He had previously welcomed the King in person and then changed his allegiance.

Cromwell defeated a lowland force at Dunbar in September 1650 and then moved into Edinburgh and proceeded to subject the nation to a harsh military rule. In July 1651 the Highlanders were defeated at the battle of Inverkeithing with the MacLeans suffering devastating losses. After Charles received reinforcements from the Macleods, MacKinnons, Mackenzies, MacKays, Frasers, MacGregors and the MacNabs he decided to bypass Cromwell's army and march to Worcester in England which had been a royalist stronghold during the civil war. No support materialised and the demoralised Scots were defeated in the ensuing battle and among those killed was erstwhile hero, Ian Mor ***(Smooth John)***, the chief of the MacNabs.

Charles had to flee for his life, using various disguises, until eventually escaping to France. He was never to return to Scotland and left his gallant Scots to their fate. Cromwell moved a large number of troops into the Highlands establishing strongholds at Inverlochy and Inverness with the intention of breaking down the authority of the clans. Cromwell was appointed Lord Protector and ruled the British Isles until his death in 1658.

After Cromwell there was a power vacuum and a mood for change which resulted in the English Parliament inviting Charles II to assume his father's throne in 1660. After Cromwell's austere regime the people felt liberated and Charles was able to establish his authority as the new monarch of the United Kingdom. Symbolically he had Cromwell's corpse exhumed on 30th of January 1661 – the twelfth anniversary of his father's death and put through a ritual of execution and the severed head displayed outside Westminster Hall. The devious Marquis of Argyll was also arrested for his many crimes which included treason and the murder of Ciotach. His son pleaded for his life exhorting that -

"Many horrid insurrections and rebellions of Islanders, remote and mountainous men, had been crushed by the Campbells!"

Not known for his valour the Marquis of Argyll was dragged to the Scottish guillotine which was called The Maiden and beheaded in May 1661. Ironically his head was displayed on the same spike above the Tolbooth that had been occupied by Montrose.

When a clan war between the Campbells and the MacLeans spread troubles across the Western Highlands Charles sent his brother James to manage affairs in Scotland. James was openly Catholic and took the view thay he should be supporting the Catholic clans who had long backed the loyalist cause against the power of the Campbells. There was much concern that the Campbells would lead a protestant revival. James further inflamed the situation by trying to force Argyll to sign an oath committing him to acceptance of a catholic succession to the throne. When Argyll reneged he was arrested and condemned to death but managed to escape from Edinburgh Castle and fled to Holland. In his absence, as had happened to the Lords of the Isles, the power of the Campbells was broken when their lands were forfeited to the crown.

In 1685 Charles II died of a stroke without an heir, despite siring several children with his mistresses during his famously debauched life. He was succeeded by James who in turn was opposed by the Duke of Monmouth which provided Argyll an opportunity of redemption. He returned from exile in Holland to support Monmouth's claim but their enterprise was savagely put down. Argyll was then left to face the clans that had long suffered under Campbell tyranny and with no support he was captured and executed.

When James became King he continued to favour the Highlanders, seeing them as a bastion of support for his religious beliefs. Cameron of Lochiel had become a royal favourite particularly after chasing Cromwell's men out of Inverlochy. The English courtiers considered Lochiel as the King's ***tame savage.*** When James decided to knight him he could not draw out Lochiel's sword because it had become stuck in its scabbard. Lochiel, himself then freed it and the King patronisingly remarked -

"Lochiel's sword obeyed no hand but his own."

Cameron of Lochiel was a legendary figure and a great warrior who reputedly resorted to barbarism in a fight and was rumoured to have killed an English officer by tearing out his throat with his teeth.

Unlike Charles II, James was an overt Catholic which led to a national crisis. His Declaration of Indulgence granted Catholics freedom of worship. Converts like James Drummond, the Earl of Perth thought he was being helpful by applying the thumbscrew to recalcitrant Covenanters. James was at best tolerated in the hope that he would be succeeded by his protestant daughter Princess Mary and her husband William of Orange. However the birth of a son also called James, changed that perception. The continuation of a catholic monarchy was unacceptable to the predominately protestant population.

The English Whig Parliament was staunchly Presbyterian and lost no time in inviting William of Orange to England. James responded by summoning his Scottish troops and Graham of Claverhouse also known as ***Bonnie Dundee*** hurried south with two divisions. On joining the royal army at Salisbury he discovered that whole regiments had defected to the protestant Duke of Marlborough. Even the English navy could not leave harbour due to a ***protestant wind.***

When William of Orange landed unopposed in Torbay in November 1688 and James realised that his position was untenable. Before fleeing to France he defiantly threw the Great Seal of England into the Thames. Back in Scotland the parliament was in turmoil and those who favoured James became known as the Jacobites and resolved to fight for the return of their King. ***Bonnie Dundee*** went to join Sir Ewen Cameron of Lochiel who had summoned the Jacobite clans to meet him in Glenroy. A council of war was held at Blair Atholl where the clansmen were joined by about three hundred Irish who were also concerned about the usurpation of their catholic monarch.

Rob Roy and his father Donald McGregor joined the gathering. They came from their farm in Strathyre and were staunch Jacobites having experienced a rise in the fortunes of their clan since the demise of the Campbells. The Jacobite army now numbered about two thousand four hundred men and set out to meet the pursuing government force of three thousand five hundred men, under General Hugh MacKay, on favourable ground.

Bonnie Dundee chose the steep slopes of the Pass of Killiecrankie where his men could lie in ambush among the trees and wait for the government forces to march up the narrow road alongside the river. On 27th of July 1689, General MacKay became aware of the Jacobite presence on the ridge above his column and the battle started late in the afternoon. With no hope of mounting an attack, Mackay deployed his musketeers, who fired their volleys until sunset with little effect. Then out from the gloom the Highlanders charged, giving the government troops insufficient time to fix their bayonets. At the time they were fitted into the barrel of the musket which prevented reloading and therefore had to be fixed at the last moment. So fast was the charge many were unable to defend themselves and were -

"Swept away by the onset of the Camerons."

The battle was fierce and bloody with about two thousand government troops killed and the rest running for their lives. One desperate soldier famously jumped across a chasm to escape his pursuers which latterly became a tourist attraction called the ***Soldier's Leap.***

An eye-witness reported that MacKay's men –

"Were cut down through the skull and neck to the breasts, others had skulls cut off above the ears like nightcaps; some had bodies and cross belts cut through at a blow; pikes and small swords were cut like willows."

It was not an easy victory. A third of the Highlanders killed and Graham of Claverhouse was mortally wounded when a musket ball pierced his left eye. The drama of the encounter is encapsulated by a poem written by Robert Burns called -

The Braes O' Killiecrankie.

Extract -

Whare hae ye been sae braw lad?
Whare hae ye been sae brankie, O?
Whare hae ye been sae braw, lad?
Cam ye by Killiecrankie, O?

An ye had been whare I hae been,
Ye wad na been sae cantie, O.
An ye had seen what I hae seen,
I' the Braes o' Killiecrankie, O.

I faught at land, I faught at sea,
At hame I faught my Auntie, O.
But I met the devil an' Dundee,
On the Braes o' Killiecrankie O.

Without the leadership of the charismatic ***Bonnie Dundee,*** the rebellion stalled and the advance was ended at the Battle of Dunkeld. By this time MacKay had invented a ringed bayonet which allowed for continuous musket fire and the Highlanders were cut down in the streets with repeated volleys. In the aftermath most of the survivors, including Rob Roy, drifted away and attended to their harvests.

James looked to the native Irish to help him regain his crown. They had suffered under Cromwell and were in no mood to give up their catholic King. It was a pivotal moment in history with the Irish seeking to regain their lands, their freedom of religion and their civil rights. The Protestants had to fight for their very survival. The Jacobites numbered about twenty four thousand including six thousand French troops, cavalry consisting of mainly dispossessed Irish gentry and infantry that were mostly poorly equipped peasantry, some of which only carried farm implements. William commanded about thirty six thousand men drawn from many countries. The Irish Protestants composed less than half of the army which was reinforced with well-equipped troops from the Netherlands, Denmark, England and Scotland.

On the 1st of July 1690 both armies faced each other across the River Boyne at a ford near Drogheda. But there was no inspirational leader like Alasdair MacColla present; James was an indecisive man, prone to panic attacks. The diminutive William of Orange was merely a figurehead in a sectarian war. Before the battle began about a quarter of the protestant troops were sent up river to try and outflank the Irish while James sent about half his force to counter the move. However both groups could not engage each other due to a swampy ravine between them and were left to sit out the battle.

Downriver the Dutch infantry began the action by forcing their way across the ford using their superior fire-power against the Irish foot soldiers. They were driven back with successive attacks by the Jacobite cavalry. William's army was not able to advance across the river until his badly mauled horsemen finally managed to hold off the Jacobites. At this stage William's second in command, the Duke of Schomberg was killed. The Jacobites were then able to regroup and resisted the advance. After gaining an advantage and with no good reason, the Jacobites were ordered to retire which they did in good order due to the successful rearguard action of their cavalry. Out of a total of about sixty thousand combatants only about two thousand had died and there was still plenty of fight left in the Irish. Demoralised they marched to their stronghold at Limerick and James fled back to France.

James's loss of nerve was blamed for the Irish withdrawal and they did not accept there had been a military victory. He is forever pilloried for their subsequent misfortunes and was derisively nicknamed –

"Seamus a' chaca" (James the Shit)

By far a more conclusive and bloody battle took place at Aughrim near Limerick on 12th of July the following year.
An eyewitness said –

"Their bodies covered the hill and looked from a distance like a flock of sheep"

"It is at Aughrim of the slaughter where they are to be found, their damp bones lying uncoffined"

"Our friends in vast numbers and languishing forms, left lifeless in the mountains and corroded by worms"

Hostilities ceased with the treaty of Limerick in 1691 which ended all hope of the Irish reclaiming their planted lands. Subsequently, penal laws were introduced against the Irish Catholics, preventing ownership of weapons and not allowing them to work in the legal profession.

FOR HIS WEE BIT HILL AND GLEN

Clan McGregor were a noble clan whose patrimony could be traced back to King Kenneth MacAlpin. Their fortunes were dealt a fatal blow after the Battle of Bannockburn when the victorious Bruce awarded the Barony of Loch Awe to Neil Campbell for his steadfast support during the campaign. The area became a Campbell stronghold and the McGregors were forced to leave their lands and live in the wilds of Glenstrae. Many of them became outlaws and cattle rustlers and contributed to the general unrest in the western highlands. Trouble flared in 1589 when John Drummond, the keeper of the Royal Forest of Glenartney, cut off the ears of a party of McGregors that had been caught poaching. The McGregors responded by killing Drummond before bursting into his sister's house and demanding bread and cheese. They then unwrapped a parcel containing Drummond's severed head and crammed the food into its mouth to protest about their starving clansmen. A few years later two Colquhouns had their throats cut when they caught some McGregors rustling cattle. Encouraged by the Campbells, the Colquhouns took action against the troublesome McGregors. This resulted in the battle of Glen Fruin which took place in 1603 when five hundred Colquhouns, with three hundred on horseback marched on the McGregors. They were opposed by four hundred men who split into two columns on either side of the glen. The Colquhouns were lured into the soft moss of Auchingaich where their horses floundered and stuck in the mud. The McGregors then attacked from both sides and massacred the entire troupe. So confident had been the Colquhouns that a party of students were allowed to watch the action but during the blood lust of battle they were also consumed in the slaughter.

The death of the students added to the outrage and King James VI was determined to punish the McGregors. McGregor of Glenstrae gave himself up to the Earl of Argyll on a promise of safe passage to England to beg clemency from the King who had by this time moved to London. He was taken over the border and by a treacherous arrangement re-arrested and bought back to Edinburgh and hanged. Robert Birrel who kept a diary of events describes what happened -

"McGregor wes convoyit to Berwick be the Gaird to conforme to the Earl's promise: fir he promesit to put him out of Scottis grund. Swa he keipit ane Heiland-manis promes: in resoect he sent the Gaird to convoy him out of Scottis grund; But thei were not directit to pairt with him, but to fetch him back agane! The 18 Januar, at evine, he come agane to Edinburghe; and upone the 20 day he wes hangit his awin hivht aboune the rest of his freindis".

And so the McGregor was hanged high above his comrades at Mercat Cross. Today the spot is marked with a mosaic dedicated to the Heart of Mid Lothian. In 1617 the Scottish Parliament passed an act abolishing the name of McGregor and that any person assuming the name should incur the pain of death. Many were persecuted, some changed their names into such as King, Murray and Grant others just became ***Children of the mist*** with no permanent home.

Rob Roy McGregor was born 1671 with flaming red hair, the son of Donald McGregor, a recognised chief of the clan. As a young man he would have taken part in the call-to-arms drill considered essential so that the men of the clan could take up arms at a moment's notice. There was an ever present danger of being attacked. The weapon inspection or ***wapinschaw*** usually took place at Lendrick and be followed by games. The leading men possessed a ***claidheamh mor*** - a two-handed sword with a double-edge blade more than five feet long. A weapon much favoured by big men like MacColla. Young men would have a claymore or broadsword the best of which were made by Andrea Ferrara, a sixteen century Italian/Spanish swordsmith -

"Rob was taught first to take position – body upright, the feet and legs positioned in different ways for best balance and speed of action. When that was mastered, he was taught the cuts made from seven angles, and seven guard positions below and above breast level. Only when these had been thoroughly learned would he be shown the three thrusts, made with straight wrist from eye, breast and hip level, and finally three engaging guards."

Donald must have been pleased with Rob's progress as he took him to fight for the King at Killiecrankie when he was only eighteen.

Rob became a famed tracker and his services were called for by the Lord of Breadalbane after the MacRaes of Kintail had taken a herd of cattle from Finlairig at the head of Loch Tay. The thieves had a two day start but Rob found their trail through the Mamlorn Forest, over the Rannoch hills and into the Badenoch Mountains. He finally ambushed the MacRaes at dawn and after a bloody fight the cows were recovered. The incident increased Rob Roy's fame and the Lairds of Lennox and Mentieth sought his protection.

Following the settlement of his Irish troubles King William's attention was mainly taken up with the grand affairs of Europe and he sought to placate the Scots by making the Presbyterian Kirk the official Church of Scotland while not accepting the Covenant. His conciliatory approach to the Highlanders was compromised by the zealous actions of the Campbells who continued to hound the renegade Jacobites that included the various MacDonald sects and clan MacGregor. The Campbells were responsible for inflaming Jacobite sympathies by massacring the MacDonalds of Glencoe as punishment for merely being late with an oath of loyalty to the new King.

On receiving orders on the King's behalf, Captain Campbell of Glen Lyon saw the opportunity for sweet revenge as he had suffered raids on his farms. Before executing his secret order he enjoyed the hospitality of the MacDonalds for ten days. At the dawning of the next day the hundred and fifty men of the troop fell on their unsuspecting hosts. Thirty eight were killed and at least three hundred escaped into the hills where many more died due to exposure in the freezing conditions. Alastair MacIan was treacherously murdered as he rose from his bed but his sons escaped. It was a botched operation and insignificant in comparison to the many other massacres in the history of the Highlands but it became symbolically important for the rebellious Jacobites. It was not so much the slaughter that was offensive but the breach of highland honour and the abuse of hospitality.

As Rob Roy rose to prominence Scotland became preoccupied by economic problems. When the harvest failed for four consecutive years half of Scotland's population of approximately one million people were starving and feared for their lives. Many were desperate and took to emigrating others succumbed to rampant diseases. The great land owners were not immune having their cattle dying on the hills and crops rotting in the field. So with eyes on the success of the English East India Company, Scotland was drawn into global economics by the Darien Scheme. Much of Clan Campbell's wealth had been lost during the restoration years and although they had regained favour under William's protestant regime, many were envious of the profits made by the English in their colonies. William Paterson, one of the founders of the Bank of England, persuaded the new Earl of Argyll to help with the funding of a Scottish colony in Darien, a Spanish territory on the Panama isthmus. The plan was to set up a lucrative trading post which would link up the trade between the Pacific and Atlantic oceans. Four thousand colonizers flocked to join the enterprise and the beleaguered land owners rushed to invest. Dreaming of riches the Campbells persuaded the Scottish Government to back the scheme. Money poured into the venture and a Campbell regiment was financed to provide security for the expedition.

When they set sail from Leith in July 1698 few realised they were travelling to a disease infested jungle. During the journey to New Caledonia more than one hundred died and when they arrived in Darien their food rotted in the hot damp climate. Within a short time all the senior navy officers died. A determined military officer managed to bring the survivors to Jamaica but most had yellow fever and were refused entry and left to starve to death.

A second attempt to colonise Darien was also plagued with disease as well as attacks from the Spanish garrison. Colonel Alexander Campbell of Fonab was sent out to take command. Without wasting time he led a party of about two hundred Scots and thirty Indians through the mangrove swamps and over the mountains to attack the Spanish fort of Toubacanti. Despite having to survive on rotten biscuits and decaying fish they managed to storm the fort. However with his men dying of disease Fonab had to submit to Spanish reinforcements. With only thirty of the original four thousand surviving it was the end of the enterprise which brought monumental consequences. Clan Campbell as well as the Scottish Government was bankrupt and the latter had to virtually beg the English Parliament for assistance.

A union of parliaments was mooted which was an anathema to Rob Roy and the Jacobites. The idea represented a betrayal of their ancestors who had fought so valiantly for independence over the centuries. The arguments were swayed by a promise that the Darien losses would be met by the English Parliament. This led to a union of the parliaments in 1707 resulting in the British Isles coming under unitary control from London.

With the union of parliaments highland rebellions became a British problem and therefore vulnerable to the resources of the British army. The Highlanders were also regarded as allies of Britain's enemies by causing the diversion of British forces from other areas of conflict. When James died at the French court the catholic King of France Louis the 14th expressed his support for his son's claim to the British throne. It was apparent that the Jacobite cause could only succeed through foreign intervention and an opportunity came after William was killed by a riding accident in 1702 and succeeded by his sister in law Queen Anne. In 1708 the young James Francis Edward, referred to as the Pretender to the throne, set sail from Dunkirk with thirty ships carrying six thousand French soldiers. The flotilla entered the Firth of Forth, expecting to link up with Jacobite supporters, but none came as they had landed on the wrong side of the country. Then the British fleet was spotted coming from the South and not wishing to be bottled up in the river, the French hastily withdrew into the North Sea. One ship was captured and the others driven by storms around the British Isles, incurring many losses in the treacherous waters. The expedition had been a disaster and merely set the cause back even further.

In the parsimonious times following the Darien fiasco honest men struggled to make a living. Meanwhile Rob was able to supplement his meagre watch income by reiving cattle belonging to English sympathisers while providing security for his Jacobite friends. One of his main victims was the Earl of Atholl and as a result of these activities he was arrested in Glasgow and imprisoned in the Tolbooth. However due to his standing with the highlander gaolers he was allowed to escape to the safety of the Trossachs. Rob had now matured into a commanding but canny individual, straight talking, a good friend and a bad enemy. He was regarded as one of the best swordsmen in the country and had survived more than twenty duels. A contemporary described him as follows –

"Rob Roy was of middle height, spare and compact but with an extraordinary breadth of shoulder. His strongly muscled legs were likened to those of a highland bull, both in light-footed agility and thighs furred with red hair. No less remarkable were the length and power of his arms – he had been seen to seize a stag by its horns and hold it fast."

During this period Rob Roy had become one of the few drovers entrusted with driving herds numbering over one thousand animals, across the border, down as far as Norwich. He was financed by the Marquis of Montrose and the trade was driven with the need to feed the British Continental Army that was engaged in the War of the Spanish Succession.

Unlike his noble forebears the Earl of Montrose was an avaricious politician constantly trying to seek advantage over the young Earl of Argyll and the Earl of Breadalbane. He had aligned himself with the obnoxious Whig government in London and sought to discredit the Campbells while the young Earl was engaged in the continental war where he had established himself as a great warrior. The opportunity came when Rob Roy defaulted on a large payment due to Montrose for a cattle transaction. His chief drover, corrupted by the amount of money entrusted to him, absconded without trace. Rob promised to recover the money but needed time and although had begun to make repayments Montrose foreclosed and seized Rob's securities. While Rob was in England collecting debts his wife and son were evicted and his house burnt. One of the reasons for the hasty action was Rob's unflinching refusal to betray Argyll's covert contact with the Duke of Berwick. The latter was the half-brother of the Pretender and had been appointed a Marshal of France due to his bravery in battle. Clearly the young Earl of Argyll wished to remain in contact with the Stewarts. It was also another episode in the age-old battle between the Grahams and the Campbells that had seen both chiefs beheaded in the previous century.

Rob Roy and his family went to Finlarig Castle where he was given sanctuary by Breadalbane who was also a Campbell with Jacobite sympathies. He was given the lease of a house and land in Glen Dochart near the MacNabs. From here and under the protection of his landlord he proceeded to exact revenge on Montrose by stealing his revenues. With his band of fifty men he became an outlaw in the mould of Robin Hood. In small groups they forcibly took rents from Montrose's tenants in exchange for a receipt signed by Rob Roy declaring that the rent to Montrose had been duly paid. When rents were increased in an effort to recoup the lost revenue some of the poorer tenants were distressed. Rob responded and gained much favour by providing the poor with funds and then regaining them by robbing the rent collectors. The ferment caused by these actions suited Breadalbane which posed the question that if Montrose was unable to control his estates then how could he control the entire country as Secretary of State.

In January 1714 the western clans including Rob met on the occasion of the funeral of Campbell of Lochnell to discuss the national situation. The union was not popular and resulted in many Jacobite toastings and drunken brawls throughout the land. A motion in the House of Lords aimed at dissolving the Treaty of Union failed by only four votes. The Jacobites decided that they would only rebel with the help of a French invasion. This was not forthcoming after the treaty of Utrecht where it was agreed that France would not come to the aid of the Jacobites. Establishing peace also meant the return of the British Army to deal with any insurrection.

Another opportunity presented itself when Queen Anne died without issue in 1714. Once again the Jacobites were outraged when James Edward's succession was bypassed in favour of a distant relative. At the invitation of the Whig Parliament, George of Hanover was crowned King in August 1714, mainly because he was a protestant. The Jacobite cause was taken up by the Earl of Mar who made his way to Aberdeen where he raised the Jacobite standard on the Braes of Mar. The muster included fighting men from the Northeast and the Lowlands but the Highlanders showing little interest in Mar's leadership and distrusted his motives. The frequent changes in his allegiance between the Tories and Whigs in the interests of personal gain indicated the calibre of the man. He was short with a hunchback and they called him –

"Bobbing John"

However, such was the level of discontent he was still able to marshal about nine thousand men. Rob Roy was in a dilemma; he had no wish to oppose Argyll whom he admired but the accession of the Pretender would restore his lands and destroy Montrose. When old Breadalbane sent out the fiery cross the MacGregors and other disaffected clans joined the rebels when they gathered at Perth.

Argyll now elevated to a Duke took command of the government forces. Unlike some of his predecessors he was a good soldier having distinguished himself under Marlborough at Ramillies and had commanded the allied troops in Spain. He was called –

"Red John of the Battles."

In contrast to Mar's levies Argyll had only two thousand five hundred regular troops and about one thousand volunteers. With Montrose reluctant to provide support he based his troops at Stirling and waited for developments.

Mar made his move on the 13th of November 1715 and encountered Argyll at Sheriffmuir. Prior to the confrontation Mar sent Rob Roy and a group of MacPhersons to secure the Fords of Frew so that his army could cross the Forth into the Lowlands. In their absence he had not expected Argyll to manoeuvre on to the open moor although it suited Argyll's well trained heavy cavalry. When Mar set out his formation he made the mistake of putting most of his light cavalry in the centre, leaving a small detachment on the right and none at all on the left. Conversely, the experienced Argyll placed all his dragoons on the wings and his infantry in the centre. He also decided that he would personally lead the charge on the right wing.

The battle started with the traditional Highland Charge but there was no charismatic leader to press home the attack. Nevertheless their superior numbers forced Argyll's left wing to give way. On the right wing Argyll used his small but experienced cavalry unit to break the charge before it reached his line of infantry. In the centre Drummond's light cavalry was unable to support the Highlanders on the other wing because they were hemmed in and continually assaulted by accurate musket fire. With one wing retreating and the other advancing the battle became a melee of confusion. When Rob Roy returned it had all but ended due to Mar's reluctance to regroup and pursue the enemy with his superior numbers. Each side claimed victory but only Argyll had achieved his objective of stopping the advance of the Jacobites into the Lowlands. Mar's failure is all the more poignant when the Jacobite casualties numbered only one hundred and fifty killed whereas Argyll had lost four hundred and seventy-seven men.

Mar retired to Perth and most of his men proceeded to melt away. When at last the James the Pretender finally arrived from France - he was too late and not being an inspiring man was unable to rally the troops. On hearing Argyll was on the march with ten thousand men, he and Mar embarked to France never to return.

Montrose sought to diminish the impact of Argyll's victory and sent his factor John Graham of Kilearn to try and bribe Rob Roy into accusing Argyll of complicity with the Jacobites, citing the low casualties at Sheriffmuir. Rob Roy refused despite a further offer of freeing him from all charges and restoring his property. His response was to raid Montrose's estates around Mentieth and Buchanan. Montrose in turn sent one hundred soldiers up Loch Lomondside with orders to capture Rob Roy. Travelling at night they came across him sleeping in the Crianlarich change house with twenty of his men in the adjoining barn. They bolted the barn door from the outside and then tried to seize Rob who was now awake due to the commotion. The door of the change house was too low and narrow to be rushed and no one could get past his flashing sword. When his men were aroused they broke through the barn door by weight of numbers and drove back the militia with their broadswords, killing some of the leaders before the rest fled for their lives.

Montrose had successfully smeared Argyll at court saying that Argyll had been lenient with the rebels. As a result he lost his command of the army in Scotland. Still Montrose was not satisfied and once again tried to entice Rob Roy to bear false witness with a new offer of amnesty. He reminded him that MacCailein Mor (Argyll) was a man that all MacGregors should hate because of the damage wreaked upon his family over the ages. But Rob realised this ***John of the Battles*** was an honourable man unlike some of his ancestors and would not betray him. Instead he turned to Argyll for protection knowing that while he may be out of favour in London he was indomitable in Inveraray. He was given leave to build a house in Glen Shira which he used as a base to continue plundering from Montrose and then at the end of the year he kidnapped Graham of Kilearn and confiscated the annual rent money that had just been collected.

The army were reluctant to send troops into the mountains where Rob's guerrilla force would make them look foolish. The commanding general wrote a note to Montrose, who seethed with rage, saying –

"Twill be difficult to gett him any way but by bribing one of his followers to betray him to a party, otherwise he will always be too cunning and nimble for soldiers under armes…"

Montrose decided to send a large consignment of arms to Graham of Kilearn for distribution among his tenants. Rob merely raided each in turn and then proclaimed that he had been re-armed at the King's expense. Montrose obtained Letters of Fire and Sword and acting on information he personally led a posse through torrential rain and darkness and surprised Rob as he lay sleeping in a house at Balquhidder. Montrose was exultant as Rob was bound with a leather belt and placed on a horse in the middle of a squadron of dragoons. On the way to Stirling they had to cross the Forth at the Fords of Frew which was in spate due to the rain. Rob's arms were released to enable him to battle the turbulent waters while tied and mounted behind a soldier reputed to be the strongest of the group. Unknown to his captors Rob had secreted a dirk under his arm and on reaching midstream slashed himself free. He then dived into the surging waters, releasing his plaid at the same time. In the gathering gloom of late afternoon the floating plaid attracted all the attention and was repeatedly slashed and fired on. Rob remained under the freezing water and swam far downstream before escaping into the forest.

News of Montrose's embarrassment spread throughout the country and a large bounty was placed on Rob's head but few conspired to collect it. Argyll laughed at Montrose's futile attempts to capture Rob Roy and when Montrose wrote to demand withdrawal of his protection he sarcastically replied –

"You feed him, but all he gets from me is wood and water."

Rob was tired and needed respite from the constant harassment and readily agreed to meet with the Duke of Atholl to discuss his surrender. He had already fought alongside his sons, William the Marquis of Tullibardine and Lord George Murray in previous Jacobite uprisings. Both sons remained in exile but Rob expected to be among sympathisers. However the old Duke still remained loyal to the Whig Government and saw the prospect of taking great political advantage over Montrose and possibly winning the release of his third son Charles who was being held in London. Once more the bargain rested on Rob's betrayal of Argyll which was steadfastly refused. Despite his submission in good faith and the offer of safe conduct Rob Roy was seized and held at Logierait. Crowing with success Atholl wrote to the King, the Duke of Montrose and others to proclaim his success. However his clansmen were embarrassed by their chief's treachery and contrived to spare their honour.

Always convivial in adversity Rob entertained his gaolers with stories and by playing music on his chanter. As was the custom for a condemned man whisky was aplenty while he waited to be taken to Edinburgh. Rob wrote a note to his wife and was allowed to go to the door to pass it to his gillie. Apparently no one had noticed that the gillie had a cavalry horse and not a customary highland garron. With sudden alacrity Rob mounted the steed and rode off into the gathering gloom. Pursuit became impossible when no other horse could be found on the estate.

Atholl was apoplectic with rage and embarrassment at having been made to look like a fool. He despatched sixty men and his best tracker to capture Rob Roy, at all costs. Although none of the people would cooperate with the searchers they tracked him down to a place where he was smitten with a fever. Fortunately two of Atholl's men had pre-warned the McGregors and Rob was spirited away before he could be taken. Rob decided to write a public declaration in an attempt to counter his pursuers –

"Honour and conscience urges me to detect the assassins of our countrey and countreymen, whose unbounded malice prest me to be the instrument of matchless villany by endeavouring to make me a false evidence against a person of distinction....This proposal was handed me first by Graham of Killerne, from his master the Duke of Montrose, with the valuable offers of life and fortune, which I could not

entertain but with the utmost horrour. Lord Ormiston, who trysted me to the bridge of Crammond, was no less solicitous on the same subject, which I modestly shifted till I gott out of his clutches, fearing his justice would be no check on his tyranny. To make up the triumvirate in the bloody conspiracy, his Grace the Duke of Atholl resolved to outstrip the other two, if possible, who, having coy-duk'd me into his conversation, immediately committed me to prison, which was contrary to the parole of honour given to me.....The reason why the promise was broke to me was I boldly refused to bear false witness against the Duke of Argyll... Were the Duke of Montrose and I left alone to debate our own private quarrel....I would shew the world how little he would signify to serve either King or Countrey. And I hereby solemnly declare what I have said in this is positive truth and that these are the only persons deterr'd me many times since my first submission to throw myself over again in the King's mercy; and I can prove most of it by witnesses."

When Rob recovered from his illness he started raiding Atholl and Montrose once again which encouraged them to come together and plan concerted action. Atholl sent his best tracker, Donald Stewart, to accompany his men while Montrose went to Edinburgh to demand a troop of cavalry in a determined bid to capture Rob Roy. Atholl's men were run around by the misdirections given by Rob's loyal supporters. As they rested in a cave above Loch Earn, Rob came down upon them in the middle of the night, seized their arms and then let the chastened men go. But unknown to Rob a fast troop of cavalry was on its way and with fresh tracks available Stewart was able to surround him before his informers could pass the word. Rob was duly arrested and put on horseback and placed in the middle of the troop which made all haste for Stirling before retaliation could be organised.

Their route took them along the steep slopes on the shore along Loch Lubnaig just west of Callander. The track was about one hundred feet above the water, towards St Bride's chapel. Fearful of falling, the troopers had to pay close attention to their horses' footing and there was only room for a single file. When one nervous animal caused a commotion by refusing a craggy traverse Rob saw his chance. He leaped off his mount and disappeared into the misty wilderness before the soldiers could load their muskets. As a result the commanding general advised the Government that regular troops should not henceforth be used against Rob Roy in the Highlands, where their ineffectiveness would only encourage the disaffected clans. He had come to the same conclusion as had the Romans when they tried to pursue the ***Scotti***.

In July 1718 war broke out between Britain and Spain. Hostilities had built up due to the disputed Spanish Succession and the ongoing trade wars in the Caribbean. A plan was conceived for an invasion of Britain involving dissident Jacobites which included the exiled Earl of Seaforth, chief of the Mackenzies and the Marquis of Tullibardine. A Spanish army was to land in England while the disaffected chiefs would land in Kintail and raise a highland army. Against his better judgement Rob Roy decided to support Tullibardine for the assistance given by the Atholl Jacobites during his recent escape.

The Jacobites landed at Gairloch with three hundred Spaniards and occupied the castle of Eilean Donan on Loch Alsh. Tullibardine assumed command and was joined by his brother Lord George Murray, members of Clan Ranald, the Camerons and Rob Roy came with fifty McGregors. News was then received that the main Spanish fleet had been wrecked by a storm off Cape Finisterre. Before the Scots group could abandon their part in the enterprise three English Frigates sailed up Loch Alsh and destroyed the two Spanish ships that lay at anchor. The frigates then pounded the castle and captured the garrison.

Had Rob been in charge the men would have disappeared into the hills but Tullibardine was imbued with youthful gallantry and decided to make a stand hoping to receive reinforcements from the wily clansmen. While he waited in vain General Wightman marched west from Inverness and up into Glen Shiel. Tullibardine positioned his men at the gorge near the Bridge of Shiel with Murray and his Highlanders on the south bank. The Mackenzies and Rob Roy's men were placed high up on the north bank. The Spaniards were on a hill in the middle of both flanks. The battle started with the mortar bombing of Murray's position while the dragoons attacked the Spanish. Both groups held on bravely until the superior numbers of Wightman's infantry managed to outflank the Mackenzies and Seaforth's arm was shattered by a musket ball. This caused them to withdraw further up the hill which enabled the Government force to take their vantage point and rain down withering fire on Murray's position. Eventually Murray was wounded in the leg and forced to retreat in the face of repeated attacks from all sides. The Spanish, under Don Alonzo de Santarem, bravely held on and fought throughout the night before surrendering to Wightman in the morning. Their action allowed the others to escape. Rob Roy sought refuge in Glen Shira while the chiefs escaped back into exile. The local Mackenzies were so impressed by the Spanish bravery that they named the mountain on which they fought –

Sgurr nan Spainteach (The peak of the Spaniards)

Montrose complained to the Privy Council about Argyll's protection of Rob Roy but the balance of power changed when Sir Robert Walpole became Prime minister. Walpole favoured young Argyll and once again power rested with the Campbells when Argyll's brother was appointed Minister of State for Scotland. In 1723 Daniel Defoe published a romantic tale called ***The Highland Rogue*** based on the exploits of Rob Roy. Although the stories were more fanciful than factual, Rob became a national hero. Even the King was amused and instructed Argyll to reconcile Rob with his enemies which led to a royal pardon in 1726. Rob knew he was coming to the end and was more interested in God's pardon after his tumultuous life. He was drawn to the Catholic faith where an act of confession could lead to the forgiveness he craved. He took council from the Drummond family and it is reputed that Father Alasdair Drummond blessed himself many times after hearing Rob's first confession. On the 28th of December 1734 Rob summoned his piper and asked him to play ***Cha till me tuille*** and while listening to the refrain he died in a peaceful reverie.

Rob was buried at the auld Kirk in Balquhidder and his memory is celebrated in the town of Callander where his statue stands in front of the local church, the place where the parade initiating the Callander Highland Gathering begins its march.

THE JACOBITE REBELLION

After the debacle of Glen Shiel the Jacobite cause seemed to have no future. Furthermore under the astute leadership of Sir Robert Walpole the Alliance with France was maintained and both countries were able to develop their colonial interests and so there was little incentive for intervention in Scottish affairs. However internal discontent still simmered. The ***Glorious revolution*** which followed the demise of the Stewarts purported to give power to the people and religious freedom but the transfer of power from the King to the Whig Government proved to be even more authoritarian. The union of parliaments had brought little benefit to Scotland and instead of profiting from trading opportunities they were increasingly subjected to unpopular taxes to fund colonial wars. The financial losses due to the bursting of the South Sea Bubble in 1721 caused much distress then the imposition of a malt tax on a whisky dependant nation caused a riot. Also many Scots hated being ruled from London and the embers of nationalism were easily inflamed.

The Pretender found refuge in Rome under the Pope's patronage. In 1720 he married the grand-daughter of the king of Poland, who presented him with a son named Charles Edward Louis Philip Casmir Stewart to curry favour with the kings of France, Spain and Poland. The young prince carried the papal hope that one day he would bring back the Catholic Faith to Scotland.

While Charles was being groomed in Rome the Jacobites in exile continued to plot. It was not until 1739, when Walpole had to take Britain to war with Spain following a dispute in the Mediterranean that they were able to find some traction with France. In 1740 the War of the Austrian Succession began and by 1741 Britain and France were again on opposite sides. A plan was agreed to land twelve thousand men at Maldon in Essex and three thousand in Scotland. Secrecy was of paramount importance in order to catch the British unawares while their troops were engaged elsewhere in Europe. However by the time Charles arrived at Dunkirk, British agents had become aware of the plan and a British squadron intercepted and drove off the French fleet at Dungeness. French barges carrying about ten thousand men were also caught in a violent storm and seven of them sank with all hands, others were wrecked on the rocks. After a second attempt also failed the mission was cancelled.

Young Charles was bitterly disappointed committed himself to what he considered his destiny – the restoration of the Stewarts. He turned to a privateer called Antoine Walsh who was willing to help Charles go it alone. When Cameron of Lochiel, the grandson of the once famous warrior, heard of the plan he called it a -

"Rash and desperate undertaking."

Charles landed at Eriskay in the Outer Hebrides with an entourage of seven persons; the most notable was the Marquis of Tullibardine elder brother of the Duke of Atholl, who had remained in exile since the Battle of Glen Shiel.

Within a few days he moved to the mainland and found only a few bemused Highlanders. His arrival was a complete surprise, even to his supporters, but was well timed as most of the British army was on the continent. The first to arrive in support were the staunchly catholic men of Arisaig and Morar and then the MacDonalds of Keppock and Knoydart accompanied by the McGregors. These were wild men who lived by stealing other people's cattle and saw an opportunity of winning booty by rebelling against the Government. Some of the great chiefs including MacDonald of Sleat and MacLeod of MacLeod refused to join in what they considered a reckless venture. With only a few rogues and thieves at his side Charles held his resolve and refused to return to France with Antoine Walsh.

His regal bearing and sophisticated appearance fascinated the wild Highlanders. He radiated a petulant arrogance and was not inclined to take any advice that would not serve his purpose.

Charles's spirit lifted when he heard the distant refrain of the bag pipes, increasing in volume as the minutes passed. Then on the crest of a hill Cameron of Lochiel appeared with eight hundred men, followed by another four hundred from Glengarry. The young Lochiel, so called because his legendary father was still alive, was referred to as –

"A man who had understood fighting and killing and stealing and not much else."

Not all of the Highlanders favoured the Jacobites. MacLeod of MacLeod was averse to a rebellion and took it upon himself to inform the Hanoverian Government that Charles had arrived. General Cope was ordered to march from Stirling to quell the insurrection before it had time to develop. Meantime troops were sent from Fort Augustus to reinforce Fort William but were ambushed near the High Bridge and forced to surrender. Morale was boosted when the prisoners were paraded at the raising of the standard. Not a single man had been lost during the action which encouraged others to join the revolution.

Although Lord George Murray was pardoned for his part in the previous Jacobite rebellion he had remained in exile and had fought for the French with considerable distinction and received the following accolade from Chevalier de Johnstone,–

"A natural genius for military operations, and was indeed a man of surprising talents, which, had they been cultivated by the study of military tactics, would unquestionably have rendered him one of the greatest generals of the age. He was tall and robust, and brave in the highest degree, conducting the highlanders in the most heroic manner, being always the first to rush sword in hand into the midst of the enemy. He used to say when he advanced to the charge "I do not ask you, my lads, to go before, but merely to follow me". He slept little, was continually occupied with all the manner of details, and was altogether most indefatigable, for he alone had the planning and directing of all our operations; in a word, he was the only person capable of conducting our army."

With such a distinguished soldier at his side Charles immediately appointed him Lieutenant General of his army.

The Jacobites crossed the Forth at the Ford of Frew to avoid Stirling Bridge which was protected by the cannons of the castle. They quickly moved through Linlithgow and on 16th of September 1745 the gentle citizens of the nation's capital awoke to find a fierce army of wild looking men, who spoke a foreign language, camped outside the city walls. One observer remarked –

"They were strong, active and hardy men....of a very ordinary size; the kilts shewed their naked limbs, which were strong and muscular. Their strong countenancers and bushy uncombed hair, gave them a fierce, barbarous and imposing aspect."

In contrast to his men Charles was tall, fair and imperious looking, dressed in a short, tartan coat and a blue bonnet. The women certainly approved of what they saw and the crowd cheered as he made his way to Holyrood Palace. There was still considerable resentment about the loss of Scottish independence among the populace and had Charles decided to declare for Scotland the course of history may well have been significantly different – but he had loftier ambitions when he proclaimed that his father was the King of Scotland, England, and Ireland.

When Cope landed in Dunbar he was well armed compared to the rebels with the infantry boosted by cavalry and a battery of cannon. The Jacobites were mainly on foot, some armed with firelocks, others with broadswords and a few only having pitch-forks and scythes. The crucial difference was the calibre of the men.

Cope advanced to Prestonpans and assembled his troops for battle across a recently cropped field bordered by the Firth of Forth to the north and a bog to the south. It was an ideal position for a regular army as they awaited an assault from the west.

Lord George Murray advised against a frontal assault with his poorly armed troops. He had the southern morass reconnoitred but could find no way through the ditches and swamps. Then a recruit called Robert Anderson, the son of a local man who had taken part in the last rebellion, came forward. He knew a way and was willing to lead them through the bog during the hours of darkness. As dawn broke, the Highlanders attacked through the morning mist, giving little warning of their rapid approach. The hastily assembled cannon was only able to fire one volley which caused no disruption to the highland charge -

"Every front man covered his followers; there was no man to be seen in the open."

When the cannons were overwhelmed the Dragoons turned and fled. So quick was the charge that the infantry having discharged their muskets, had no time to reload before the fury was upon them. The action lasted no more than ten minutes.

Success at Prestonpans encouraged many of the vacillating clans to declare for the cause and shortly after the battle Cluny MacPherson and his men arrived in Edinburgh. The Jacobite numbers were now about five thousand and the priority was to march on London before the British continental army returned to defend the realm.

The Government's southern army had stalled at Lichfield after their commander Sir John Ligonier fell seriously ill. With the on-coming danger no time was lost in bringing back the King's son, the Duke of Cumberland from the British army in Flanders where he had distinguished himself as a brave and competent soldier. When the English troops learned of his appointment they –

"Leaped and skipped about like wild things."

The wily Lord George Murray made a feint by leading his troops as if making for Wales where there was some Jacobite sympathies. The ruse worked, Cumberland placing his army near Newcastle-under-Lyme with the intention of intercepting the invaders. The way was then clear for Charles to enter Derby unopposed.

After a long, hard march in a strange, unfriendly country, many of the weary Highlanders began to desert and few English Jacobites had come forward. By this time, the British army had returned from Flanders and was massing for the defence of London. In addition, two battle-hardened armies, both superior in number to the rebels, were closing in pursuit. Lord George Murray seeing a disaster looming, forced his reluctant Prince to begin retreating back to Scotland and bravely offered to command the rearguard. Charles fell into a rage as he had never been countermanded in his life but wiser heads prevailed.

Cumberland led his cavalry and a thousand mounted foot soldiers in a dash for the border. They were ambushed by the rearguard just south of Penrith which enabled the main Jacobite force to cross the border. By the time Cumberland relieved Carlisle at the end of December it was time to pause due to the onset of winter while the rest of the British army was deployed to repulse a possible French invasion. On 18th of December a convoy of eleven ships sailed from Calais resulting in two being captured and another sunk. At daybreak the next day a convoy from Dunkirk, consisting of sixty ships loaded with arms and ammunition, was sighted and immediately attacked. At least seventeen transporters were destroyed or taken to Dover with the remainder forced to return to port. On the 20th of December the British admiral attacked the escorts of another convoy making for Boulogne and all the transporters were driven ashore and wrecked. Following such grievous losses the French lost heart and ***The Great Enterprise*** was abandoned.

Lord George Murray had made the right decision by enforcing a retreat back to Scotland.

Cumberland was recalled to England to take command of the British army in the event of an invasion. General Hawley was then sent from Newcastle with a new professional army, confident that he could defeat the Jacobites. He had fought at the debacle of Sheriffmuir and was convinced that the Highlanders could not withstand a cavalry charge. He was a severe man and on one occasion in Flanders a contemporary related –

"After a deserter was hanged before Hawley's window, the surgeons begged to have the body for dissection. He reluctantly parted with the pleasing spectacle and demanded that the skeleton be hanged up in the guard-room."

Charles set up his headquarters at Bannockburn and laid siege to Stirling Castle while Lord George Murray reconnoitred the ground for the coming battle. Hawley had spent three days hauling heavy cannon from Edinburgh to Falkirk and set up his camp to the west of the town. Charles brought his men together at Plean Muir and held a council of war where Lord George proposed that the Highlanders take the offensive instead of waiting to be attacked. His strategy was to establish his vanguard on the Hill of Falkirk, a four hundred foot high ridge, to the south west of the town. At this location, cannon firing from the boggy ground below, would be rendered useless. Part of the plan was to distract the Government's army by sending units down the main road in full sight of the enemy while the main body filtered through the Torwood undetected.

As the Jacobites approached Hawley feasted at Callendar house, convinced that the Highlanders would not attack his superior forces. When the plan unfolded desperate efforts were made in an attempt to stop the Highlanders reaching the top of the hill. The Hanoverian cavalry was ordered to race up the steep slope followed by infantry that struggled in vain to keep up with the horses. They were also hampered by torrential rain driving into their faces and mud under foot. Lord George and his Atholl men were waiting for the arrival of the cavalry and when they broke the crest, assaulted them with a withering volley from point blank range. This gave time for the Jacobite army to form their ranks in favourable positions. Their right flank was protected by a steep cleft in the hill and the left flank by a swamp on the bank of the Glen Burn.

While both sides fired at each other across the gully, Hawley ordered Ligonier to regroup his cavalry and attack the right flank. George Murray waited until they had come to within ten paces and opened fire. About eighty dragoons immediately fell dead and in the confusion that followed the Highlanders set about the survivors -

"The most singular and extraordinary combat immediately followed. The Highlanders, stretched on the ground, thrust their dirks into the bellies of ther horses. Some seized the riders by their clothes, dragged them down, and stabbed them with their dirks; several again used their pistols; but few had sufficient space to handle their swords. MacDonald of Clanranald….assured me that whilst he was lying on the ground, under a dead horse, which had fallen on him, without the power of extricating himself, he saw a dismounted horseman struggling with a Highlander; fortunately for him, the Highlander, being the strongest, threw away his antagonist, and having killed him with his dirk, he came to his assistance, and drew him with difficulty from under the horse."

The MacDonalds raced after the retreating cavalry who in their haste galloped over their own infantry, causing further disruption. Most of the Highlanders bore the old type of musket which did not use cartridges and therefore could not be reloaded due to the heavy rain. Instead they pulled out their swords and swarmed down the hill into Hawley's struggling infantry. Soon the whole Government army was in full retreat, running for their lives towards Linlithgow.

After the battle had been won Charles feasted on Hawley's supper and the Highlanders relished the great number of hampers and wines which had been abandoned by the fleeing enemy.

After Falkirk Charles split his army into two main groups with the intention of regrouping at Inverness. Lord George Murray took the lowland regiments and the cavalry on the circuitous route via Montrose and Aberdeen hoping to receive supplies from French ships. When Charles approached Inverness his army was straggled throughout the Highlands. Little regard had been given to the activities of Lord Louden who had collaborated with the MacLeods of Skye to gather a northern force in support of the Government. Aware of the danger, Lady MacIntosh diverted Charles from Inverness and provided quarters for him and his entourage at Moy, the seat of the MacIntosh clan. When Lord Louden was informed that Charles had only about five hundred men in his company he seized the opportunity of ending the war and bringing great personal acclaim. In the middle of the night on 16th of February 1746 Louden marched with fifteen hundred men from Inverness. Lady MacIntosh had been informed by secret letter and without saying a word to her sleeping Prince she despatched her blacksmith and personal staff to encounter Louden's troops. On hearing their approach they fired repeated volleys and ran about making a great noise, shouting the names of Lochiel and Keppock, as if the renowned warriors were among them. The sudden barrage from the darkness of the night seemed that the whole highland army was on the attack. Louden's men panicked and many were trampled to death as they ran back to Inverness.

On hearing of what had happened Charles assembled his troops and marched on Inverness in pursuit of Louden who lost no time in making good his escape via the Kessock Ferry to seek refuge in the depths of Ross-shire. Louden had the sense to commandeer all the boats to prevent being followed. Lord Cromarty was then sent, accompanied by the MacKinnons and the McGregors, on a man hunt that took them all the way to the Western Isles.

Charles set about consolidating the Highlands and sent Lochiel down the Great Glen to capture Fort Augustus and Fort William. Lord George Murray turned his attention to relieving Atholl which had been occupied by Government forces which included the hated Campbells. He was joined by Cluny MacPherson as he travelled through Badenoch. The men were divided into several raiding parties and departed into the night leaving Lord George and Cluny with twenty five men at a rendezvous near the Bridge of Bruar. When the day broke they were informed that Sir Andrew Agnew was approaching with a strong force of Government troops. Most of the small group was for escaping into the hills but Lord George had a different opinion –

"If I quit my post, all the parties I have sent out, as they come in, will fall into the hands of the enemy."

He deployed his men behind a dyke and spread them out before unfurling the colours of the MacPhersons and the Atholl regiment. All the pipers were ordered to play their noisiest pibrochs as soon as the Government soldiers came in sight. On a given signal everyone drew their swords and brandished them above their heads with their customary blood-curdling roar. As the blades glinted in the morning sun from the wide spread location it appeared there was a large group of Highlanders eager for a fight and commanded by the best warriors in the country. Sir Andrew took a minute to gaze at the spectacle and then ordered his men to march back to the safety of Blair Atholl Castle.

Cumberland resumed command of the Government army and was reported to have crossed the River Spey. Charles summoned his widespread army to a muster at Culloden House. Lochiel lifted the siege at Fort William and Lord George withdrew his men from their assault on Blair Atholl Castle. Cluny and the MacPhersons were still in Badenoch and Lord Cromarty's regiment, with the MacKinnons and McGregors, were still far away on the other side of the country searching for Lord Louden. As the army started to arrive in dribs and drabs Lord George proposed that the highland army should occupy the broken ground on the other side of the river Nairn which would provide more cover than an open field. He realised that the era of the Highland Charge was coming to an end due to advances in weaponry used by the enemy. Drawing musket fire before charging was no longer an effective tactic due to the use of cartridges which enabled rapid reloading and volleying.

The Prince came up with his own, ill-advised but grandiose plan, whereby the Highlanders would march through the night and surprise the enemy at their encampment near Nairn. This was the strategy that had proved successful at Prestonpans and he saw no reason why it should not work for a second time. Lord George reluctantly agreed being aware of the overwhelming problems. Many of the soldiers were still in far off locations and those that had arrived were hungry and tired after making long hasty journeys. With little food available a large number was forced to move on to Inverness and forage for supplies. Lord George realised that it was necessary to implement the plan without delay to have any chance of success. Therefore, with only about half the army available with the remainder commanded to follow on arrival, Lord George Murray led his troops through the dense muddy forest. Progress was slow, having to travel a long circuitous route to avoid enemy outposts and in the darkness of the night there were many obstacles. When the first rank eventually reached the edge of the forest the sun was beginning to rise and the broken column stretched to the rear for many miles, in no condition to attack. The strategy had failed and on hearing a bugle sound the call to arms, they realised their presence had been detected. There was no option but to retreat back through the woods.

The highland army got back to Culloden in the early hours of the morning. After another night march the men were exhausted and famished. Crucially before the Jacobite army had time to recover a message was received that Cumberland was marching towards them. The dispirited highland army was frantically recalled, some did not respond. Lord Cromarty along with the MacKinnons and MacGregors were still in Sutherland and Cluny with his MacPhersons had still not arrived from Badenoch. Other than run away there was no option but to confront the cream of the British army with a depleted and demoralised force.

Ironically Cumberland was able to choose the field of battle and halted his formation where the firm ground came to an end.

Lord George Murray's concerns about the battle ground were to prove crucial. Cumberland had taken the initiative by occupying the firm ground, forcing the Jacobites to occupy an area between two walls with the southern end extending on to a turf dyke. This restricted freedom of movement; furthermore advances from the Jacobite left flank, where three MacDonald regiments had been assembled, were blocked by the presence of a swamp between the front lines. Cumberland realised that the lie of the ground would encourage the battle to skew towards his left flank and placed the redoubtable Colonel James Wolfe and his musket men behind the turf wall to await the onslaught.

The weaponry was also crucial – the Highlanders mostly had old French muskets which required the application of a powder horn before firing whereas Cumberland's men could maintain a rapid volley using cartridges. Also the efficient use of their cannon compared favourably with the disorganised Frenchmen who manned the few Scottish cannon. The Highlanders still depended on a rapid highland charge and close quarter engagement with the enemy.

When Prince Charles did not give the desired command to attack, his men were exposed to withering gunfire. The delay was put down to the Prince's young messenger being decapitated by a cannon-ball. On the other side Cumberland -

"Finding his cannon rapidly thinning the Jacobite ranks, without experiencing any loss in return, had no desire to attack."

As the Highlanders waited impatiently the enemy gunners changed to grapeshot and –

"Swept the field as with a hail storm and the Highlanders only partially inured to artillery, were greatly surprised and disordered by it."

Seeing their line being greatly thinned the Mackintoshes broke ranks and charged, followed by the men from Atholl.

An English soldier described the attack -

"Their spirited advance lasted but a short time and they shifted away to our left. They came up very boldly and fast all in a cloud together, sword in hand. They fired there pieces and flung them away; but we gave them so warm a reception that we kept a continued close fire upon them with our small arms: besides two of our cannon gave them a close fire with grapeshot which galled them very much."

"Like wildcats their men came down like in swarms upon our left wing and began to cut and hack in ther natural way without ceremony."

Some managed to burst through the front line but none made it to the second.

The MacDonald regiments did not take part in the attack being unable to move forward due to the ground conditions with some knee high in the mud. They had also suffered severe losses as they stood waiting for orders and despite the urgings of the Duke of Perth they started to fall back. Seeing this, Cumberland's cavalry moved to outflank and pursue them as they started their flight. Some of the MacDonald officers refused to retreat and Keppock exclaimed to the heavens –

"O my God has it come to this, that the children of my tribe have forsaken me!"

He then charged, sword in hand, towards the enemy lines. His brother Donald, in his eagerness to be the first to engage the enemy, was among the first to be shot down. Keppock also fell with a ball through his arm and after receiving a second wound his officers entreated him not to throw away his life. Their efforts were in vain and he died on the battlefield.

Most of the chiefs who led the attacking line were killed. The chieftain of the MacLeans turned back to look for his two missing sons and was intercepted by two troopers. He rushed on them; killing one and wounding the other but three others came and cut old MacLean to pieces. Cameron of Lochiel, at the head of his regiment, fired his pistol and slashed with his sword until he was wounded by grapeshot in both ankles. When Cumberland came across the wounded Fraser of Inverallochy, the young colonel refused to ask for quarter and defiantly declared his loyalty to Prince Charles. Cumberland then ordered Colonel James Wolfe to shoot him but the future conqueror of Quebec refused to be an executioner and the order was carried out by another officer.

Lord George Murray, leading the men from Atholl, had his horse killed from under him and in the hand-to-hand fighting that followed lost one sword and broke another. He received several cuts and was covered in blood. Realising the desperate situation he forced his way back and led the second line into the fray to support his hard pressed men.

In spite of their bravery, the Jacobites had lost the day to a superior force and with presence of mind Lord George retreated in good order. Those that retreated towards

Inverness were relentlessly pursued and cut down, leaving a trail of bodies for nearly four miles. Many fatally wounded men crawled into the woods to die rather than wait to be murdered.

Prince Charles was aghast that his hitherto invincible army had been routed. He was mindful of charging forward to rally his men but his bridle was seized and he was reluctantly led away. Realising all was lost Charles made his final order –

"Let every man seek his own safety the best he can."

Following the disaster it was said –

"Had Prince Charles slept during the whole of the expedition and allowed Lord George to act for him, according to his own judgement, there is every reason for supposing he would have found the crown of Great Britain on his head when he awoke."

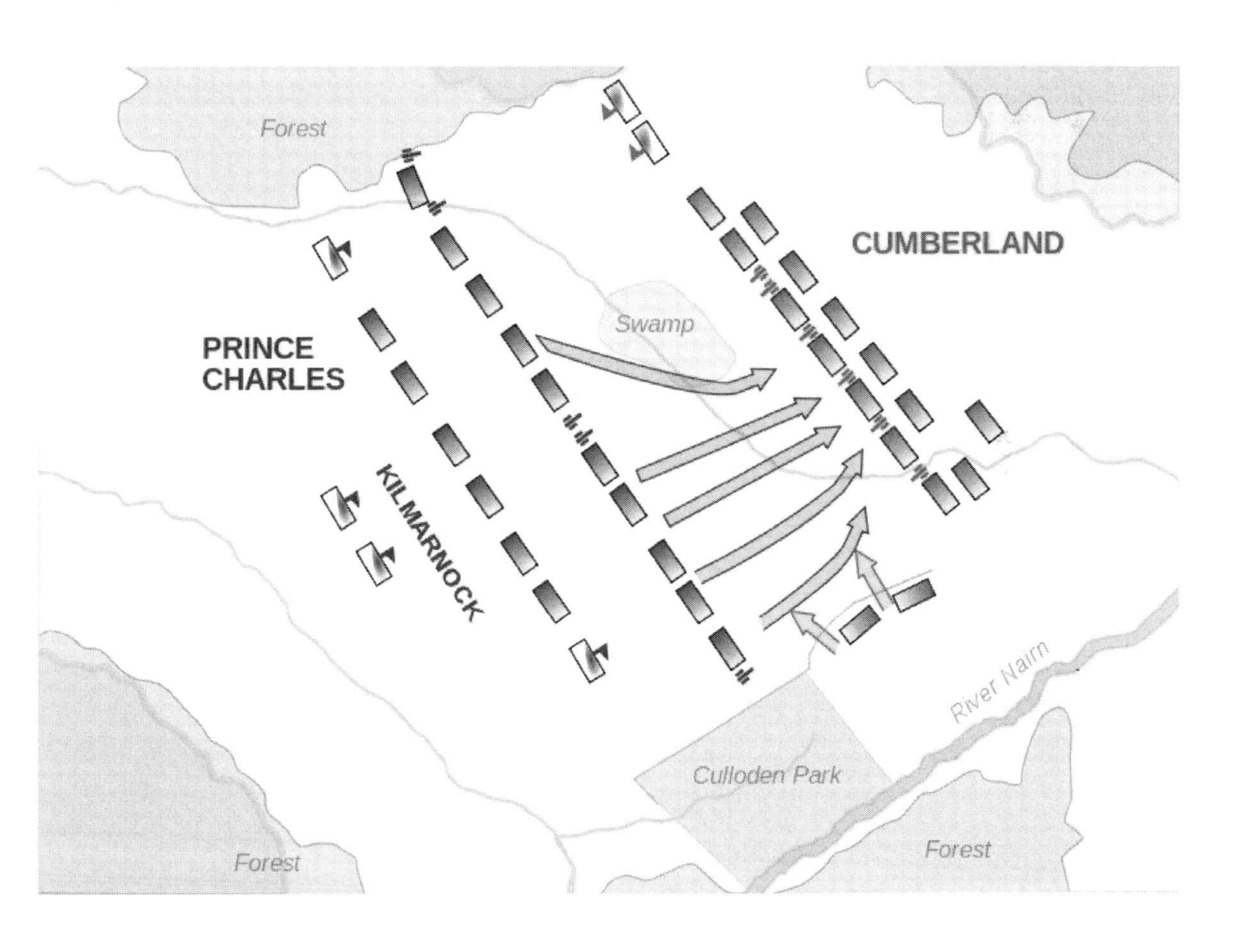

The saga of Prince Charles' escape says more about the highland character than the Prince himself. His exploits are fine examples of true loyalty with no possibility of personal advantage. Here was a man who disregarded the advice of his friends and left them in great peril. Still they acted to protect him and even the ordinary people continued to risk their lives on his behalf.

Following his escape from Culloden, Charles changed his clothes and was escorted through the night to Invergarie near Fort Augustus. He was left with two faithful companions who took him to Borradale where the local MacDonald chieftain procured a boat. He was rowed across the Minch during a dark and stormy night, landing near Benbecula the next morning.

When Cumberland learned of Charles' presence in the Hebrides he sent more than a thousand men to search for him. They brutally combed the entire group of islands as far as St Kilda. The hebrides were surrounded with cutters, sloops, frigates and war-ships, allowing no passage to anyone without a passport. An act of gallantry occurred when Charles was about to be captured by his pursuers. A young man blocked their passage declaring that he was the Prince and confronted the confused soldiers allowing Charles to escape. Not sure of their conquest they severed the young man's head and sent it for identification. The only person who could reliably do so was his former hairdresser, a man named Morris who was incarcerated in Carlisle. By the time the ripened head reached the gaol it had decayed beyond recognition.

When a young woman called Flora MacDonald was told about the distress of Charles, she at first, did not want to be involved but on seeing his poor condition her heart softened and agreed to try and bring him to Skye. She managed to gain passports for what she described as her man servant and maid from Captain MacDonald, the chief of the local militia. Charles then became Betty Burke, an excellent spinner of flax, and. dressed in woman's clothes he was taken back to the mainland.

The MacDonalds of Glenaladale took charge of Charles and resolved to bring him through the line of sentries posted across the glen. When it became dark they could see the soldiers continually moving between the fires that were burning at each post. With careful timing they led Charles up the channel of a small river that flowed in a hollow between two of the posts and moved forward when the sentries' backs were turned.

They decide to set out for Ross-shire in the hope that they would find safety among loyal Mackenzies. On the way they were obliged to call at the house of Christopher Macraw being sorely in need of food and shelter. Although comparatively rich Macraw came from a barbarous people, among whom there were few gentlemen. He made them pay dearly for his services and demanded to know their identity and Charles was passed off as a young chief of Clan Donald. When the whisky had mellowed Macraw's temperament he railed on about the Highlanders that had taken up arms for Charles and said –

"Those who still protected him were fools and mad-men; that they ought to deliver themselves and their country from distress, by giving him up, and taking the reward which the government had offered."

Charles expressed his wish to go Badenoch where Cluny MacPherson and Lochiel were believed to be in hiding. On the way they crossed the great hill of Corado and heard of seven brave and faithful men living in a cave high up in the crags. They were broken, desperate men some of whom had fought in his army. When the Prince came upon them they fell on their knees to honour him and welcomed him to feast on the beast they had killed that very day. There was no question that they would betray his presence.

"Charles staid in the cave with these men five weeks and three days; during this long abode, either thinking he would be safer with gentlemen, than with common fellows of a loose character, or desirous of better company, he told MacDonald of Glenaladale that he intended to put himself in the hands of some of the neighbouring gentlemen; desiring him to inquire about them and learn who was the most proper person for him to apply to. Glenaladale talking with the Highlanders about the gentlemen in their neighbourhood, and inquiring into their character, they guessed from his questions what was the intention of Charles; and conjured him to dissuade the Prince from it, saying that no reward could be any temptation to them; for if they betrayed the Prince, they must leave their country, as nobody would speak to them, except to curse them: whereas £30000 was a great reward to a poor gentleman, who could go to Edinburgh or London with his money, where he would find people enough to live with him, and eat his meat and drink his wine."

Such was the code of honour among the broken Highlanders.

Following a close encounter with a government patrol the cavemen were required to fire their muskets revealing their location. Charles knew he had to move on and find Cluny or Lochiel. On the 29th of August they moved into Badenoch and joined Cluny MacPherson and Lochiel in a specially constructed hideout called the *cage* which was camouflage by trees on the face of a steep, rocky part of the mountain.

Charles left with Lochiel on the 19th of September 1746 when word was received that French ships were coming to rescue them and the Stewart dynasty ended for ever.

REVIVAL

It was the common man that suffered most in the aftermath of Culloden when Cumberland's troops systematically dismantled their way of life. The Hanoverian Red Coats scoured the country rooting out all vestiges of Jacobite support. Houses were burnt, women raped and about twenty thousand cattle seized. More than three thousand five hundred men were captured and found guilty of high treason. Most were transported to the colonies for life; some were executed and others were hung drawn and quartered. An Act of Proscription was passed which enabled all weapons to be confiscated, the wearing of tartan and the kilt were banned and the Gaelic language forbidden in schools and churches. All designed to break the spirit of the indigenous people by taking away the things that installed a man's pride. Many Highlanders were forcibly recruited into the British army and sent for service overseas. Within a few years after Culloden twenty- two regiments were formed which denuded the Highlands of their young warriors. Some fought under General Wolfe during the conquest of Quebec others in the American War of Independence and the highland regiments became legends during the Napoleonic Wars.

The most damaging action was the confiscation of estates owned by the Jacobite chiefs and the abolition of the right of tenure for those living on the land. Management of the estates fell to commissioners in Edinburgh who were only interested in opening up the land for profit. Ordinary people could not afford the new rents and were forced out of their homes. The chieftains that had been loyal to the government also looked on with envious eyes at the money being earned by the vacated properties after they had been turned over to large scale sheep and cattle farming. They no longer valued their tenants as warriors and their wives and daughters wanted to emulate the soft life of the southern gentry.

The Duke of Sutherland decided it was his patriotic duty to improve the yield of his land and employed agents to clear his estates for large scale grazing. In 1801 Sutherland was a wild country populated by a hardy insular race, part Gael and part Viking, numbering about twenty-five thousand. With delusional magnanimity he sought to remove his people by offering them land holdings on the coast, proclaiming that –

"They might harvest the sea with more profit than the earth."

The people of Sutherland were not interested in land improvement or the rewards of industry and were content to operate their illicit stills, sing their psalms in Gaelic and believe in the evil eye. Their forced removal resembled the treatment meted out to the natives of North America, Africa and Australia by uncompromising colonists. When the English and Lowlanders arrived to survey the valley along the banks of the Kildonan river they entered the traditional land of Clan Gunn who were a dour race more Norse than Gael. They made their living by distilling whisky and were not interested in becoming fishermen. When the eviction orders went out the men of Clan Gunn marched down the coast towards Golspie threatening to hang the Duke's factor and burn Dunrobin Castle. They assembled at the Inn of Golspie to listen to the ranting of the local sheriff and the threat of eternal damnation from Church of Scotland ministers who were sponsored by the elitist regime. As the tirade was in English they drifted away more confused than afraid, followed by a powerful army group that had been forced marched from Fort George.

The ***Year of the Burnings*** started in the cold of January 1814 when many square miles of muir-pasture was burnt to enrich the next season's grass for the coming sheep. This left the local raw–ribbed black cattle to search in vain for food, leaving many to die of starvation. The barns that protected the cattle were destroyed and the houses of those that refused to move were put to the torch and people driven away like animals.

A few lairds resisted the temptation to accept offers from the rich farmers from the South. Chisholm known as ***The Fair-head,*** from Strathglass, listened to his graziers at an all-night meeting and sent the sheep farmers away in the morning. The Chisholm was then carried away on the shoulders of his clansmen with his piper playing a rant of triumph. The reprieve did not last long as the old man died in 1793 and although his wife protected the people until her death in 1801 she was succeeded by the twenty-fourth Chisholm who lost no time in dismantling the clan. Within two years five thousand emigrants left Fort William for Antigonish in Nova Scotia.

The next to succumb was Alistair Randalson McDonald who was proud of his family's history and sensitive about his honour and like nothing more than to parade at the head of his clan. As a matter of personal honour he engaged the grand-son of Flora McDonald in a duel and killed him. He instinctively disliked the sheep farmers and tried to stop them burning their pastures in the spring, killing the Birch and Oak trees that had cloaked the hills in his youth. However his debts mounted and he had to move with the times and when his brave regiments returned from the Napoleonic Wars they found that their parents had been evicted and forced to move to the other side of the world.

Following the repeal of the Act of Proscription several Highland Societies came into being in various parts of the country with the purpose of promoting highland culture, music and traditions. A great nostalgia swept the country and many elitists groups supported the ***Highland Improvements***, seeking to wallow in past glories. At a time when there was scant regard for the common man, they glamorised his primitive plaid and made it compulsory attire at their grand meetings and on social occasions. It was also a period of great anxiety for the Government as Britain had just lost the American War of Independence which gave way to radical thinking and aspirations of democracy. Then in 1789-99 the French Revolution erupted, leading to the bloody elimination of the French aristocracy. There was a real fear that the same could happen in Britain but the subsequent patriotism engendered by the Napoleonic Wars in 1803-15 kept the nation together.

When the Continental War ended the cessation of military supplies and the return of thousands of soldiers resulted in an economic downturn, culminating in the rise of the Scottish Radicals in 1820. The weavers from Fife led an artisan strike aimed an uncaring government. They marched to the Carron Ironworks in Falkirk with the intention of seizing weapons but were made to disperse by the Hussars. One of the ring-leaders was John Wilson of Strathaven who later, famously, marched to Cathkin Braes to organise a major assault on Glasgow but his supporters were ambushed and he was subsequently hanged and decapitated at the Glasgow Tolbooth. Others were seized and hanged in Stirling. When John Baird and Andrew Hardie stood on the scaffold they made defiant and stirring speeches which ignited the cause of trade unionism in Scotland. The Government pushed through the Scottish Reform Act in an endeavour to pacify the people. This enabled the citizens of Glasgow to elect their first member of parliament and the hated Corn Laws were repealed.

It was a time when the country had to regain its pride and unity and many sought to do so by stimulating the social activities of the past. Trying to emulate his famous ancestors led Alistair Randalson MacDonald to persuade a number of highland gentlemen to form what he described as –

"A pure Highland Society in support of the Dress, Language, Music and Characteristics of our illustrious and ancient race in the Highlands and Isles of Scotland, with their genuine descendants wherever they may be."

He organised a gathering at Inverlochy in 1815, on the same grass field where Alasdair MacColla had destroyed Clan Campbell in the bloody battle that had taken place one hundred and seventy years before. His purpose was essentially self-aggrandisement using the common man employed as a source of amusement. It began with the gentry engaged in a grand hunt in which the deer fell ***at the height of their speed.*** The hunt lasted three days and was confined to the guests of the Laird. Afterwards they celebrated their exploits and took pleasure in their clansmen competing in the ancient traditional sports. Randal NaCraig McDonnell was expected to win the stone lifting but was reported to be short of his normal vigour.

The events contested at the first ever recorded Highland Games were as follows -

Stone Lift - won by Donald MacCalman from Lochy Side.

Putting the Stone - won by Angus More Kennedy from Ballistaire.

Standing Putt - won by John Roy McDonnell.

Standing Leap (over the bar) - won by Angus More Kennedy.

Running Leap - won by Duncan McDonnell from Glenmorriston.

Throwing the Hammer - won by Randal NaCraig McDonnell

Pulling the Stick – won by Donald McDonald from Knoydart.

Such was the enthusiastic feeling engendered by the games that a noble gentleman by the name of McIntyre, in the ***Garb of Old Gaul,*** was moved to take his silver mounted dirk and presented it to the young heir of Glengarry. When the young man at first refused he sent a message to his father saying that the McIntyre claimed the chief of the MacDonnells as the chief of his blood line and the author of their race.

A footnote in the report mentioned that a canal labourer in low country dress asked to be allowed to contend for the Stone Lift and was answered –

"The world to the worthiest."

To the man's mortification after straining and turning the stone several times he could not raise it from the ground.

At the second grand hunt on the following year the winners at the games were –

Putting the Stone – Randal NaCraig McDonnell.

Lifting the Stone – Angus More Kennedy.

Throwing the Sledge Hammer – Angus More Kennedy (56ft 5ins)

Another footnote mentioned that Randal Na Craig was the approved man at the Stone and Hammer since 1793 and therefore the first recorded champion of the games. His main rival since 1809 had been Angus More Kennedy who was now expected to maintain a very respectable place in those athletic feats.

Alastair Randalson's Highland Games also had an element of blood-lust. In 1822, following the grand hunt, the competitors were required to display their prowess by killing cows with a hammer and then tearing them to pieces.

The Inverness Courier described the event -

"Another of our ancient sports, namely following on a cow, in the dead thaw, and manfully tearing the still reeking animal limb from limb, by dint of muscular strength. Some people were, we saw squeamish enough to be shocked by this exhibition, and did not scruple to use the epithets of brutal and disgusting and so forth…Even the most expert of the operators took from four to five hours in rugging and riving, tooth and nail before they brought off the limbs of one cow."

The prize money was paid at five guineas per joint.

It was also reported that the competition to lift an eighteen stone boulder over a five foot high bar was won by a humble stone mason after having foiled all the ***pretty men of Glengarry.***

Walter Scott praised Alistair Randalson for his flamboyant Scottishness which he considered to be a re-kindling of the pride of a nation. In contrast Robert Burns despised him for neglecting the true needs of his people. Families were starving to death, living in the open with their only source of sustenance coming from gathering shell-fish. Those that were able left their native land for the colonies.

A major effort was under way to raise the spirits of the people by instilling a mood of patriotism. By far the most significant occasion was the visit of George IV to Scotland in 1822. The grand affair was engineered by Sir Walter Scott, consisting of a parade of kilted highland regiments followed by a ***Grand Ball,*** which was attended by all the peers of Scotland. The mandatory dress for the occasion was full highland regalia. In the van of the ***Great Parade*** was none other than Alistair Randalson MacDonald followed by the men from Glengarry wearing a brightly coloured tartan of dubious origin. The crowd roared their approval when the Germanic King appeared in a bright red and green kilt and claimed to be of Stewart lineage. The specially made tartan later became known as the Royal Stewart and it was the pivotal moment when the kilt became the national dress for the whole of Scotland.

Many had admired the Highland Games that had taken place at St Fillans in 1819 and in 1827 they were taken over by the St Fillans Highland Society.

"The games emphasis on strength relates to the redefinition of the Highlander in the second half of the eighteenth century – having been a Jacobite rebel he had become a valuable recruit for the British Army."

For the talented, participation in the games was a lifeline with prize money providing for the well-being of their families.

The actual events depended on the implements that were available such as a tree-trunk, a blacksmith's hammer, and a rounded stone or cannon ball. Wrestling was popular, occasionally stick fighting, archery and stone lifting. Standardisation did not come until later and for the putting event a smooth stone was used at Inverness, a rough iron ball at Luss and a lead ball with finger holes at Aboyne.

In the remote area of Glenisla the locals recalled the exploits of Donald McCombie otherwise known as McCombie Mor due to his prodigious strength. His reputation was such that around the year 1660 the Earl of Atholl implored him to come and be his champion. The pride of the clan was at stake when a gigantic Italian appeared and challenged the best man the Earl could produce. He was a famed professional swordsman and none had come forward. At first McCombie was reluctant until the Italian lifted his kilt and smacked his buttock with the flat of his blade. With a flourish McCombie pulled out his sword and killed the Italian on the spot.

As well as being a warrior McCombie farmed sheep on the high plateaus of the Grampian Mountains. It was common practice in those days for shepherds to live in rough shelters next to fresh water springs, forming little communities where they would engage in social activities. McCombie was famous for wrestling bulls when they proved troublesome and his prowess at stone putting was the subject of legend. He would have attended the shepherds market by Braemar, considered the crossroads of the Highlands due to the convergence of the glens. There would have been an autumn meeting to discuss the affairs of the day followed by traditional sports. It was not until 1832 that the Braemar Highland Society decided to regulate the games and the sum of £5 was donated for prize money. This was on the occasion of Queen Victoria's visit and she was so impressed that she bestowed Royal Patronage and they became known as the Royal Braemar Highland Games.

The Games became so popular that their number grew from about two dozen in 1840 to over a hundred by 1900. The champions became superstars of their generation and some of the names that emerged are reminiscent of ancestral warriors. The games at Skye started in 1877 after a meeting between Lord MacDonald of the Isles and MacLeod of MacLeod with the intention of burying past differences. A committee was formed with the purpose of creating games to match those at Inverness and Oban. A member of the committee was Harry MacDonald who had spent most of his life in India and kept his love of Scottish culture and language. He was a huge man who had a special bath made to accommodate his bulk.

Following the mass exodus in the earlier part of the century the ex-patriot Scottish communities began to flourish and Caledonian Societies were set up as an overseas version of Highland Societies. Many were anxious to proclaim their Scottishness and were keen to show off their prowess. Among the overseas athletes that have carried the MacDonald name with distinction are Harry MacDonald and Doug MacDonald. Both born and bred in Canada, reflecting the cream of the youth that were lost during the ***Clearances.*** Harry was also an exceptionally large man who would not have been able to settle in a normal bath tub.

The Antigonish Highland Society in Nova Scotia sponsored Highland Games in 1863. At the time the 78th Highlanders were stationed at Halifax and they travelled to Antigonish to provide a pipe band for the games. Just after the First World War and one of their champion athletes was Dan R Chisholm whose name echoes the migration of his clan from Strathglass during the Clearances. A year later a Highland Games and Celtic festival started up in Victoria, British Columbia, reflecting the deep Scottish roots in that distant community. Over the next century the Highland Games spread throughout Canada including small venues such as Callander in Ontario and the three day event at Fergus, Ontario that attracts up to fifty thousand visitors

In contrast to the hard conditions found in Canada by destitute emigrants things were different in Australia. Most were welcomed and found work in the sheep stations which had been deserted due to the gold rush and Yorkshire merchants positively encouraged the migrations to keep their mills supplied with Australian wool. Once again the Scottish settlers transplanted their culture within the new settlements and in 1857 Geelong held its first Highland Gathering, featuring the age old games. Later in the century Scottish families also settled in New Zealand and founded the City of Dunedin which is the Gaelic name for Edinburgh. Many of its districts were named in memory of their homeland capital, such as Corstorphine and Morningside and at the present day they also have thriving Highland Games.

STALWARTS

The people of Aberdeenshire largely escaped the deprivations suffered by the Highlanders during the Clearances and remained a sturdy race. In 1837 Donald Dinnie was born near Aboyne. His father, Robert Dinnie, was a man of great physical strength, the champion wrestler of Deeside and became known for his ability to lift heavy stones. In his memoir Donald Dinnie tells the story of one of his father's feats which has since become legendary

"On the granite stone bridge that crosses the River Dee at Potarch there were, and still are, two large stones weighing about 8cwt the pair, placed in a recess. In the early 1830s massive iron rings were placed in them, to which ropes were fixed so that the scaffolds could be attached for pointing the bridge. Now, one of these stones was somewhat heavier than the other. Very few strongmen of that day could lift the heavy one with both hands, but my father could raise one in each hand with apparent ease, and could throw the heavier stone on to the top of a parapet wall of the bridge.

On one occasion, I have been told; he took one stone in each hand and carried them to the end of the bridge and back – a distance of 100 yards. This achievement has been pronounced the greatest feat of strength ever performed in Scotland."

Donald joined the Perth Highland Society in 1856 and gave a vision of the old style games before standardisation was attempted. Gladiatorial events took place as well as exercise with irregular implements. Swordsmanship was one of the leading contests using a basket handle and a three foot long cane, an event in which James Paton was unbeatable. Back-hold wresting occurred at every major Highland Games and the iron weights thrown were locally available implements such as a blacksmith's hammer and those used for measuring farm produce. Dinnie also boasted of his father's prowess at the ***Swee Tree,*** now called the swingle tree where two protagonists sit on the ground, each opposite the other, grasping a stick with the intention of pulling the other over.

Dinnie is credited with introducing the around the head hammer swing in place of the old figure of eight style which was more akin to swinging a two-handled sword. He helped to standardise events so that records could be established, one example being the introduction of a four foot long, wooden hammer shaft. As a result he became the undisputed Scottish Champion by putting a stone weighing 16lbs a distance of 49ft 6ins and throwing a 16lbs Hammer a remarkable 130ft 6ins which was almost 10ft further than his closest rival. He was also never defeated at Back-hold Wrestling.

During his prime Dinnie did much to popularise the Highland Games. Being a grand champion he excited the population that came in droves to witness his great feats. He was called on to appear and promote inaugural events that established many of the prominent games that have continued to the present day. In July of 1867 he became a founder member of the Aboyne committee and at the first games achieved nine firsts and one second. Today in the lounge bar of the Huntly Arms, where the first meeting took place, there is a stained glass window with an image of Donald Dinnie competing at the games. Dinnie also went to the first games at Skye in 1877 and was acclaimed as follows -

"Donald Dinnie, the Stonehaven athlete whose presence had so elevated the first year of the Games and who had helped more than anyone from outside the district to get them underway."

The following year he took his friend George Davidson to Skye and they shared all the prizes for the Heavy Events.

In 1870 Dinnie was invited to Boston where he met and defeated the greatest athletes in America and was proclaimed the World Champion. He then went to Toronto where he duly won all the traditional highland events but the crowd was disappointed that the expected clash between Dinnie and a local man from the quaintly named town of Glengarry did not take place. His name was Rory McLennan whose grandfather had emigrated from Kintail in 1802. He preferred to give exhibitions of his new running and turning style of throwing the hammer and although Dinnie was more inclined to extol his own efforts he acclaimed McLennan as the greatest hammer thrower he had ever seen. During the exhibition McLennan threw a 24lb hammer with a stiff handle 130ft 4ins. Later, in 1872, at Chatlottentown, he threw the 16lb hammer over 180ft and the wonder of his innovation led to the modern Olympic wire hammer throwing style.

As well as being a great all round heavy event athlete, Dinnie was almost invincible at leaping and sprinting but was primarily a warrior who feared no man. When he was sixteen he beat the best wrestlers in Scotland. In later years he faced up to Jem Mace who was recognised as the best pugilist in Britain after objecting to Mace's insulting remarks about ***Scotch Folk.*** In the ensuing confrontation he managed to avoid Mace's punches by slipping behind, lifting him into the air and then smashing him, face downwards, into the ground. When the Englishman eventually got his breath back he behaved in a very civil manner.

During his tour of America he was challenged by Clarence Whistler, the wrestling champion of America. The match took place in the Kansas City Coloseum and during the fight Dinnie threw his opponent so hard that he dislocated his arm. When a doctor put it back in place Dinnie then proceeded to dislocate Whistler's knee joint. The beleaguered American Champion later killed himself during a tour of Australia when his party trick of drinking champagne and then eating the glass went horribly wrong.

In 1883 Dinnie was booked to appear at the Dunedin Games in New Zealand where the committee paid him £50 for the privilege of advertising his name. People came from all parts of the South Island to see him and he won all eighteen events that he participated in. The wrestling was left to a Cumberland man called William Hudson who became so exalted that he challenged Dinnie to a match two weeks later. After two rounds Dinnie hurt his opponent so badly that he had to retire. His feat so impressed the Christchurch Caledonian Society that they organised a special event so that Dinnie could demonstrate his prowess. This involved wrestling a giant Maori who had won at Dunedin for fifteen years in succession. When Dinnie ended the big man's successful run he was thought to be invincible.

Donald Dinnie was a large, athletic figure with a proud, regal bearing and reported to have eyes like an eagle. He was selected to represent the image of William Wallace, the much lauded Scottish freedom fighter by a famous Australian sculptor. The eight foot high, white marble statue can be found in the Ballarat Botanical Gardens, west of Melbourne.

DONALD DINNIE

The next best to Dinnie was George Davidson, born in 1853 from Cromar in Aberdeenshire. Although younger that Dinnie by sixteen years he continued to throw the hammer using the old pendulum style and still managed more than 100ft. In 1881 he broke Dinnie's long standing record at Aboyne by putting the 22lb Stone a distance of 37ft 1.5ins. George was also a strongman who frequently accompanied Dinnie at his weightlifting exhibitions. One of his feats was to press two 56lb weights simultaneously, achieving a record of fifty-two repetitions. When he accompanied Dinnie on a trip to America some of the local athletes tried to have them banned because they were taking all the top prizes. The idea was considered an abomination. Ironically the great champions of the past would have spun in their graves if they knew that some of today's Scottish competitors were trying to restrict prizes being awarded to overseas challengers. Fortunately our modern champion – Gregor Edmunds ridiculed the idea and said –

"Let them stand tall and defiant like our ancestors – we should fear no one!"

After Dinnie, Alexander Anthony Cameron of Lochaber dominated the scene. At the beginning of the twentieth century he was referred to as the ***Mighty MucComber*** at the Aboyne Games in 1901 and was undisputed champion from 1903 until 1914. In 1901 he beat Dinnie's record at Aboyne with the 22lb Stone by putting 38ft 9ins and improved the record in 1904 with 39ft 5ins. Cameron also established Braemar records in the Light Hammer with 117ft 10ins and in the Heavy Hammer with 92ft 8.5ins. His most significant feat was achieving 32ft 9ins with the 28lb Stone using a mandatory standing style. His record stood until 1962 when it was bested by Arthur Rowe, a former European Shot Putt champion, who managed to throw the awkwardly shaped stone a distance of 33ft 6ins.

Cameron's natural strength impressed the legendary George Hackenschmidt who was also known as the Russian Lion. After a wrestling exhibition he described Cameron as the strongest man he had ever met and offered to take him on a world tour. The big Scotsman replied –

"Aye, I'll be going – back to Lochaber."

He just could not bear to leave his highland home and the farm that he loved.

After the first World War Jim Maitland from Cullen rose to prominence alongside Bob Starkey and Jock Nicholson. At Braemar in 1926 Maitland won both Hammers with 112ft 10ins and 90ft 6ins and also won the 56lb Weight for Distance and the 28lb Weight for distance with 32ft 1ins and 62ft 8ins respectively. Starkey won the putting the Heavy and Light stones and Nicholson won the Caber. Maitland also managed to beat Cameron's heavy hammer record at Aboyne with 93ft 0ins.

It was an age when the giants of the games became national heroes by exciting the imagination of a depressed populace in the era between World Wars. In 1928 a huge audience packed into the London Coliseum to see some of the outstanding Highlanders of the day. They included Maitland, Starkey, Nicholson and a MacGregor and the cheering crowd inspired Maitland to achieve a new world record in the 56lb Weight for Height with 15ft.

The Nicholson family established a remarkable record in the amateur circuit. Between 1901 and 1939 the four Nicholson brothers featured in the first three of the Scottish Shot Putt Championship. Andrew Nicholson representing the Glasgow Police won the title eleven times in succession. At Ibrox in 1904 Tom Nicholson broke the British record for the ***American Style*** hammer throw with 169ft 8ins which was less than two feet behind the world record. Tom was fourth in the 1908 Olympics and in 1920 he arrived late and missed the qualification. He was so esteemed by the other athletes that they refused to compete unless he was re-instated. Despite the kafuffle he managed a credible sixth place and the American champion, Matt McGrath, said he would have beaten them all had he gone to America for coaching.

The Duke of Atholl was amazed on presenting the Camanachd Cup to the victors of the national shinty championship when he learned that seven of the team were brothers called Nicholson.

A contemporary wrote –

"The Nicolsons were men of their day. Their talent was a natural one, largely unharnessed by any rigorous training or coaching. Their life was a busy one. The call of the farm and beat were persistent and demanding. Life was too busy for too much of a commitment to athletic pursuits."

The turn of the century was also a period when the other part of the Gaelic Nation in Ireland still seethed with resentment over the English colonisation and protestant plantations. Some saw the advent of athletics as a an extension of their native sports and an opportunity to regain national pride –

"The athletic pastimes we seek to revive, have, from earliest ages, been a main characteristic of our native land, and the means by which the muscular superiority and fame of her people were established"

There was little interest in competing at the Olympics because Ireland was compelled to compete under the British Flag and were content to show their superiority over the English at the AAA Championship. One was Denis Horgan who won the shot putt seven times between 1904 -12 achieving a record of 44ft 11ins. Others crossed the Atlantic and competed for America including Limerick man John Flanagan who won three Olympic titles in the 16lb Hammer in 1900-4-8 and established a world record for the Olympic turning style of 170ft 4ins. The Clan-na Gael society of New York exploited the prowess of the Irish by staging athletic events that attracted huge audiences and used the money for the ongoing struggle for Irish independence. Such was the strength of feeling at the time that an Irish American regiment travelled to support the Boers during their war against ther British.

It was not until after Ireland gained its independence that an Olympic Gold medal was won by an athlete representing the old country. Six generations later after the death of Alasdair MacColla his reputed descendant, the son of Jack O'Callaghan of Derrygallon, became known as Paddy the Whaler. He was a noted Gaelic footballer and weight thrower and would run against horses for money. His nickname came from his skill and repute as a salmon- poacher. The youngest of Paddy's sons was born in 1906 and grew to become Ireland's greatest Olympian. He was also an extremely bright child, entering school at the tender age of two. When he was sixteen he won a place at the Royal College of Surgeons in Dublin and became Dr Pat O'Callaghan when he was only twenty years old – too young to practice in Ireland but he was able to serve in the Royal Air Force Medical Corps.

While at university he became interested in hammer throwing and collected an old cannon ball from Macroom castle, had it made into a wire-hammer at a foundry at Mallow and started to train at the family farm. In 1926 he won the Munster title in throwing the 56lb Weight for Distance, the Shot Putt and won the Irish Hammer title the following year. He was selected for the Olympics in Amsterdam and threw 168ft 7ins beating the Swedish world record holder, Ossian Skjold by four inches to become Ireland's first Olympic Champion. Pat's brother Con O'Callaghan competed in the Decathlon and Shot Putt and also won the Irish Championship in throwing the 56lb Weight but not enough to beat Pat's record of 8metres 48cm set in 1931. Shortly after returning from the Olympics Pat set an Irish record at the ***Tailtean Games*** with a throw of 170ft 2ins.

Pat O'Callaghan's achievements are all the more remarkable as they were done under the most basic of conditions. At that time throws were made from a grass circle wearing spiked shoes. When he came to compete at the Los Angeles Olympics he belatedly discovered that the throwing circle had the new-fangled cinder surface. He was not allowed to change his shoes during the competition and struggled to qualify for the final. During the interval he managed to find a hacksaw and sawed the spikes off his shoes. With one throw left in the competition he lay second behind the Finnish Champion, Ville Porhola and with typical determination hurled his last throw beyond the leading mark. With a distance of 176ft 11ins he achieved the accolade of becoming the only man in Irish history to win two Olympic gold medals.

He was the favoured to retain his title at the Berlin Olympics but political disputes intervened. Pat was proud of his heritage and after his win in Amsterdam he proclaimed –

"I am glad of my victory, not of the victory itself, but for the fact that the world has been shown that Ireland has a flag, that Ireland has a national anthem and in fact that we have a nationality."

Up until the Los Angeles Olympics in 1924 the concept of an all Irish home nation under the Tri-colour was recognised. However the embers of the old animosities were still aglow. Troubles flared when the unionist politicians in Belfast started lobbying for a separate identity for Northern Ireland within the umbrella of the British Amateur Athletic Association. The concept chimed with the efforts behind moves to partition the North from the South. The existing governing body stuck to the traditional position of an All-Ireland home nation. No compromise could be found and at the instigation of the British the southern Irish authority was suspended from international competition. As a result some Irish athletes immigrated to America and established a great Irish heavy-weight athletic tradition in their new country. Pat O'Callaghan chose to remain in his beloved Ireland and was therefore denied a place in the 1936 Berlin Olympics where he would have surely won another gold medal. In 1934 he had already set a European record with a throw of 186ft 10ins and after missing the Olympic Games he broke the world record with a throw of 195ft 5ins in Fermoy, Co Cork. However, with the suspension still in force, the International Amateur Athletic Federation refused to ratify the record. Ironically this ensured the record of his compatriot, Patrick Ryan, who competed for America, remained in place.

After an accident when a flying hammer killed a child he took up professional wrestling in America. With his high profile and good-looks he was offered the film role of Tarzan by Sam Goldwyn. He was a larger than life character standing 6ft 1in and sixteen stone and revered as a humble, charming and jovial man.

PAT O'CALLAGHAN

In 1928 the town of Crieff held the Highland Games Heavyweight Championship of the World which was won by a Dundee policeman called Ed Anderson with Starkey in second place. This began an new era with challenges coming from the likes of George Mitchell, Bob Shaw, Jock McLennan and a promising youngster called George Clark.

George Clark from Banff began competing in 1924 and rose to prominence in the early thirties. He was a dour, irascible and irreverent character. According to one old judge -

"He jokes wi' deeficulty."

He sometimes tossed the caber wearing his ***bunnet and breeks*** in contrast to his brother–in-law, the tall handsome and immaculately dressed Jack Hunter of Dunecht. As a result, when George won at Braemar, Hunter was the one presented to the King. George was known to surreptitiously swig his bottle of whiskey from under a towel and inquire if the King was looking. On one occasion he was asked for a receipt to justify his claim for expenses and having slept in a tent had none to present. He responded by saying that he had wiped his ***erse*** with it and would try and find it if necessary. Fair play was not in his nature and had a well-known ploy of placing a towel on the stop board then sweeping it up if he touched down after a throw. It was of course a foul but most of the canny judges chose to give his the menacing presence the benefit of doubt. George was not the type that extolled Corinthian principles and during one of his wrestling bouts was heard to say to an aspiring young athlete –

"Sit doon or a'll brak yer bak."

George was a good weight thrower and set a new record when he threw the 28lb Weight a distance of 76ft 4ins at Aboyne in 1934 and later the same year improved to 80ft 6ins at Pitlochry. He was also credited with throwing the 56lb weight over 15ft but was never ratified because he allegedly cast the implement into the River Clyde before it could be weighed. .

George was the first to toss the famous Braemar Challenge Caber, a feat that was not repeated until the arrival of Bill Anderson. He was also one of the best ever Cumberland and free style wrestlers and went to America where he defeated Dan O' Mahoney the acclaimed world Champion. George knew every trick in the book and a few that are not in the book. He was prepared to mix it and out brawl anyone that upset his scientific approach.

Jack Hunter won the Scottish Championship in 1950-2. He was followed by Alexander Anthony Cameron's namesake and distant relative, Ewen Cameron OBE, who continued the Lochiel legacy by winning the Scottish Championship at Crieff in 1953. Ewen established the Highland Games at Lochearnhead and the water skiing centre on the loch. He became renowned for recovering fallen skiers with a mighty sweep of one hand while holding his boat steady with the other. Ewen is fondly remembered for his portrayal of Sgt

Hunter in the classic movie ***Geordie*** which tells a romantic tale of a young Highlander being discovered at the Highland Games and going on to win a gold medal at the Melbourne Olympics.

Bill Anderson first appeared at the Highland games at Alford in 1956 and by 1959 showed his potential by beating the Scottish hammer record with a throw of 131ft 11ins. Bill's early success was an anathema to George Clark who was in his declining years. It was reported that, when the eager young Bill arrived at Blackford after a long journey from Aberdeen, he was met by George, who as usual, was holding court with his fellow heavies. Among them were Sandy Sutherland, Bob Aitken, Sandy Gray, Eck Wallace and Jay Scott.

George took great pleasure in confronting Bill and saying –

"Ye cannae compete – you've got to enter first. Aye, ye better awa hame laddie, ye're no getting to compete."

To his credit Bill did not rise to the bait even although he was a tough customer in his own right. He was not averse to engaging in wrestling which was common practice for the ***Heavies*** of his era. When he toured Japan early in his career, the big man received a challenge from a Japanese Sumo champion which he readily accepted. During the engagement Bill sought to apply the highland wrestling technique of lifting his opponent off the ground before throwing him on his back. Bill amusingly recalls the experience –

"I grabbed the mannie under his belly and lifted it high over his head but the wee mannie inside remained on the floor!"

Bill became the greatest grand champion of his era by emerging victorious after an epic struggle with Arthur Rowe, considered to be England's greatest ever field athlete. At the behest of George Clark, the European Shot Putt champion first arrived at the Aboyne Games in 1962. His initial success galvanised Bill into the defence of his realm. Over the next few years the popularity of the games soared as many thousands sought to witness the mighty confrontation. Perhaps their greatest contribution was to make the world aware that the Highland Games had reached the highest echelon of sporting achievement.

According to Jack Davidson's research the best recorded performances of the period were:

EVENTS	**BILL ANDERSON**	**ARTHUR ROWE**
Light Putt 16lbs	**52ft 4ins (Strathpeffer '67)**	**57ft 91/2ins (Aboyne '64)**
Heavy Putt 22lbs	**41ft 3ins (Invergordon'64)**	**48ft 9ins (Crieff '67)**

Light Hammer 16lbs	**151ft 2ins (Lochearnhead '69)***	**149ft 0ins (Lochearnhead'69)**
Heavy Hammer 22lbs	**123ft 5ins (Crieff '69)**	**123ft 0ins (Crieff '68)**
Weight for Distance 22lbs	**87ft 2ins (Crieff'66)**	**83ft 9ins (Auchterarder'66)**
Weight for Height 56 lbs	**15ft 8ins (Aboyne '70)**	**15ft 7ins (Aboyne '68)**

*** World record**

Arthur Rowe, Brian Oldfield & Bill Anderson
Braemar 1973

After finally disposing of Arthur Rowe, Bill was presented with a new challenge in the form an American named Brian Oldfield. He was like superman and looked ready to fly away at any moment. He was recognised as the best shot-putter in the world. In 1973 he arrived at Aboyne and shattered the Stone Putt records by throwing 61ft 7ins with the Light Stone and 49ft 0ins with the Heavy Stone. He then created a sensation at Braemar by established world records in the Light Stone with 63ft 2ins and 40ft 7ins with the 28lb Braemar Stone. Despite Oldfield's incredible display Bill Anderson still won the overall championship.

When Bill started to dominate, Arthur Rowe famously remarked,

"I am torn between greed and pride"

THE WAY WE WERE

The self-confidence and sagacity of Alasdair MacColla are some of the necessary attributes of a warrior. Such were present in spades within my remarkable friend George McHugh who displayed traits of a superiority complex.

During my formative years my constant companion was George. We were both rivals and firm friends and despite the apathy and oppression of our teachers while incarcerated at boarding school we pushed each other to physical excellence. The regime intimidated many and forged a mental toughness in others. They tried to suppress our individuality by forcing us to engage in team sports instead of pursuing individual success. We were only allowed to play rugby during the autumn term and when we were both called up for national trials we had not played for four months and lacked match fitness.

Without George my later involvement in Highland Games and developing the sport of Strongman may not have happened and the world would have been a different place. When we were 14 years old he defiantly brought a 16lb shot putt into the school only to have restricted access as we vied against each other. Fortunately we caught the attention of Tony Chapman the chairman of the Scottish Sports Council following a newspaper article which labelled us as the "***Unbeatables***" due to our rugby exploits. This paved the way to being able to compete in the Scottish Schools Championship and after winning the titled I returned to school where George beat me at a domestic event. Tony also introduced us to David Webster who became instrumental in starting my weightlifting career which led to three national championships. When I left for university George remained behind. By this time he had grown into a formidable presence and decided to extract retribution. They were unable to expel him because they feared the very real threat of physical violence and his knowledge of many dark secrets.

On completion of my first year at Glasgow University I managed to include George and myself in a troupe travelling to the Bahamas. The intention was to play out a Highland Games scenario for the amusement of American tourists. Included in the group were Bill Anderson and Jay Scott and such was our bravado we were able to convince the organisers that we could travel as boxers although we had no experience in the noble art – we just fancied our chances. Nevertheless we acquitted ourselves reasonably well against the likes of "***Tidal Wave***" and ***"Cleveland KO Paris"***, the latter having survived twelve round with the fearsome ***Sonny Liston.***

As young men we were mainly interested in the sunshine and beautiful American tourists while the romantic kettle drums played throughout the night. Each morning we would frantically pump up our muscles before parading down Bay Street hoping to attract the attention of our glamorous prey.

During our time in Nassau we befriended a big black fellow called Tony Carroll who was later to win a Mr Universe title and become the model for ***He Man*** toys as ***The Beast Man***.

On one occasion all three of us swam out to a buoy, far out from shore, marking the shipping lane. While we frolicked, waving at the giant liners, Tony noticed a black shadow hovering under the swaying buoy to which all three of us precariously hung. It was a large barracuda intent on finding a meal. As time passed we all became increasingly nervous and at precisely the same moment George and I concluded that Tony would have to be sacrificed. The round orbs displayed by his eyes suggested that he harboured a suspicion. Fortunately a fishing boat spotted the beast lurking beneath and came to the rescue. Before we were able to jump aboard the barracuda savagely attacked the white hull indicating that white flesh was the preferred option.

My first foray into the world of Highland Games was at the age of seventeen when I competed in the Police Sports at Ibrox Stadium in 1961. The Glasgow ***Polis*** had traditionally harboured many of the big Highlanders including George Davidson, Alexander Cameron and James Morrison, the latter having won the Scottish Heavy Events Championship in 1901. Being policemen they were required to take part in the amateur circuit because betting and the exchange of money was frowned upon by the legal establishment. On the day I was introduced to a burly fellow named Nicholson, also known as the Strangler because of his novel way of arresting rowdy Glaswegians. He was a relative of the famous family from Tighnabruaich in the Kyles of Bute. Another method of ensuring peace in his domain was his penchant of hammering a ***"thruppeny bit"*** into the wooden surface of a public bar with the pounding of his mammoth fist. Also present was Jim Brown from the Hoover AC whose massive presence seemed to darken the sun.

At Ibrox I managed to win the top prize in the Shot Putt much to the chagrin of Sandy Sutherland from Golspie who was the junior sensation of his day. Admittedly my success was due to a handicap system that disadvantaged talented athletes but on receiving a forty eight piece dinner service which delighted my mother, I was smitten and the games were to become a large part of my life. Sandy was one of those hairy Highlanders that matured at an early age and I was able to take his record the following year when I won the Biles Memorial Trophy at Glasgow University.

My advancement in athletics was inhibited with the hard regime of study that had to be maintained to have any chance of success in the old Scottish universities. Priority was to seek bragging rights in rugby, weightlifting, boxing and athletics in the hope of securing possession of a beautiful woman. Such distractions did not prevent me from breaking the Scottish native record in the Shot Putt in 1967. In the same year I lost my weightlifting title to Grant Anderson from Dundee despite achieving a military press of 320lbs.

Happy hunting grounds were the amateur Highland Games at Gourock, Shotts, Bridge of Allan, Rothesay and most importantly at Cowal. I managed to win the championship at all of the venues but not consistently, with honours being shared with Laurie Bryce and Ian McPherson. When Laurie Bryce won the coveted Sutherland trophy in 1967, laden with prizes, he asked Ian McPherson to carry the heavy trophy down through the crowd-lined streets all the way to the harbour. This he willingly did with great aplomb, receiving and accepting cheers and congratulations – Ian had the jib of a champion while Bryce was left to stagger behind with the rest of his cumbersome burden.

Well to the forefront of throwing events is the Field Events Club (Edinburgh) and their astute coach Bob Watson is shown during a coaching session dwarfed by four of Scotland's leading throwers: (L to R) DOUG EDMUNDS (Shot & Discus), CHRIS BLACK (Hammer), LAURIE BRYCE (National Hammer Record Thrower) and SANDY SUTHERLAND (Shot & Discus). PHOTO: Scotsman Publications

I first met Ian McPherson when I was nineteen, in a bus on my way to the Scottish Athletics Championship which was to be held at Westerlands in Glasgow. He wore a flamboyant Blue Blazer, awarded by the University of Aberdeen for sporting excellence. To me this glowing figure represented the solution to my shy awkwardness, bred in the confines of boarding school. In the days of youthful chutzpah and immaturity an attitude of ***there are nane like us*** prevailed. Young men strove for prominence using any talent available to them, much like a wild animal seeking a mate. The less gifted indulged in tribalism and assumed a group identity associated with supporters clubs. Those who were fortunate to be sportsmen at least had a harmless way of expressing themselves. And so it was with my peer group whose arrogance masked a deep rooted uncertainty. The blazer represented a means of sitting in humble repose while proclaiming one's greatness.

A blue blazer had to be achieved at all costs and worn at every opportunity.

IAN McPHERSON

McPherson originated from Lairg in Sutherland and his heart lay in the Highlands. He proudly asserted that his father resembled famous film stars such as Randolph Scott and Robert Taylor and it was easy to imagine that his ancestors were Cluny MacPherson's clansmen. Like many Highlanders he possessed a clear, analytical mind and was invited to study for a doctorate in physics at Strathclyde University. Resident in Glasgow his favourite happy hunting ground was the Highlander's Institute. It was a place where Gaels could socialise and engage in tartan frolics away from the malevolent gaze of ***Glasgow Keelies***. Many bright eyed girls from the northern isles gathered there, hoping to find a suitable young Highlander. I was always impressed with their wild beauty and piercing eyes that suggested an ability to see over long distances. We were not surprised when Ian eventually married Rachel McRae, a fluent speaker of the Gaelic language who had been brought up on the Isle of Harris.

Ian's pride and joy was evident when he sang MacPherson's Rant which recalled the antics of a defiant highland rogue on his way to the gallows. He considered himself a kindred spirit of Jamie MacPherson who was born in 1675, the son of a highland chief and a beautiful gipsy girl. Jamie MacPherson's father was killed when he attempted to recover some cattle taken by Badenoch rivers and Jamie was brought up by the gypsies and grew -

"In beauty, strength and stature rarely equalled."

As well as possessing exceptional physical strength he was an expert swordsman and fiddler. He indulged in a life of relieving the rich of their wealth but was never known to have engaged in any atrocity. He was a man who had many enemies and was arrested many times but always managed to escape, aided by the populace and favoured by the Laird of Grant. Finally Jamie was captured at Keith Market during a fierce fight but only after a woman had dropped a blanket over him and he was disarmed before he could get free of it. He was condemned for being an Egyptian and a vagabond and sentenced to be hanged at the Cross of Banff. While waiting for the executioner he composed the song called MacPherson's Rant. In keeping with his natural bravado he defiantly played his song and danced below the gallows tree and in a symbolic gesture to the ending of his life he ended by breaking the fiddle across his knee.

The legend of MacPherson's great strength gains credence from the size of his sword which is still on display in Duff House at Banff. His bones were also found to be much stronger and larger than those of ordinary men and the broken fiddle can still be found at the Clan MacPherson Museum in Newtonmore.

"Ach, little did my mother think,
When first she cradled me
That I would turn a roving boy
And die on a gallows tree.

Chorus –

Say rantingly. Say wantingly,
Say dauntingly gaed he;
He played a tune, and danced aroon
Below the gallows tree.

Farewell, yon dungeons dark and strong,
The wretches destinie,
Macphersons time will not be long
On yonder gallows tree.

O what is death but a parting breath?
On many a bloody plain
I've dared his face, and in this place
I'll scorn him yet again.

Untie these bands frae o' ma hands
And gie tae me my sword
There's no a man in a' of Scotland
But I'll brave him at his word.

He took his fiddle into both of his hands
And he brak it o'er a stone
Said, na neither hands shall play on thee
When I am died and gane.

Ian McPherson's warrior spirit was partially satiated by winning a black belt in Judo and with his passionate participation in the Highland Games. He was a big man for his day weighing about fifteen stone in his prime. He had inherited the muscular legs of his forebears that had carried them quickly over mountainous terrain where enemies found it impossible to pursue. His shoulders were of lean, flexible muscle, perfect for swinging a two-handed claymore. The power of his legs helped him to propel the shot putt nearly fifty feet enabling him to win the national title in 1963. His true prowess was with the Scots Hammer and we could only watch in amazement as he threw well beyond our best efforts. Without the help of shoe spikes and the longer hammer used in the modern games he achieved a remarkable distance of 131ft-2ins. He will be long remembered for his tussles with Alec Valentine at the Cowal Games, where he came out on top in many occasions. Alec was also a great athlete who had competed at the Commonwealth Games and played rugby for Scotland.

IAN McPHERSON winning 16lb Hammer Cowal Games 1965

We were once invited to the Spartan's Club in Edinburgh, a preserve of meritocracy where admission was reserved to those with a sporting pedigree. This is where I met Neil MacDonald and was impressed with his vociferous bravado despite the affliction of a terrible stutter. No matter the pressure he always insisted on finishing a difficult sentence with the staccato of a machine gun. It was also amazing to witness that the more intoxicated he became the more fluent was his speech. Neil was a pugnacious character who was never far from a battle and he appreciated the presence of his new young friends which deterred his enemies. He was a few years older and had become a successful dentist, largely at the expense of Irish labourers. In an age where tooth decay was prevalent it was easy to persuade itinerant workmen to have all their teeth removed at a single visit to avoid future problems. Another ploy was to fill as many teeth as possible whether needed or not. Not surprisingly he had a Rolls Royce to impress the ladies and an E-Type jaguar which was useful for escaping detection during a drunken spree. We were greatly amused when we heard that after a high speed chase over many miles, the police finally captured him and he was breathalysed. Everybody was surprised when he passed the test - none more so that Neil himself. He also tried to explain his escapade by saying that he had thought he was being pursued by his enemies.

Neil MacDonald had been a modest wire hammer thrower but when the Commonwealth Games came around he was determined to be in the limelight. To everybody's surprise he reinvented himself and beat Laurie Bryce at the Scottish Championship in 1970 with a new games record, as a result was selected for the Edinburgh Commonwealth Games.

Neil was always a good and generous friend and provided his notorious Rolls Royce for my wedding carriage. I lost touch with Neil when I went off to Africa. In later years, when the adrenaline days had gone and the burden of age started to stifle his fire, he decided to leave in his typically impetuous way by committing suicide.

In time I realised that the blues blazer was a deterrent and that preening should be left to the fairer sex. However modesty does not come easily to a warrior and seems to fly in the face of natural selection. The blazer was ultimately purged of its dignity when my father decided to wear it to the Odeon Cinema. He had the look and demeanour of Burl Ives as portrayed in the film ***The Big Country*** down to his trousers being held up with some kind of rope. With his workman's bonnet and corpulent twenty-six stone frame, he was a mighty sight for the proud denizens of Glasgow University.

The MacPhersons were indeed a warrior clan but it was not until later travels that I met arguably their greatest champion. I was informed about the great man by an American athlete with the heroic name of Beau Fay after he had competed at the Newtonmore games which was presided over by the Chieftain who was none other than Tommy MacPherson, the most decorated living war hero in the British Army.

Formally known as Sir Thomas Stewart MacPherson, he was born in 1920. His mother was the daughter of the Reverent Archibald Cameron and with such blood lines he was destined to become a warrior. His elder brother Phil attained the status of being one of Scotland's greatest ever rugby players and the young Tommy had sat on the knee of Eric Liddell, the legendary Olympian and was also inspired by characters like Herbert Waddell and Dan Drysdale who played for the British Lions. It is not surprising that the game of rugby helped forge his strength of character and steadfastness that was to serve him well during the coming World War. His early years at Fettes College in Edinburgh were blighted by a bone condition called osteomyelitis. Undaunted he could still beat some of his friends despite his crutches and also used them to vault over the occasional fence. When he finally recovered he went on to equal the school record for the half mile race with 2mins 8secs and broke the mile record, winning the cup for the best athlete. Tommy's natural fitness and fleetness of foot saved his life during his subsequent military career.

Tommy was a school boy contemporary of Euan Douglas who became the British record holder in hammer throwing with a throw of 192ft 6ins in 1955. Euan was an impressive posh boy that I had the privilege of meeting in my youth, an inspirational figure who had an unconventional code of ethics. Laurie Bryce kept in touch with Euan and eventually took his Scottish record in 1967 with a throw of 194ft 0.5ins. Fettes College was also the rendezvous for the Scottish Schools Athletic team in 1962 in which I represented Scotland against the best of England and Wales at Houghton-le-Spring. These were my first tenuous connections with the history of Tommy MacPherson.

When the War broke out Tommy joined the Cameron Highlanders and then volunteered for a new force called the Commandos inspired by Churchill's admiration for the Afrikaner Commandos he had fought against during the Boer War. The Commandos were to be irregularly organised, highly mobile and able to set Europe ablaze behind enemy lines. They first saw action at the battle of the Litani River in Lebanon during the campaign to eradicate the Vichy French from Syria who were supporting the Luftwaffe raids on the Suez Canal and a threat to the vital oil reserves in Iraq. The plan was to land north of the Litani bridges and secure them before the main column advanced from Israel. The Qasmiyeh Bridge was blown before it could be taken leaving the Commandos to occupy the enemy until the river could be crossed. Tommy, now elevated to a captain under the overall command of Captain Ian McDonald, was ordered to take the remaining Kafr Badda Bridge. The objective was hotly defended by a number of armoured cars but eventually they managed to overcome the mainly Algerian and Senegalese troops who were not inclined to lay down their lives for their colonial masters. The number that surrendered almost overwhelmed their captors and at one point a Vichy French sergeant broke ranks and tried to stab MacPherson and managed to lacerate his arm before being despatched by an alert trooper.

Tommy's next assignment was to reconnoitre a suitable landing place on the north African coast for a commando assault on Rommel. The small troop of four men found themselves abandoned when their recovery submarine failed to appear. They decided to try and walk to Tobruk and split into two units. Tommy kept to the coast while the others tried to follow the desert road and were quickly captured. Interrogation revealed the presence of two folbots hidden in a cave indicating the presence of another unit. On the second night their pursuers used a big Doberman to track them and when the animal became agitated it was released. In the growing darkness its black body was almost invisible and as it came upon them its huge white fangs caught the fading light. Not wishing to fire a shot MacPherson had the presence of mind to silently despatch the creature with his commando knife as it sprang for his throat. The episode reminded me of the effort made to protect my family in a junk yard in Lagos Nigeria after a savage dog emerged, racing towards us with evil intent. It occurred that it might be rabid but I stood my ground and as it pounced, met it with a mighty punch which struck its frothy incisors and propelled it backwards. Afterward the wound on my hand caused some worry when the local doctor informed us that there was no cure for rabies.

After a couple of days avoiding enemy patrols MacPherson and his companions were extremely hungry having run out of their meagre rations. By chance they had come across a German encampment. After studying the sentries they concluded that they would be easy to evade then at nightfall. MacPherson boldly strode into the camp and slipped into a tent that was full of sleeping Germans. He was able to snatch two lengths of French bread before the alarm was given. With all hell breaking loose he quickly ran up the hill and disappeared into the darkness.

With only fifty miles to go they hid under a bridge to avoid a passing truck and found a major telephone line which they immediately sabotaged. This proved foolhardy as it drew attention to their location and in the silence of the night a patrol of Italians on bicycles surrounded them. MacPherson managed to remove the magazine from his gun and put it in his pocket before surrendering the weapon. Back at the camp, after a heated interrogation, one of the officers ordered Tommy to show him how the gun worked and handed it over. Tommy immediately reloaded and held them all up. He planned to steal their staff car and make good his escape but when he stood up his legs spasmed with cramp and as he fell the Italians jumped on top of him.

MacPherson was incarcerated in the medieval fort of Gavi until September 1943 when Mussolini was deposed and the Italians signed an armistice with the Allies. The Germans then appeared and surrounded the castle. Within few days the prisoners were taken to the railway station for shipment to German concentration camps. Guards were placed every ten yards along the platform. Inevitably the prisoners refused to cooperate with the loading process, diverting the attention of the guards and MacPherson made a dash for freedom. Running as fast as he could, he zigzagged up the village hill, dodging bullets that kicked up the dust all around him. An elderly man crossed his path and was wounded in the leg; a startled dog gave chase only to be shot dead. There was no cover and he was finally overhauled by a German motorised vehicle. An irritated sergeant emptied his gun around his feet and when they got him back to the station he was stood up against a wall and ordered to be shot. Fortunately an officer countermanded the order. When MacPherson reached a transit camp in Austria he teamed up with two officers from New Zealand and with the cooperation of French labourers boldly marched out of the camp and made for the mountains. After a hazardous journey avoiding patrols and climbing steep precipices they arrived back in Italy. When they reached the town of Chiusaforte near the Yugoslavian border they decided to clean up and pretend to be itinerant workers. One of the New Zealanders brazenly walked through the town without incident. When MacPherson and his companion followed all went well until the door of a local tavern burst open and suddenly they were surrounded by enemy soldiers. Using his language skills Tommy almost managed to persuade his captors that they were Croatians on their way to Ljubljana to work in the locomotive sheds. However when they were searched they found the New Zealander in possession of a letter from his wife and their cover was blown.

They were sent to Stalag 20A in Poland where they found that most of the prisoners had been incarcerated since Dunkirk and had developed a strong hold over the guards by bribing them with Red Cross parcels containing items like chocolate, coffee and cigarettes which were impossible to obtain in the Polish civilian world. The escape committee was also in touch with the local black marketeer and an escape plan was worked out. Using manikins to fool the roll call MacPherson and three others managed to escaped from the camp before being picked up by a character called ***Gangster Joe*** and driven to Gdynia. After engaging in a dangerous cat and mouse game under the direction of the Polish resistance they eventually found a ship bound for Sweden. To avoid detection they buried themselves under a cargo of coal and remained concealed until given the all clear. On reaching Sweden they were welcomed by the Vice Consul who provided them with a hot bath, clothes and gave Tommy his first drink of milk since leaving the United Kingdom, almost two years before.

Within days of arriving home Tommy MacPherson was ordered to join the Jedburghs. This was a newly formed group of ***Special Forces*** consisting of elite soldiers drawn mainly from the Brits, French and Americans. After being intensively trained in demolition, unarmed combat, communications and weaponry they were to be dropped into occupied territory prior to the D-Day landings. Their purpose was to rally the resistance and hamper German troop movements as much as possible. There was also a secondary purpose and that was to coordinate the supply of arms and increase morale by fighting alongside them attired in a British military uniform. Much of France was riven by fear and treachery due to a Germany reign of terror. Execution of hostages was commonplace as reprisal for acts of sabotage. Typically when a railway line was blown up near Agen, twenty hostages were strung up on meat hooks alongside the line and left to die.

Before his departure Tommy was promoted to major and awarded the Military Cross.
In high spirits, he and two friends visited a fortune teller. He was told that the three of them were going into action and that he would be the only one to return which eerily proved to be correct. He was also ushered into the presence of General de Gaulle who told Tommy that he disapproved of his mission and reluctantly provided his written authorisation to impress the French Resistance – which, according to Tommy it didn't. Churchill once said

"The greatest cross I have ever had to bear was the cross of Lorraine."

MacPherson was parachuted into German occupied France alongside his French number two and a radio operator. Being a proud Highlander with a disregard for personal safety, he landed wearing the full Cameron Highlander uniform including a tartan kilt and Sgian-dubh. In a later interview with the Scotsman newspaper he recalled his reception by the Maquis Resistance .

"Just as I arrived I heard an excited young Frenchman saying to his boss, Chef, chef, there's a French officer and he's brought his wife!"

His orders were to delay the advance of the 2nd SS Panzer Group by blowing up bridges and destroying road and rail routes. In one attack he trapped three hundred Germans and one hundred of the French Militia in a railway tunnel for several days. On another occasion after MacPherson had booby-trapped the barrier arm of a level crossing, he managed to bring the arm crashing down on a German staff car decapitating the local Kommandant. He was also involved in many deadly episodes of hand to hand fighting and starting with a group of twenty seven daring men twenty of which were killed during these operations.

While the Allies were trying to secure a beachhead in Normandy two young Frenchmen on a motorbike, roared into the yard where MacPherson had his centre of operations. They brought news that the 2nd Motorised SS Infantry Division was racing to Normandy. This was a battle hardened group that had fought with distinction at the Russian Front and it was essential they be slowed as long as possible. One of the boys was despatched to tell the resistance fighters at Bretenoux to hold the river crossing while MacPherson sabotaged the route further along the road. The column of tanks and half-tracks stretched as far as the eye could see and the ensuing battle of Bretenoux Bridge proved to be the bloodiest battle fought by the resistance in the entire war. Holding up one of Germany's most formidable fighting units was considered crucial in the success of the D-Day landings.

When the Germans eventually succeeded in crossing the bridge they came across two large trees that had been brought down to block the road. MacPherson had also placed his one and only anti-tank mine in the dust before the obstacle and strapped it to a large chunk of plastic explosive. When the halftracks proved unable to move the trees a heavy tank with a mine sweeping blade moved forward and blew up as it passed over the mine. The vehicle slewed across the road making it completely impassable. Hours later, the Germans came across another set of toppled trees. This time they carefully checked for land mines, not realising the branches had been booby trapped with grenades which caused further carnage. As dawn broke the following morning the almighty start up of the column masked the explosion which brought down a third set of trees. This time the sabotage group withdrew leaving the second boy, at his own discretion, to spray the German troopers with his Sten gun and was sadly killed by return fire.

Not surprisingly MacPherson became well known not least because he always wore his kilt during military operations. The German's put a 300,000 franc price on his head to encourage the French traitors to seek him out. While enjoying a glass of wine a maid rushed in and said

"The Germans are here!"

MacPherson managed to escape through the back door but three of his colleagues chose the front door and were gunned down in the street. After another operation the Germans scoured every house in the village where they took cover. Simone Courtiau, the local infant school teacher risked her life by hiding MacPherson and his companion in the school store. Fortunately the school was the only building not to be searched and charmingly in later years when Tommy was chieftain at the Newtonmore Highland Games he was astonished when Simone turned up to greet him.

On 14th of August 1944 a force of two hundred thousand American and French troops landed in the south of France between Marseilles and Cannes to open a second front. At the same time General Patten was moving south from the Normandy beachhead. The Germans responded by beginning to withdraw northwards to consolidate the defence of the German border. MacPherson then decided to blow up a series of bridges and power lines south of the Massif Central to deny passage to the retreating Germans. As a result those who did not sympathise with the Allied cause referred to him as –

"That lunatic Scotsman who keeps blowing up bridges."

Knowing that Major General Erich Elster was under pressure Tommy enacted a daring bluff. In a modern equivalent of a ***Highland Charge*** he commandeered a recently captured German Red Cross vehicle and accompanied with a French officer, a German doctor and a driver decided to dash through the German lines, straight to Das Reich Division headquarters. After driving through the night being strafed by machine gun fire they managed to arrive intact. They were met by the General and an SS colonel and Tommy set about convincing them that there was no escape from the encircling troops. Appearing in full Highland uniform complete with hat lent credibility to his assertion that he was a bona fide representative of the Allies. He maintained that he was in touch with the RAF who were preparing to massacre his German troops as they marched along the unprotected roads of the Loire valley. The support of vengeful French troops was embodied by the presence of Major Sarazan at his side. The Germans were eventually duped leading to the surrender of twenty three thousand troops; consequently thousands of lives were saved by Tommy's brazen act of courage.

When the battle for France was won Tommy MacPherson was honoured by a full military parade and had the ***Croix de Guerre*** pinned on his chest.

Tommy was transferred to the Italian theatre of war to continue harassing the retreating Germans while the Allies advanced up the spine of the country. He reported to the SOE headquarters in Bari to await orders. After months of hardship he threw himself into the hot spots in newly liberated Rome and found himself desperately seeking transport back to Bari. He fell in with a pilot due to take a group of senior officers to a conference, obviously the worse for wear as he staggered towards his plane. Tommy occupied the co-pilot's seat and as soon as the plane took off the pilot gave him brief instructions and promptly fell asleep. After experimenting with the steering wheel he found himself singing happily in the clear sky, unconsciously pulling back on the high notes and pushing forward on the low notes creating a wave-like motion during the entire journey. When the pilot landed he apologised to the distressed officers stating that there had been a bit of turbulence and none was the wiser. The story reminded me of my time in Zambia when I was handed the controls of a single engine plane carrying our weightlifting team the five hundred miles from Chingola to Livingston. The pilot then fell asleep much to the consternation of my companions. I managed until we hit a thick bank of cloud and then amidst much screaming the plane dropped like a stone. The pilot slowly aroused himself and merely explained that the air pressure was lower in the clouds and all that was needed was a bit more throttle and promptly went back to sleep.. Eventually I was able to swoop down on the wild herds and continued to terrify my friends. As we approached the Victoria Falls I insisted that the pilot took over and the tough Afrikaner then dived through the spray of the ***Mosi-oa-Tunya*** and we all thought we were going to die.

MacPherson was parachuted into northeast Italy near the summit of Monte Canin. Encouraged by the success of the Allies the Partisans had banded together and tried to liberate a few villages. The Germans reacted by destroying most of the villages and many hostages were left hanging from street lamps. It was Tommy's job to reorganise the disillusioned resistance and teach them how to operate a guerrilla war with a main task of disrupting the German retreat through the Alps. He joined the Osoppo group who were the mortal foes of the communist Garibaldini. The Germans were the common enemy and occasionally both groups cooperated in a common cause. However the Garibaldini had aligned with Tito's Slovenes with the intention of seceding Trieste to Yugoslavia in return for supporting a communist takeover of Italy at the end of the war. MacPherson was determined to resist this eventuality and the Garibaldini tried to get rid of him. In an operation reminiscent of the ***massacre at Glencoe*** a party of Garibaldini and two Slovenes arrived at the Osoppo base in bad weather looking for shelter. During the course of the evening they enjoyed the hospitality of their host while at the same time looking for MacPherson. When he could not be found they slaughtered the Osoppo and ripped out the teeth of their leader. There were many narrow escapes and acts of treachery and bravery. One of Tommy's saboteurs was a man named Berto who was betrayed and tortured in an attempt to have him reveal the location of an arms dump. He broke when they threatened to mete out the same to his girlfriend. Knowing the dump was booby trapped and in the knowledge that they would be executed regardless, he used his girlfriend to draw in the Germans, ostensibly to help lift the heavy lid and they were all blown to smithereens.

Partly due to the blocking tactics employed by Tommy and the blowing up of vital bridges, the German forces in Italy capitulated. The Slovenes then tried to invade and engaged in fierce fighting with the local Italians. MacPherson arrived at the scene dressed as a Major

General, purporting to represent the Eighth Army and was thus able to get both sides to sign an agreement to stay on their own side of the river. During his time in northern Italy he was instrumental in saving the life of the Bishop of Trieste and the Archbishop of Udine and the Pope bestowed him with a Papal Knighthood and the Star of Bethlehem. Once again using an outrageous bluff he was able to negotiate the surrender of twenty thousand Cossacks who had fought for the Germans. They were the same group that became involved in the famous international incident when Churchill had them repatriated to Stalin's Russian where they faced certain execution.

When Tommy MacPherson returned at the end of the War he took up a scholarship at Oxford where he was able to indulge in his beloved sports and became a member of the Achilles Club, the equivalent of the Spartans club in Edinburgh. He was a friend of the great Roger Bannister, the first man to run a mile in under four minutes and actually defeated Roger in an 800 metre race. He represented Britain at the Universidad World Championship and was in the frame for the London '48 Olympics but was foiled by injuries and business commitments. He played rugby for Oxford University and frequently turned out for London Scottish where he enjoyed the company of many international stars and made life-long friends. Like his elder brother he was a talented player and a named reserve for the Scottish national team. During the London Scottish annual dinner where all had to be attired in full Scottish regalia, he decided to attend the Achilles ball at Ganders, later the same evening. ***Suitably relaxed*** he announced his arrival by jumping on to a table and performing a highland jig, revealing a bald leg that had been treated for injury alongside his hairy original. This caught the attention of a particularly beautiful woman who had come to the ball on the arm of Roger Bannister. The cheeky chappie was an engaging character and she left on the arm of Tommy.

I discovered that Tommy and I had shared similar sporting experiences. We had both been British University Champions and in different eras played rugby against the British Army in the Berlin Olympic stadium. Our business careers had taken us to Nigeria and I smiled when I heard that the piece de resistance at a banquet given by a local chief was a cooked monkey. It looked as though it was asleep and when he courageously sunk his teeth into a bicep its fingers flicked to and fro, much to the horror of our hero. I resolved to give him a laugh by sending him my book, ***The World's Greatest Tosser,*** to remind him of his sporting adventures.

At the time of writing Scotland was facing a referendum to decide the case for political independence. It is fair to say that a country that can breed the likes of Tommy MacPherson should have no fear for the future.

SIR TOMMY MacPHERSON

ANOTHER CHALLENGE

Following our adventures in the Bahamas I returned home to resume my studies while George McHugh decided to stay behind and live on his wits. Showing amazing initiative for a nineteen year old he decided to slip into a high society party at an exclusive resort. Using his good looks and impressive physique he soon attracted an admiring audience. This led to his becoming a rich man's companion who paid for his services as a protector and a procurer of beautiful women, involving frequent trips to Miami. The growth in his self-confidence led him to seek employment in the Italian film industry. It was at a time when Steve Reeves was making his Hercules films and George had all the credentials. Unfortunately the genre changed to spaghetti westerns and the cloying presence of gay admirers had become more than irritating.

During my time at University George and I wandered around as if we owned the streets of Glasgow and looked after each other during many nefarious adventures. For example on one occasion I was asked to eject a troublesome fellow from a party. Just as I was about to throw him down the stairs a body was hurled over my head, bouncing off the wall of the stairwell en route to the bottom. An assailant was about to strike me on the head with a bottle only to be seized under the crotch and yanked overhead before being hurled into oblivion.

While I studied, George immersed himself intro a ferocious training regime, developing his physique to such an extent that he became arguably the strongest man in Scotland. He easily captured the title of Mr Caledonia and I envied the splendour of his appearance. I persuaded him to accompany me to ***Paisley's Outfitters*** after being awarded my blue. Much to the consternation of the wee tailor, who came forward to carry out the requisite measurements, George was presented as my surrogate. The ultimate shape of the garment was something I could aspire to.

George's next enterprise was the introduction of the Bunny Girls to Edinburgh where he caught the attention of the casting unit for the new James Bond to replace Sean Connery. He possessed the required good looks and suave Scottish accent but had amassed 20 stones of muscle. The role of ***Oddjob*** was suggested but the required accent was a problem. So George returned to the domestic scene and following my lead entered the Highland Games. He made an appearance at the Edinburgh International Games in 1968, very powerful but with little technique. I managed to beat him by a mere ½ inch in the Putt but he was the only man able to toss the heavy caber. In 1968 I established a new putt record at Gourock with 51ft 4ins but to my chagrin in 1969 while consumed with the rigours of completing a doctorate, George McHugh increased the record to 53ft 1ins which remained unbeaten for more than thirty years. Later that year George was selected for the triangular international against England and Wales and managed 54ft 6inches.

GEORGE WITH BUNNY GIRLS

By this time he had developed into a colossus, bench pressing more than 500lbs and establishing a new record in the bicep curl with 220lbs. He then joined Carnegie College in Leeds under the tutelage of Mike Lindsay who had attained 5th place at the Rome Olympics. On receiving some proper coaching he moved towards the 60ft mark and caught the attention of the Commonwealth Games selectors.

We all looked forward to George's appearance on the world stage. To everybody's surprise a slim version of the original behemoth appeared at my wedding. Like Samson before him he had succumbed to female wiles. He had met the beautiful Janet who did not appreciate his bulging presence and so he shed four stones while seeing off the opposition by threatening to break his neck. He was a Frenchman so there was little sympathy.

George was my best man when I got married in the University Chapel in 1970. The event was celebrated as the "***Weightlifter's wedding***" with my bride lifted high on one hand with George dutifully ready to catch should the wind tip her over. The occasion was photographed and appeared as the front piece of a national newspaper which subsequently won the photograph of the year award. Afterwards I sailed off to Africa leaving my old friend behind

Much to her credit Janet had tamed the beast by having him shed much of his muscle mass and imbuing him with a spirituality that moved him to champion the weak. Instead of despatching rough justice to miscreants by hanging them from coat hooks, hurling them towards a radiator or by driving them headfirst through the ceiling, he saw his future in the teaching profession.

Displaying an extraordinary self-confidence he presented himself at Millfield College and persuaded the owner to appoint him as a house master. Despite his lack of experience he had charmed himself into arguably the most prestigious school in England and taught the likes of Sean Connery's daughter and Omar Sharif's son. George's personal experience at boarding school had taught him that suppression and violence resulted in rebellious resentment and damaged goods. He set about instilling the pupils with pride and a belief in themselves. Sometime this required individual mentoring but most of all a role model they could aspire to and emulate. George did not suffer fools and his philosophy was reinforced by the brooding menace of his intellect and physical attributes.

He became one of the youngest headmasters in the public sector and quickly gained a reputation for taming wild schools that had become unmanageable. The education authorities persuaded him to take charge of Wellfield comprehensive in Durham as it was destined for closure due to the falling role caused by student anarchy. George set about establishing himself as a heroic role model. In front of the whole school with the popular ***Jimmy Young Show*** in attendance he set about establishing eleven British weightlifting records. Afterwards he was whisked away in a new Aston Martin as had appeared in the James Bond film. The students were proud of their headmaster, the school returned to wearing school uniforms and there was not a sign of graffiti anywhere.

George moved on to tame other establishments and became a Super Headmaster when he was simultaneously in charge of three large secondary schools. On one occasion he had to take over a school after the headmaster committed suicide.

Later he became principal of one of the new City Technical Colleges which were promoted by the conservative government and fell afoul of the local labour party which saw it as an elitist establishment. With little regard to political correctness he stated that –

"To stand up before your school and say that there are no winners and losers is dishonest and does not serve these youngster at all"

He was invited to Downing Street for a congratulatory meeting with Mrs Thatcher the conservative Prime Minister and when the school became increasingly popular with the aspiring working class, his efforts were later commended by the new labour Prime Minister - Tony Blair

The Rt Hon Tony Blair MP
Prime Minister and Leader of the Labour Party

Mr George McHugh
Washwood Heath Technology College
Burney Lane
Birmingham
B8 2AS

23 March 2005

Dear Mr McHugh,

I very much hope that you enjoyed the evening at Number 10 recently. I was very pleased to meet so many of you.

I think it is important that we recognise the positive impact people such as yourselves are making to your communities. Without your contribution, the improvements we have seen in public services would not have been possible.

I want to place on record my thanks for the great work you are doing.

With best wishes,

Tony Blair

P.S. Are you still breaking records?!

Later in his career George was put in charge of the military school in Kuwait at the time when Saddam Hussein was planning an invasion. He was advised that he should be chaperoned due to the growing instances of westerns being kidnapped for ransom.

Typically this was rejected and he relished the idea of someone trying to kidnap him only to be confronted by the beast. On the other hand he championed the cause of a young serving girl who was being force into being a sex slave. He threatened the entire community with exposure and confronted the Sheik in person. He succeeded in saving the young lady's virtue but was subsequently taken to the airport under gunpoint - despite the vagaries in his life George was always valiant.

When I left Scotland for Africa I thought I was finished with my beloved Highland Games. At that time there was a vibrant, young expatriate population in Zambia, numbering about three hundred thousand which was greater than the population of Iceland. Although they were mainly Afrikaners, Scotsmen could be found everywhere. Even the General Manager of the mining complex where I worked was a MacDonald. At first I dabbled in the local weightlifting club run by Harry Rose, a red-haired Scot who originally hailed from the Kingdom of Fife and had represented Zambia at the Commonwealth Games. The local scene was dominated by indigenous strongmen like Godfrey Iron Man Mwansa who publicly challenged a character called Tarzan City Guy to a strongman contest. Mwansa taunted Tarzan saying he merely boasts to the public and had no real power. He said the only people whom he respected to have real power were Charles Madondo and Doug Edmunds. Inevitably I was pitted against Madondo at the Zambian Power-lifting Championships, organised by the Livingstone Amateur Weightlifting Club.

A headline in the ***Times of Zambia*** read - .

"Edmunds beats Madondo in showdown."

The importance of this was to gain the respect of the local black people who christen me ***Makuba Bwana*** and when I became friends with ***Zantar the Mighty Kananda*** my family was protected from harassment by the ***Thief men.***

The main expatriate sport was rugby which I indulged in with a passion. I was proud to be selected as tight head prop for the national team against the mighty Penguins which was a British selection of international players. In rugby parlance I was able to win twelve strikes against the head which enabled me to claim a few pints of beer from my peers.

Rugby is a game for warriors originated by the English and spread throughout the world mainly by Celtic migrations. There is a predominance of Irish names among the Wallabies of Australia. Granite-faced Scotsmen, whose ancestors moved to New Zealand and mixed with the savage Maoris, produced the All Blacks who are consistently the best team in the world. One of the most famous residents of Zambia during my time was Andy MacDonald, a man that Alasdair MacColla McDonald would have been proud to have had by his side. He held the distinction of being the only non-South African to play for the Springboks and became a legend when he killed a lion with his bare hands. Having no weapon he choked the beast by shoving his arm down its throat while it slashed at his exposed torso.

I was surprised when a visitor from the old country arrived at my door. His name was Colin Balchin, an athlete that I had known from university days. Together we resolved to run a Highland Games when we heard that the regalia from the former Northern Rhodesia Pipe Band was held in store by a local Scot who could also play the bagpipes. My talented wife became one of the highland dancers and we also had the availability of a local Scottish Country Dance Club. Most of the Heavy Event athletes and wrestlers came from the rugby club; others included Harry Rose and Zantar the Mighty. In addition Caledonian Airways were persuaded to bring Donald Clark from Elgin who was the current Scottish amateur champion.

Africa being Africa we were presented with a new problem. On the eve of the games we received a prohibition notice from the District Governor's office on the basis that the event was racist. Balchin was a cool and persuasive individual but it took him to the limit of his powers to have the order rescinded by meeting with the Governor in person. So in 1971 we ran the first Zambian Highland Games.

The ***Times of Zambia*** carried the headline –

"Scouts celebrate feastival."

A great day became a special day when Zantar the Mighty became the first black African to toss the caber.

The second games were held on the following year and attracted crowds from all over the country. They included Colin Bryce, the brother of my great friend Laurie and uncle of the present day organiser of the World's Strongest Man competition – his namesake Colin Bryce.

When I returned to Scotland at the start of the 1975 season, Laurie Bryce, Willie Robertson and I decided to cross the great divide and join the professional ranks. With the arrival of ***the big three amateurs***, as we were called by a newspaper, Bill Anderson was presented with yet another challenge.

Laurie Bryce showed his mettle by beating Bill with the 28lb Weight at their first confrontation at Blackford and I won the shot putt at Markinch the following day. Bill responded by winning all the other events and some years later improved his personal record in the heavy putt to 44ft 11ins at Tobermory and threw the 56lb weight over 16ft at Aberdeen.

Laurie Bryce was a determined character and during his university days was compared to Jake LaMotta who was known as Raging Bull after winning the World Middleweight Boxing Championship. With little training Laurie was persuaded to take part in the British Universities Boxing Championship. He battled his way to the final where he was plainly outclassed. However, bloodied and bruised, he relentlessly came forward and in the end knocked out his assailant who was no less than the reigning British A.B.A. Champion.

LAURIE BRYCE

Prominent among our new opponents were John Freebairn from Kilsyth, Alec McKenzie from Ross, James Macbeth from Caithness, Geordie Donaldson from Forfar, Gordon

Forbes from Buckie and two gentlemen from Kelty in Fife referred to as the ***Toon Toughs.*** Later in the season we encountered the American trio of Fred Vaughan, Ed McComas and Tom Johnston as well as Colin Matheson and Billy Binks from Australia.

Willie Roberson was a man of substance who had competed internationally for Scotland in the wire hammer and at three Commonwealth Games as a wrestler and was a proven warrior. Ever bellicose, Laurie and I persuaded Willie and the biggest of the Kelty giants to engage in a battle behind a shed during the Cowdenbeath Highland Games. We had collected a prize purse of £50 and both combatants were willing but wiser councils prevailed.

The mighty Brian Oldfield again arrived in Scotland in 1975 with the newly formed International Pro Track and Field Team. He was accompanied by Randy Matson who had won the Olympic Shot Putt title. The pride of Scotland rested with Bill Anderson, Laurie Bryce and I. We challenged the American giants to participate in a Highland Games competition. When Randy Matson declined he received a playful kick in the arse from Brian Oldfield for his alleged cowardice. We responded by refusing to putt the shot and declared that our event was Stone Putting.

On a cold evening at Meadowbank Stadium in Edinburgh Oldfield putt 73ft 1ins which was far beyond the official world record at the time, leaving Matson about six feet in his wake. Unlike Matson, Oldfield had no qualms about competing in the games. They called him Crazy Horse and after his demonstration he bounded over to join us in our highland fest. Bill easily won the Hammer but had to draw on all his resources to beat Oldfield with his final throw in the 28lb Weight. Bill and I managed to beat him in the caber mainly due to our technical ability while Brian revealed his enormous power by managing to turn the difficult stick from a horizontal position.

In 1975 I moved to Dundee and became friends with Grant Anderson, a giant of a man who had won a bronze medal in weightlifting at the Commonwealth Games. It did not take much persuading to tempt him out of his gloomy, damp gym which resembled a dungeon. When Laurie Bryce heard that I had started to train Grant he called me to warn that I would be creating my own ***Frankenstein Monster.***

Grant showed his potential at Oxton in 1976 when he became the first man to clear 16ft in the 56lb Weight for Height. When George Clark heard about the new man he surprisingly made an appearance at one of our training sessions accompanied by his attractive daughter. It seemed to me that his intention was to engage with Grant as part of his never-ending quest to find somebody to defeat his former nemesis – Bill Anderson.

Later that year I was amazed at old George's effrontery when he was judging the heavy events at Tomintoul. After completing my last throw in the Light Stone I was a few inches behind Bill Anderson and I could see that George was disappointed. After a few minutes thought, he said to me –

"Hae another yin, I could see ye werena ready."

My extra putt made no difference and Bill just shook his head and smiled.

On my first visit to Oldmeldrum I encountered living history in ther form of Sandy Gray from Alford. He had first emerged from his farm in 1949, went on to established the heavy hammer record at Crieff with 100ft 4ins and won the Scottish Heavy Events title in 1954. In his prime he was an excellent weight thrower and was credited with the world record for throwing the 56lb Weight for Height with 15ft 10ins – a record that lasted until 1976. He was a big man, standing about 6ft 6ins with enormous hands and feet. His shoes were a size fifteen and his small cheery face belied his looming presence. I had great difficult in understanding his ***Doric*** dialect and he was reputed to be extremely parsimonious, in keeping with the reputation of an Aberdonian. On one occasion an esteemed official called George Halley took it upon himself to travel the weary hundreds of miles from Blackford in Perthshire to rural Alford to see Sandy. After hours in his presence not even a cup of tea was served. On his return Halley remarked –

"He seemed to be living aff neeps."

After we had finished behind the leaders at Oldmeldrum, Sandy presented me with his great calloused hand to demand fifty pence which was his share of the prize which we had won in the weight over the bar contest.

During the rest of the decade Bill and I shared honours in the putting events and sometimes I mastered him in the caber but I never beat him overall. The highlights of my career were victories in the World Caber Tossing Championships against legendary champions. The first was in 1976 against Bill Anderson, Colin Matheson and Charlie Allan and then in 1978 against Bill Anderson and Grant Anderson. The latter was to become the next grand champion and the man to finally take the place of his namesake. Bill Anderson's dominance was also shaken with the arrival of Hamish Davidson at Oldmeldrum Games in 1978 where he established his credentials by beating Bill's world record for throwing the 28lb Weight with a distance of 88ft 10.5ins.

Another great moment was encountering the mighty Bill Kazmaier at Braemar who was indisputably the strongest man in the world. Winning the title that day by beating Bill and Hamish Davidson helped to establish the respect of my peers before I returned to Africa for the next chapter of my life. As it was in Zambia one is never alone if you are a Scotsman. In my new role as National Sales and Marketing Manager for IGL Ltd. in Nigeria I considered it a useful ploy to raise my business profile by introducing the local community to the grandeur of a Highland Games. Helping in the enterprise was an incorrigible fellow named John Rudden who hailed from Helensburgh and a former winner of the wrestling prize at Luss Highland Games and to my surprise Colin Bryce, who had also moved to Nigeria. Valuable support was also provided by Larry Crilly who was to become a life-long friend and the godfather of my son Gregor.

Taking the place of Zantar the Mighty was a colossal police superintendent called Chris Okonkwo who had competed in the Munich Olympics. His friendship helped to preserve my family's safety in a dangerous and vibrant country. Chris became so impressed by Bill and Grant Anderson that he named his new-born son Anderson Okonkwo. Another one of my friends had a fearsome reputation. He was a great rugby player whose team had triumphed during the final selection process for the Scottish national team. Despite his obvious talent, he was the only player not to progress because his fiery temper drove him to render an opponent unconscious during the course of play. True to his nature, he was at the centre of a huge street fight in the middle of Lagos where the oppressive heat and chaos inflamed the best of people. It ignited when stuck in a traffic jam he glared at a sullen Nigerian in an adjacent vehicle and was greeted with a burning cigarette butt being flicked on to his lap. Bob Haldane was typical of the Highlanders that had proved so crucial to the success of the British Army.

Once again Caledonian Airways provided crucial support by flying out the best athletes in the professional circuit. The group included the mighty Geoff Capes, Grant Anderson, Bill Anderson and Hamish Davidson. At that time they were the best heavy event athletes on the planet. Capes had established a new British record in the Shot Putt with 71ft 4ins, Grant had taken over the mantle of grand champion from Bill with new records in the Heavy Hammer and 56lb Weight for Height and Hamish had beaten them all at an exhibition in Princes Street Gardens.

The games took place in November 1980 and were such a success that I decided to stage a World Heavy Events Championship the following year. In Lagos in 1981, with David Webster present as commentator, perhaps the first authentic championship took place with all the ***big hitters*** present. The line-up was -

Bill Anderson – Scotland

Grant Anderson – Scotland

Geoff Capes - England

Hamish Davidson – Scotland

Douglas Edmunds – Scotland

Dave Harrington - Canada

Bill Kazmaier – USA

Chris Okonkwo – Africa

Fred Vaughan – USA

Inspired by Colin Bryce who worked for Taylor Woodrow, the company with the famous tug-o-war logo, we were able to produce sixteen international tug-o-war teams, representing almost every ethnic group employed in Nigeria. The back-hold wrestling was supervised by John Rudden who was the only white man to engage the African warriors. Not surprisingly the foot races were dominated by the Nigerians but the ***Hash House Harriers,*** renown for beer drinking, made their presence felt in the road race. Kazmaier displayed his enormous strength by lifting a 900lb barbell and was then challenged by the entire Woman's tug-o-war team. Even the belated assistance of Capes failed to spare his blushes. The dancing was led by Jean Swanson from Logierait near Blair Atholl and the pipe band was none other than the Lagos Police Pipe Band.

Geoff Capes came out on top after dramatically beating Kazmaier in the 56lb Weight for Height with a world's best of 17ft 2ins.

It was a grand affair presided over by Sunday Dankaro the Nigerian Minister for Sport.

The Lagos Line-up

The boys all had a great time during their stay in Nigeria and some of the escapades are described in ***"The World's Greatest Tosser".*** Many of them expressed concern over my hip injury that plainly hampered my prowess. They encouraged me to retire and organise events when I returned to Scotland. So I formed a partnership with David Webster and a friend called Colin Finnie and we proceeded to promote our brand of Highland Games and help establish an annual World Heavy Events Championship.

From a Highlander's point of view the only problem with Geoff Capes was that he hailed from England. Like Arthur Rowe before him he made a big impact on the circuit establishing many field records and was the first man to exceed 90ft with the 28lb Weight for Distance.

GRANT ANDERSON

Scotland needed a champion to protect its honour and ***cometh the moment cometh the man*** in the person of Grant Anderson from Dundee. He had succeeded Bill Anderson as the best hammer thrower, establishing a world record with the Heavy 22lb Hammer by throwing 123ft 5ins. I believe he was also the greatest caber tosser evidenced by his display at Kilbirnie in 1983 when the organisers produced an enormous challenge caber. Only three athletes were able to toss the difficult qualifying caber namely Grant Anderson, Geoff Capes and me. Even the mighty Bill was left in its wake along with the top Americans. I was unable to balance the giant challenge caber and Geoff's best effort was a rise of about thirty degrees. Incredibly Grant tossed the stick with relative ease.

Grant Anderson wrested the World Title from Capes at Musselburgh in 1982 and famously won the Crieff Championship in 1983 which was filmed by the BBC during the production of a programme called ***The Heavies.*** Capes responded by winning the title at Carmunnock, dominating the circuit during the eighties and enhancing his reputation by winning the World's Strongest Man title on two occasions. Like Donald Dinnie before him, he popularised the games by raising overall standards as his opponents strove to beat him. When I surprisingly won the caber at Luss in 1983, beating both Grant and Geoff, I felt like the King of the World.

Hamish Davidson was always able to beat Geoff in hammer throwing before injuring his leg in a freak training accident. He permanently ruined his knee when he fell into a rabbit hole as he ran up a hill while carrying a railway sleeper on his back. The episode was typical of his barbaric training methods. He then resorted to the introduction of outrageous new events in an effort to foil the big man. One was throwing a bin full of concrete which weighed about fifty kilograms but Geoff still managed to win. However he had to capitulate when Hamish brought forward an ancient barbell for an overhead lift - Geoff managed 370lbs whereas Hamish lifted 440lbs.

Geoff finally lost his title in 1988 when Jim McGoldrick from California won the Championship in Aviemore. His demise was complete in 1990 after Alistair Gunn from Halkirk beat him in the Shot Putt at Inveraray. Typical of his breed he gleefully taunted Geoff and wounded the great man's pride. Geoff left the scene before the games had ended and never returned.

ALISTAIR GUNN

Alistair Gunn came from the defiant family that had survived the clearances. His grandfather had won the Hammer at Halkirk every year between 1920 and 1928 and his father was the champion of the far north strongman circuit. Alistair became one of the most outstanding athletes of his age and some say the best that has ever been when taking his stature into account.

He won the World Championship at Kilmarnock in 1995 beating among others Francis Brebner and the famous strongman Magnus Ver Magnusson from Iceland. He was also in the vanguard of a golden era in Scottish hammer throwing. During his career he threw the light hammer over 150ft on a number of occasions while his great rival Stephen King established new world records at Inveraray in 1998 with 153ft 2ins in the Light Hammer and 125ft 1in with the Heavy. Then in 2000 at Aboyne, Bruce Aitken from Auchenblae improved the Light Hammer mark to 156ft 8.5ins.

Alistair established himself in the pantheon of honour by winning the Scottish Open Championship at Crieff on eight occasions; an event regarded as the ***blue riband*** of the circuit. He was also a remarkable caber tosser and won the challenge caber at Braemar, in front of the Queen, eight times which still stands as a record.

BRUCE AITKEN

Bruce Aitken also salvaged our national pride by wresting back the World Heavy Event Championship at Concord, New Hampshire, in 2004.

Bruce Aitken's father was the popular Bob Aitken who competed in the same era as Sandy Gray and Bill Anderson. He was reputed to be the finest hammer throwing technician of his generation. In response to inquiring Americans endeavouring to discover the mysteries of hammer throwing, the boys from Forfar would say,

"Ask Bob Aitken. He kens!"

Bruce often competed alongside his brother Steven Aitken who was arguably the best all-rounder of the two and together they were the most successful brothers in the history of the sport.

When Bruce Aitken retired he took over the management of the Drumtochy Arms which was once owned by Donald Dinnie.

Following my retirement in 1984 I proceeded to organise games at Carmunnock, Blair Atholl, Callander, East Kilbride and later, among others, at Aviemore, Killin, Glasgow and Glenarm. I also became involved in competitions on a worldwide basis in such diverse locations such as Iceland, China, Finland, Korea and Brazil. Other milestones were the British Garden Festivals and the 1986 Commonwealth Games pageant.

Since I had first introduced highland games to Iceland during the Jon Pall era, Hjalti Arnason popularized the culture and established an eight-game circuit. Scottish visitors to the Land of Ice and Fire found it both strange and heart-warming to see young Vikings proudly wearing their kilts, albeit with locally-designed tartans. Since the early days many Icelanders have come to Scotland to compete in the games and some have excelled in world championships.

Alistair Gunn finally ended Jim McGoldrick's reign as World Champion at the games held in Kilmarnock in 1995. Close runner up was Francis Brebner, only a half point behind. They were bitter rivals and there was little love lost between them.

FRANCIS BREBNER, KEVIN THOM & ALISTAIR GUNN

Accordingly, when I received an invitation from Hjalti to take a three-man team up to Iceland, Alistair and Francis were automatic choices. The third member was Kevin Thom from Dumfries, arguably the best heavy event athlete to come out of the South of Scotland. They were to face a powerful Icelandic team which included the talented Gunner Huseby and the mighty Saemundur Saemundsson who many thought would be the new Jon Pall. The third member if the Icelandic team was Audunn Jonsson, a silver medalist in the World Power lifting Championships.

Having fond memories of Iceland I decided to take my wife and good friends, Colin and Margaret Finnie so they could see for themselves this enchanting land and its wonderful people. Andres Gudmundsson met us at the airport with his craggy and strangely handsome face. I had not seen him since we had been in Sun City, South Africa for the World's Strongest Man competition and he still bore his almost permanent mischievous grin. He booked us into a hotel and left a high-wheeled Nissan Patrol at our disposal. There was no hire charge as my Viking friends were chieftains in their own land.

ANDRES GUDMUNDSSON

The games took place at the village of Mosfellbar, about five miles to the west of Reykjavik where Jon Pall's family lived. I was sad to learn that his mother still grieved for him after his passing in 1993. This induced me to give an emotional speech during the opening ceremony in honour of the great man's memory.

Gunnar won the Shot-Putt with a throw of around 54ft then Francis responded by winning the 28lb Weight for Distance. No one could challenge Alistair in the Hammer as he was the best in the world at that time. Saemundur was spectacular in the 56lb Weight, clearing 17ft 6ins and narrowly failing at 18ft 3ins in an attempt to break the world record. Reflecting the lack of trees in Iceland the caber was a long rubber oil pipe and controlling the wobble proved difficult. It took all of Francis's experience to come out on top and Scottish pride was saved.

Afterwards I took a trip up the hill that overlooked the games to visit Jon Pall's grave. The snow had gone and flowers bedecked the little churchyard where a tall, black, volcanic rock marked the place. The harrowing reality was made more poignant by the photograph encased in the stone. It showed Jon Pall at the peak of his powers with the twinkle in his eye I knew so well. Colin left me alone to have a word with my old friend. Meanwhile, Linda was pottering around a flower shop by the roadside. On hearing her accent the shopkeeper started talking about her friend in Scotland and Linda realized that she was talking about me. She turned out to be Jon Pall's sister and she gave my little flower girl a bouquet of dried flowers to remember her by.

As is their want the boys had to check out the nightlife, which they found surprisingly vibrant. They were more than enchanted when a group of girls started to chat them up. Our highland lads shied away from the natural progression of buying them a drink. Alistair had the reputation of being ***fly and crafty*** while Francis was well known for being ***grippy.*** This left Kevin our gallant lowlander to make the offer and his eye-watering bill provided a source of great mirth to the others.

The following evening Alistair and I were made honorary Vikings at the Sgorukrain, a medieval ale house in the old part of the city where Icelandic folklore was enacted. The Gudmundsson brothers were out in force, Petur the Olympic shot-putter, Andres the stone lifter and the diminutive Hilmar. Many of the Vikings that had competed in Scotland were there. As well as Hjalti they included Magnus Ver Magnusson, Valbjorn Jonsson, Saemundur, Gunnar and Magnus Best, the bodybuilder. All responded with gusto to the frequent toasting of our induction by drinking the dreaded ***Black Death*** from drinking horns. The clamour rose to a crescendo when we were hustled out and made kneel in front of the Chief Viking. He was clad in ancient battle garments and traditional horned helmet. We were then beaten with his sword and prostrated while devilish incantations were made. The bondage was interlaced with commands, which obliged us to quaff entire drinking horns in one gulp. When suitably sanctified we were released into the night's festivities.

Alistair displayed unusual bonhomie and continuously offered to get me a drink. Later I discovered he had also been buying himself a drink and signing my name on the tab.

The next morning saw a grim struggle to escape the sour grip of the ***Black Death*** as we prepared to embark on an adventure trip into the wilderness. The Vikings talked about ***The six rivers*** and our dull brains did not grasp what was in store. Our guide had a four-wheel drive vehicle fitted with enormous wheels. We followed him through the tortured countryside and across the giant flood plain where only a few months before a spectacular of wall water and mud had raced to the sea. This had been the outcome of a volcano erupting under the glacier ice and bursting out with awesome power.

After a while we were obliged to stop and observed a white-faced Alistair hurrying from one of the vehicles. It was a moment to cherish after his antics at the Sgorukrain and Francis was beside himself with glee when he videoed his rival's miserable convulsions.

On leaving the road we drove towards the Seljalandsfoss waterfall. Unlike the well-known Gullfoss Falls, the Victoria Falls and even Niagara where the water roars into a boiling chasm, we could look up and admire its gentle splendor. The water was easily blown by the wind and the rays from the low-lying sun glinted against the torrent, inducing a brightness that was difficult to gaze on. We were unaware of the fine spray that wetted our faces and little rainbows abounded in every direction.

We had entered the Rangavallasysla nature reserve where a myriad of rivers rushed away from the melting glaciers that thrust out between the black mountains. Due to the previous night's festivities, I was pleased that Linda had volunteered to drive and was oblivious to her kamikaze approach to impending dangers. The little convoy plunged into the first river and crossed with little difficulty. On progressing further the torrents increased in strength and depth. The big truck then made the first probe and after a successful crossing stood in rescue mode should the others get into trouble. The game was on, testing the skill and fortitude of the drivers while passengers cowered in helpless terror. Being swept into the nearby lake was an ever present danger and had happened to hapless adventurers the previous week. When we got stuck and water washed over the windscreen Linda crunched the gears and bucked us to safety. Finally as we lurched through the deepest and most dangerous river the Vikings stood cheering and gave Linda a standing ovation.

This was the first time a woman had successfully negotiated all the rivers.

The Highland Games held at the Commonwealth Stadium were significant in that they were the first occasion when amateurs and professionals were brought together. Arguably the most significant result of our efforts was the Callander Highland Games which grew to be a testing ground for the new burgeoning sport of Strongman and as a setting for a series of World Heavy Event Championships. The Games were regards by many as a pilgrimage to the very roots of their sport. Competitors travelled to Callander past the battlefields of Bannockburn and Stirling Bridge. Their warrior hearts stirred at the sight of the William Wallace monument, standing like a sentinel on the other side of the river valley that overlooks the ancient massif of Stirling Castle. Turning west they pass near the Falls of Frew before entering the Trossachs where Rob Roy spent most of his life. On reaching the old town of Callander they were ensconced in the ***Dreadnought*** hotel once owned by the McNabs. The corner buttress of the building carries the image of severed heads to remind a visitor that just a few miles beyond is Loch Earn where Smooth John meted out his special brand of justice.

My son, Kristian with Callander stalwarts MATT SANDFORD (World Champion) BEN PLUCKNETT (American Discus Record Holder & JOE QUIGLEY (Commonwealth Games Silver Medalist)

In recent years the status of Highland Games in Scotland has diminished due to a lack of financial support and publicity but they still play an important role as a major tourist attraction. A lot of people think that the Highland Games are merely a quaint Scottish pastime but as can be seen from the nationalities and calibre of the athletes listed in the Callander Role of Honour (see appendix), the games belong in the highest echelons of sport. Many counties now take part and there are hundreds of events outside Scotland, for some unfathomable reason the expatriate is much more patriotic than the homeland breed. Seeing smiling athletes with strange sounding names, proudly wearing the kilt indicates a widespread desire to be part of the Scottish Diaspora.

Despite our best efforts the games needed more enhancements. A meeting was called in Edinburgh by a member of the law firm Todds Murray to discuss what might be done for our national sport. Present were David Webster and Willie Baxter, the latter being responsible for resurrecting Celtic wrestling. Others included David Dinsmore the director of the Royal Highland Society, a representative of the Scottish Highland Games

Association, Willie Robertson, Gregor Edmunds and a phalanx of Event Scotland officers – most of who had never been to a Highland Games. Not surprisingly the meeting was inconclusive so I decided to take unilateral action. My response was to try and return the games to their original format by including gladiatorial and strength events to reflect the participation of warriors. With my experience, described in ***Giants and Legends,*** I was able to bring together the best of the world's strongest men and the most elite Highland Games athletes with the intention of producing a grand champion. Our team included the garrulous Colin Bryce as presenter and a gifted television director called Will Clough, who had been successful with the World's Strongest Man programme. I was then able to negotiate nationwide television coverage with Channel 4.

The new concept was called ***The Highlander Challenge.***

Blair Atholl was chosen to host the first of the new enhanced games. What better place than the centre of Scottish medieval history and the seat of Lord George Murray, the last Jacobite hero?

No less a personage than Dr. Ian McPherson agreed to drive his old friend around some relevant historical sites to provide links for the television programme. We left the motorway about ten miles north of Dunblane, passed through Braco and turned left at the Roman camp at Ardoch on the road to Comrie. Turning westwards at Comrie we passed the ominous rock pile of Dundurn Fort which was an old Pictish stronghold. When we reached St. Fillans we were joined by local historian David Birkmyre – a former Scottish javelin champion and national record holder. This was the place where one of the first Highland Games of the enlightened age took place. We also learned that St Fillans was named after a Dalriadan missionary from Ireland who helped to bring Christianity to the Picts in the sixth century. His chapel and grave are at Dundurn on the eastern end of Loch Earn. On progressing along the loch we passed the malevolent-looking McNeish Island which reminded us of when Smooth John McNab devastated a family of outlaws for stealing his family's whisky. At the north end we past the Lochearnhead games field where Ewen Cameron ruled the roost and then on to the home of Clan McNab at Killin.

There was no trace of the castle at Eilan Ran where Smooth John lived with his family. In 1613 a charter of superiority over the MacNab lands was granted to the Campbells of Finlarig Castle which was situated just across the river from Eilan Ran. When Smooth John joined Alasdair MacColla and raided the Campbell territories along Loch Tay the consequences for Clan MacNab were ruinous. Their lands were sequestered and Eilan Ran was subsequently burnt out of existence. The ruins of Finlarig Castle still stand on the shores of the river Dochart and the sight of the beheading pit bears witness to the harsh governance of the time.

On visiting the MacNab museum we were confronted with a large portrait of ***The MacNab.*** An imposing figure of manhood, dressed in full highland regalia, his name was Francis the sixteenth chief and direct descendant of Smooth John. He lived at Kinnel house and presided over the mounting family debts after failing in many lawsuits against the Campbells. Reputably of Herculean strength, he merely ignored his plight and carried on producing and drinking whisky. He reputedly terrified a bailiff by having him lavishly entertained with the whisky and then confronting him with the hanging of a debt collector. He was not to know that the execution was staged and fled without daring to serve the writ. When Francis died in Callander at the age of eighty one he left thirty-five thousand pounds worth of debts. He was buried on the magical island of Inchbuie at the Falls of Dochart in Killin. The grave yard can still be reached through a gate in the middle of the Dochart Bridge which gives access to the island.

The irascible nature of ***The MacNab*** is amply revealed in his sojourns to London where he started gambling at the new fangled craze of cock fighting. After losing his money to insufferable English dandies he pledged to return with a Scottish bird and win back his losses. No doubt they looked forward to the opportunity of fleecing him again. Some months later he returned with a wooden crate that had made the long trip by sea. As the champion cockerel strutted in anticipation of its next victim, the dandies anxiously waited to see the ***Cock o' the North.*** Out stepped an eagle, red eyed with rage and ravenous with hunger.

We finished the day by driving along the south shore of Loch Tay so that we could appreciate the herculean efforts made by the McNabs when they raided the McNeishes in 1624. Our route took us up two thousand feet to a high plateau called Glen Tarken which stretches for some ten miles before descending down to Loch Earn. We marvelled at their murderous determination as they dragged their heavy boat through the snow along the tortuous route. Nearby in Glen Boltachan a stone covered in red lichen marks the spot of a decisive battle between the two clans during the previous century. The unnatural red colour is believed to represent the copious amount of blood that was spilt. Clan McNeish was an ancient clan that had emanated from three Irish brothers when they invaded Scotland in the third Century BC, members of the fabled ***Scotti.***. In 1522 a land dispute with the McNabs erupted in a violent battle in which the chief of the McNeishes was killed and his clan almost wiped out. A few survivors managed to escape to their island stronghold in Loch Earn where they became a family of outlaws and vagabonds, preying on their neighbours for survival.

On our second trip we were accompanied by Garrett Johnson, one of the best shot-putters in America and a Rhodes Scholar at Oxford University. He had the style and demeanour of a future statesman and I was pleased to buy him a kilt. We stopped at the Wallace monument in Stirling to take a look at the replica of Wallace's sword and came across a new statue that had been placed in the car park, depicting Wallace carrying a weapon called the mace. It was not an example of fine Scottish art and resembled actor, Mel Gibson, carrying a 28lb throwing weight. The place had become world famous due to the film ***Braveheart,*** in which Gibson portrayed a romanticised version of Wallace's life.

GARRETT JOHNSON

Once again we drove through Killin, along the north side of Loch Tay and after a few miles turned left up the escarpment into Glen Lyon. It is known as the Crooked Glen of Stones with the remains of twelve castles that existed during the time of the Picts. When we reached the picturesque centre and observed the surrounded high mountains and the remnants of a dense forest it was easy to imagine their ancient stronghold. We then turned south following the river Lyon on its way to Loch Tay and stopped at a village near the Brig o' Balgie. Here we found the fabled ***Pictish Warrior Stone*** lying near its ancient pedestal. Our American friend refrained from trying to lift it being afraid of injury. Gregor Edmunds was unfazed and demonstrated his power by managing to heave it onto his shoulder. The stoutly built Will Clough insisted in having a go and strained to lift it just clear of the ground, indicating that the feat was beyond that of normal men.

On continuing our journey we passed the famous McGregor's leap. After the proscription of Clan Gregor in 1563 knives were out for Gregor McGregor, the chief of his clan. For a time he was protected by his father-in-law, Campbell of Glen Lyon known as Duncan the Hospitable. But McGregor was an adventurer and continued to trouble more senior members of the Campbell hierarchy. In 1565 Campbell of Glenorchy sent assassins to the McGregor village and killed two of his people. As chief of his clan, Gregor was bound to take vengeance. This he did by murdering the perpetrators and their accomplices, incurring the wrath of the whole of Clan Campbell. He was forced into hiding but occasionally came to visit his beloved wife and eventually servants betrayed him. He was pursued by blood hounds and managed to escape by jumping across the rocky chasm over the river Lyon. Unfortunately he was later captured and beheaded.

When we reached the end of the glen we turned towards Aberfeldy and observed the ancient standing stones that had been erected by the Picts for a purpose yet to be understood. We stopped at Menzie Castle where we were assured that a ghost still roamed around the premises. It was the house occupied by General Wade when he was building the Aberfeldy Bridge. There was also a lifting stone at the front door that was used as at the Aberfeldy Games. Gregor dismissed it as a mere pebble. Our adventure ended at Aberfeldy where our famous black friend from Florida was introduced to the Scottish staple of haggis, neeps and tatties. After quaffing a pint of shandy we returned home via the ***Sma Glen*** following the route taken by MacColla and Montrose on their march to Perth prior to the battle of Tippermuir.

The next day took us up the Aberdeen road to the plains north of Brechin where the battle of Dunnichen is said to have taken place. We visited the church yard at Aberlemno and marvelled at the ancient standing stone depicting the battle with the carvings of warriors, horsemen and mysterious symbols that were still visible. The Picts did not have a written language this was their means of communication and the stone provided the inspiration for the introduction of the Pictish Stone Carry – reminiscent of the Husafell Stone in Iceland.

On Whitson Sunday 2007 the stage was set for the first international ***Highlander Challenge*** with the assembly of an awesome group of competitors in the court-yard of Blair Atholl Castle. The iconic fortress was first built in 1269 and so impressed Queen Victoria that she granted the Duke of Atholl a charter allowing him to maintain the only private army under arms in Scotland. When the pipers had finally tuned their raging instruments the opening parade got underway. Leading the procession were the Clann an Drumma group, dressed like ancient Picts, bashing out a stirring call to arms, followed by the athletes in single file. Next in line was the Atholl pipe band at the head of the Atholl Highlanders marching with their muskets, swords and lochaber axes. Bringing up the rear was a group of soldiers pulling a cannon. They came down from the castle and on to the field where MacColla and Montrose had their momentous first encounter.

ABERLEMNO STONE

The athletes were lined up and presented to the eleventh Duke of Atholl – a mighty group of warriors -

Dave Barron: USA – American Highland Games champion and self-styled one man "A" team

Kyrylo Chuprynin: Ukraine – Olympian and Weight for Height world record holder.

Gregor Edmunds: Scotland – Scottish Highland Games and Braemar champion.

Garrett Johnson: USA – World Top Ten Shot-putter and National Collegiate champion.

Saemunder Saemundson: Iceland – National record holder for Throwing the Weight for Distance and Height.

Scott Rider: England – Competed in Commonwealth Games and Winter Olympics.

Sebastian Wenta: Poland – Former National Shot putt and Discus champion.

Mike Zolkiewicz: USA – Three times Discus National Collegiate champion

When the awe struck Garrett Johnson was interviewed he said –

"I have heard real men do the Highland Games so I've come to play with the big boys."
"It is good to be back at the roots and do the real thing."

The games started after a rendering of the Carnyx war horn whose howling tones summoned the ancient Pictish warriors to battle. Towering above the arena were the Weight for Height stands, emblazoned with the word Gododdin, as a reminder of the small group of Scottish warriors that had fought to their deaths in a vain attempt to stem the invasion of the Angles. They were the Scottish equivalent of the Spartan 300 that defended ancient Greece against the Persian horde.

Gregor Edmunds took an early lead in the Hammer until the last round when Dave Barron exceeded his mark. Fortunately the Scotsman was last to throw and like a true champion able to summon his strength when under pressure, pulled out his biggest throw of the day and won the event.

The overall standard of stone putting was arguably the best ever seen at a Highland Games with the lead changing many times throughout the competition. Finding himself in a surprising third place, it was time for Garrett Johnson to steel himself and show his mettle. He then employed his spinning technique to full effect and surpassed the field.

Next was throwing the 28lb Weight for Distance referred to as the Mace to fit with the spirit of the day, Gregor was expected to win as he had recently come near the world record for the event but Mike Zolkiewicz had other ideas and established a lead in the last round. However once again by digging deep Gregor managed to produce a fantastic throw maintaining his pride and taking him back to the top of the Leader Board..

As expected, Kyrylo Chuprinin excelled in the gladiatorial events. With his ice-blue, expressionless eyes and the demeanour of a member of the Russian mafia, he was an intimidating character. The games commentator described him as –

"A big, scary looking man."

We could not find out what he did for a living, avoiding answers with a laconic smile. When I was on a trip to Kiev, I marvelled at his big wheeled vehicle with its high chassis, he then proceeded to demonstrate its ability to jump over the parapet of a motorway with the intention of avoiding a police road block.

In the first round of the Pole Push the savage Viking instincts of Saemunder Saemundson startled Sebastian Wenta who weighed more that 160kgs and stood 6ft 7ins. Wenta was bustled out of the ring before he could settle into the action. Saemunder then went on to challenge Gregor in the second round and found that in contrast to a relatively docile Pole he had to deal with a fiery Scotsman. A violent fight took place which ended when

Saemunder crashed to the ground. Gregor was then left to face Kyrylo Chuprinin in the final. After a mighty struggle both men were exhausted having fought to a stalemate. In desperation Kyrylo turned to his dark side and instead of continuing to push against his opponent, he executed a surreptitious tug and Gregor fell on his face. The action was against the rules but the referee failed to notice and Kyrylo was declared the winner.

Big Sebastian was chastened after his ignominious defeat in the Pole Push and was determined to win the Wrestling. He was the strongest man on the field, having achieved a second place in the World's Strongest Man competition. The men lined up facing their opponents, stripped to the waist and bare-footed. At the sight of so much naked flesh a joke was made about a housewife's choice. Unfortunately for Gregor, he was drawn against the mighty Pole and to the accompaniment of the Clann an Drumma's rousing music, was lifted off the ground and crushed against the great barrel chest. Having succumbed to the power he was thrown to the ground and left struggling for the breath that had been driven out of him. The final was contested over three falls between Sebastian Wenta and Kyrylo Chuprinin and when the latter won the first round it was as though an enraged grizzly bear had awakened from its slumber. With uncharacteristic venom Wenta made short work of the hapless Ukrainian in the next two rounds.

The next event was throwing the 56lb Weight for Height in which Chuprinin held the Scottish Highland Games Association's world record at 17ft 1.5ins, achieved at Inveraray in 2005. This is always an entertaining event with athletes exhorting spectators for support. Dave Barron was so pleased when he cleared 16ft that he performed a cartwheel with a spectacular roll of his 6ft 4ins frame. When he failed at 17ft he resorted to pulling up his kilt and flashing his bottom – the crowd loved his antics.

Kyrylo Chuprinin won by clearing 17ft with apparent ease and declared that it had been -

“No problem”

A phrase he often used due to his limited command of English.

Only three men could turn the big championship caber which was calibrated to have a caber number of more than 1000. This method of measuring the degree of difficulty is described in the tale of –

“The World's Greatest Tosser”

At the penultimate stage of the competition the Ukrainian was in the overall lead and favoured to win the championship. The last event was a brutal trial of strength and stamina, consisting of carrying a stone weighing 400lbs as far as possible. There were two four-man heats in which the challengers could goad each other into ***last man standing***. During the first, Scott Rider raced to the front in an effort to demoralise the opposition. His legs drove like pistons enabling him to carry the implement an amazing distance of 130ft. This left the big men in the second heat with a target and as they set off on the painful journey. Chuprinin collapsed in a dead faint. The dead weight had crushed his chest and prevented him from breathing. Regardless of the drama behind, Sebastian Wenta and Gregor Edmunds continued their weary journey, each trying to break the spirit of the other. First they overtook the Americans and then they staggered to a conclusion. Sebastian was just able to beat Scott Rider's gritty effort whereas Gregor just fell short. So the Englishman had become the kingmaker and Sebastian won the championship by half a point over Gregor. The unfortunate Kyrylo was reduced to third place.

Bruised and bloodied, Kyrylo warded off concerns for his welfare by saying that he had –

"No Problem."

The final results were

Champion - Sebastian Wenta

Second - Gregor Edmunds

Third - Kyrylo Chuprinin

The television programme attracted record audiences.

THE BATTLE OF SCONE

We decided to honour ***Ian McPherson*** by making him the chieftain at the second Highlander Challenge, arguably one of the greatest games of the time. Stirring music was once again provided by the Clann an Drumma and a group called the Chili Peppers who were later to become world famous. Ian was dressed as Robert the Bruce to impart the impression of a King commanding his warriors. His supercilious look could have come from the Bruce himself and the role was a natural fit.

The second Highlander Challenge was held over two days on a field below the Palace of Scone, across the river from the place where McPherson's ancestors had engaged in the bloody Battle of Perth.

Our plan was to produce three television programmes with sixteen athletes engaging in two qualifying heats and a final. So once again we had to find historical links. Nearby was the resting place of the Stone of Destiny where the ancient Kings of Scotland sat during their coronation. The original stone had been taken by King Edward 1 and placed in Westminster Abbey. It was a symbolic gesture meant to subdue the Scots but served to inflame them and ultimately led to the great victory of Bannockburn. Today a replica sits on the site which was of particular interest to Gregor Edmunds due to his family's connection with the saga of the stone.

Gregor traces his ancestors to a highland weaver named Morris who had probably come from the Hebrides during the clearances. He lived in the Kingdom of Fife which became a prosperous coal mining community during the Industrial Revolution. The weaver's family started a coal trimming business in the small port of St David's helping to fuel the great steam ships of the era. Gregor's grandfather emerged from the social exploitation of the times to become a defiant Scottish Nationalist. As a young man he ran away from his home in Rosyth and joined the army at sixteen, successfully lying about his age because of his physical stature. His refusal to take orders from those he did not respect led him into perennial trouble. Most of his national service was spent in a Gibraltar jail where punishment details included cleaning the stairs of Gibraltar with a tooth brush. Ever defiant he decided to abscond and found refuge with a prominent group of nationalists. Among them was the laureate Christopher Grieve, an academic called Douglas Young and Bob Macmillan the father of playwright Hector Macmillan. Christopher Grieve, also known as Hugh MacDiarmid, was lauded for his perceptive poem called ***A Drunk Man Looks at the Thistle*** and is recognised as Scotland's best poet since Robert Burns. Hector with similar views about social injustice wrote a famous play called ***The Sash,*** a satire about the sectarianism that has divided the nation since the Covenanters.

The group produced a seditious newspaper called the ***Freeman*** which exhorted Scotland to once again fight for independence. This was during the Second World War and considered treasonous by the British Government. To avoid being arrested Gregor's grandfather changed his name from John Morris to John Edmunds and so the family became English in name only. One of the group's projects was to take back the Stone of Destiny from Westminster Abbey and big John was given the task of carrying the heavy stone out of the Abbey into a waiting car. He trained by lifting heavy ingots at Beardmore Steelworks but before the plan could be put into action the stone was taken by a rival group indicating that the desire for insurrection was widespread.

This was Gregor's chance to honour his grandfather's memory and he was given permission to lift the stone and carry it about.

Establishing television links took us to McCombie country in the Grampian Mountains. As we neared Glenshee on the road to Braemar we turned right into Glenisla to meet the landowner, Major Gibb and his shepherd Jock Davidson. Both had helped to find the legendary stone that McCombie Mor had putted almost for hundred years ago. Clues to its resting place were given in an ancient text provided by Jack Davidson -

"The place where the feat was performed, and the stone itself, and the stance, are all remarkable. The source of the River Prosen, a right bank tributary of the South Esk, is at the west end of the slope that reaches back from the summit of the Mayar, 3043 feet, whose eastern side rises abruptly over Glen Prosen. At the west end of this slope, in two slight depressions which spreads out like a V, are gathered the head-waters of the Prosen, at a short distance from the source of the Cally, a left-bank tributary of the Isla. Between the two depressions is a comparatively level meadow of short bent grass, and from the surface of this meadow the upper edge of a fast stone, about 4 or 5 feet long, projects for about 6 inches above the surface. This projecting edge of boulder forms the stance, and about 26 feet beyond this stance is embedded, in a round hole in the ground, a round-shaped rough-surfaced stone of about 35 lb in weight, and local tradition for over two hundred years has handed down the hole, in which the stone lies embedded to about half its diameter, as the mark to which McCombie putted the stone from the stance."

We were provided with the unique opportunity of pitting a modern champion against an ancient legend. The stone had assumed the status of a relic and the television producer wanted to film Gregor throwing it from exactly the same arena as McCombie. It was reasonable to assume that McCombie used the old standing style on the short stance at the top of the misty mountain. The howling rainstorm suggested the presence of a fierce spirit who had an interest in the proceedings. Putting the Heavy Stone was one of Gregor's best events having thrown 49ft 4ins with the conventional 22lb stone. McCombie's stone was much heavier and awkward and the challenge was formidable. Steeling himself against the raging storm Gregor managed to exceed the old mark but not by much. Afterwards Gregor remarked –

"That McCombie must have been some man!"

Before we left, the Major carefully returned the stone to its ancient resting place.

Our next stop was at the gates of Braemar, the only purpose built Highland Games stadium in the world where up to thirty thousand people greet the royal family who attend the games every year – making the occasion unique in British sport. We had arranged to meet Murray Brown the local fixer and former Highland Games athlete. Murray obtained permission to pull out the famous Braemar Caber and at the insistence of our producer Gregor and I, the only father and son to have won the event, were filmed holding the historical stick. Afterwards he organised a visit into the grounds of Balmoral, the Queen's private castle. We were then able to film the stone carving on the rear wall depicting King Malcolm Canmore addressing his warriors, some of whom held implements very similar to the throwing weights used at the games.

Polish strongman, Sebastian Wenta, who had achieved second place in the Word's Strongest Man, accompanied us on the trip. The plan was to have him lift the Inver Stone and then to have a go at the famous Dinnie Stones. Unfortunately he tore a muscle in his shoulder so Gregor had to lift the stone to spare our blushes. It is said that if anyone lifts the stone from its bed and carries it to the pub across the road a free pint of beer will be provided. From there we passed through Aboyne to the inn at the Bridge of Potarch where the Dinnie stones can be found. With Wenta unable to oblige, a local man known as big Callum, was summoned to do his party trick. On finishing his pint of beer and with great aplomb he grasped the handles, lifted them clear and staggered across the width of the bridge. Once again he demonstrated his ability to carry out a feat of strength that had defied many strongmen throughout the ages. Callum was more than able to lift the stones and could carry them with two 56lb weights attached.

Sadly Callum Morrison passed away in 2011 and will be long remembered competing in the Drum Major competition at Braemar. He tossed his heavy swagger stick over a twenty foot bar and then caught it with one hand, without breaking his stride. Being completely drunk ***didnae fashe him.***

On the 19th of July 2008, commentator Hamish Davidson, self-proclaimed Knight of the Realm, set the tone with the proclamation –

"Scotland, a rugged and beautiful land with a turbulent history has forged the character of its tenacious and noble people, here at Scone another battle awaits!"

After the parade Ian McPherson thrust his sword into the ground and declared –

"I lay down the challenge for any man to take the sword from my champion – the King's Champion."

Sebastian Wenta pulled out the sword and waved it above his head and roared –

"I am Champion!"

The first heat contained most of the throwing specialists –

Dave Barron USA – Runner-up in American Highland Games Championship.

Sean Betz USA – Holder of World Highland Games Championship (2008).

Larry Brock USA – Holder of American record for throwing 56lb Weight for Distance.

Gregor Edmunds Scotland – World Highland Games Champion (2007).

Aaron Neighbour Australia – Competed in Commonwealth games in Discus and Shot Putt.

Scott Rider England – British Shot Putt Champion and competed in Olympics and Commonwealth Games.

Darius Slowik Canada – Pan American Games Discus Champion and Commonwealth Games bronze medallist.

Lucasz Wenta Poland – Polish junior champion in Shot Putt.

The competition started with the Hammer and as expected Sean Betz established an early lead but was surprised by Scott Rider who seemed to be on fire. Sean just managed to hold on to his position with the Englishman less than three inches behind. In the heat of competition Scott had achieved a personal record with a nine foot improvement on his previous best.

Aaron Neighbour was not pleased with last place which was displayed at the bottom of the score board. His Australian pride was ruffled when a female commentator remarked –

"Neighbour, the boy from down under is exactly that!"

The television link introduced the next event by showing Gregor Edmunds casting stones into a river. This recalled the use of stones as the most basic of weapons, effectively used by Robert the Bruce when he ambushed his pursuers at the battle of Glentrool.

Casting the Stone proved to be a titanic struggle between the specialist shot-putters. Lucasz Wenta employed the traditional glide technique, exhibiting his dynamic power by throwing almost 59ft. In contrast Scott Rider used the modern spinning method which enabled him to beat his rival and exceed the 60ft barrier – a distance rarely achieved with awkwardly shaped stones. Newcomer, Darius Slovak was unable to employ his normal style and had to throw Braemar Style but still achieved a creditable distance of 50ft 1.5ins. However the stone proved too awkward for Aaron Neighbour, who despite being a Commonwealth Games finalist in the Shot Putt, was once again consigned down under.

The Caber was a worthy stick about 19ft 6ins long and weighing about 140lbs, chosen to test the mettle of the challengers so that the best man wins. The view prevailed that if all could toss the Caber it would be deemed unworthy and result in a lottery. Caber tossing is a reminder that Scotland was once a heavily wooded land and stripped bare to build ships for the English navy. Great tracts of the ancient Caledonian Forest were also burnt to provide pasture during the Clearances. Traces of the original, indigenous forest can still be found in Sutherland and some parts of Argyll. Our calibration proved to be satisfactory with only three out of the eight contenders, able to turn the stick. Scott Rider came out on top with Gregor Edmunds a close second and Larry Brock the best of the rest.

At last Aaron Neighbour was confronted with an event that appealed to him. He had won the Australian Strongest Man title, stood 6ft 6ins and fancied his chances in the Stone Lift. The event consisted of lifting four field stones of increasing weight over a caber resting between two trestles. Due to Aaron's position on the score board he was required to make the first attempt which gave an advantage to his opponents by allowing them to get his measure.

While the Clann an Drumma beat rhythmically on their war drums the big Australian attacked the stones. He lifted the first three easily then after a minor struggle was successful with the fourth. Darius Slovak could only lift two stones, Lucasz Wenta struggled to lift three and Sean Betz only managed two. David Barron surprised everybody by rapidly lifting the first three stones in a faster time than Neighbour. When he was unable to lift the last he just sat down and waved to the crowd. Hamish Davidson was not impressed when Larry Brock only managed to lift one stone. Gregor was confident in the knowledge that he had once held the world record for lifting the Atlas Stones. He rushed forward and lifted all four stones as if they were pebbles, beating Neighbour's time by almost seven seconds. Scott was last to attempt the trial of strength and gamely lifted three stones but he was only good enough for fifth place.

Pitching the 20lb sheaf with a hay fork is a popular event in the North American circuit but rarely included in Scotland. So it was not surprising when the Americans displayed a superior technique and came out on top.

Our occidental friends were outside their comfort zone at the prospect of engaging in the Pole Push which demands a physical confrontation. Scott Rider appeared to relish the prospect and was compared to a pit bull terrier by the commentator. He quickly disposed of Darius Slowik, Aaron Neighbour did likewise with Sean Betz and Gregor Edmunds easily defeated Larry Brock. Dave Barron was made of sterner stuff and fiercely resisted the attacking thrusts of Lucasz Wenta. The confrontation between a Manhattan lawyer and a Polish street fighter was at least intriguing and a case of brain versus brawn. The dour Pole eventually overcame the determined American who was forced to succumb when pushed on to his knees. Rider seemed to enjoy the violence and wasted no time in the semi-final when he tore into the monolithic Australian. The latter was unable to cope with the vigour of the Englishman who repeatedly drove upwards from a low position, taking his opponent off balance and not allowing him to settle. Scott tried the same tactic in the final against Gregor who had disposed of Wenta. Initially The Scotsman had to give way and then drawing on his experience he moved like a matador and forced Scott to charge out of the ring like a frenzied bull in a Spanish arena.

Qualifiers for the final were–

Scott Rider

Gregor Edmunds

Sean Betz

Dave Barron

The second heat contained most of the strongman contingent including defending champion Sebastian Wenta –

Johannes Arsjo, Sweden – Sweden's Strongest Man

Kyrylo Chuprynin, Ukraine – Olympic Discus thrower

Neil Elliott, Scotland – Winner of Scottish national Shot Putt and Discus titles

Mark Felix, England & Grenada – Runner-up in Britain's Strongest Man.

Solvi Petursson, Iceland – Winner of Iceland's Strongest Man.

Sebastian Wenta, Poland – Defending Champion

Mike Zolkiewicz, USA – Three times All American Discus Champion.

Wout Zylstra, Holland – World record holder in Weight for Height and third in World's Strongest Man.

The first event was throwing the Mace which Kyrylo Chuprynin won relatively easily drawing from his discus throwing ability. His distance of 88ft 7.5ins exceeded the legendary Bill Anderson's best of 87ft 10ins which was the national record for many years. This was followed by the Casting of the McCombie Stone in the Braemar style. The archaic rule demands that both feel must remain planted to the ground during the course of the throw. Sebastian Wenta won with 39ft 7ins nearing the Braemar record of 40ft 10ins achieved by Geoff Capes in 1981. He celebrated his victory by lifting the lady commentator above his head with one arm, giving her the thrill of her life.

Next was the Whisky Barrel Carry, a strongman event demanding determination and grip strength. It was a head to head race along a 45metre course carrying two large barrels in a steel crate, weighing approximately 750lbs.

Johannes Arsjo from Sweden, who called himself the Viking Invader, welcomed the opportunity of displaying his power and blazed up the course. He was closely followed by Mark Felix who appeared like a block of obsidian granite, splendidly turned out in his home-made black watch kilt which perfectly matched his complexion. Third place went to the charismatic Solvi Petursson who exhorted the spectators to give him their vocal support. Only Mike Zolkiewicz failed in the brutal task of completing the course.

Tossing the Caber for Distance proved too difficult for the inexperienced winner of the Barrel Carry, demanding a technique that can only be mastered with extensive practice. The heavy stick had be lifted without assistance, balanced in the vertical position then tossed from behind a stop-board. A successful attempt demanded that the implement pass through ninety degrees and be thrown as far as possible. This is regarded as the Swedish Style and has its origins in the Island of Gotland which was a famous Viking stronghold. The annual festival, held in Visby during July, is referred to as ***Stangaspeilen*** and as well as tossing the caber for distance the stick must be lifted from the horizontal using the thighs as a fulcrum, requiring an even greater level of skill..

Despite his heritage Johannes Arsjo was unable to control the caber and ignominiously joined Mark Felix in recording complete failures. Johannes did not give up easily and committed the cardinal sin of not releasing when he lost control. While still in his grasp the far end struck the ground sending a ricochet up the stick. His arching trapezius muscles saved him from breaking his collar bone but he still caught a glancing blow on the head and fell to the ground, momentarily stunned. He recovered quickly and with great bravado, sprang up, waved his arms aloft and shouted "***Viking power!***" as if his demise had been intentional. Kyrylo Chuprinin won the event with Sebastian Wenta coming second and Wout Zylstra, considered the old master, a close third.

Everyone expected Wout to win the Weight for Height as he held the world record with a throw of 18ft 9ins but his glory years had passed with age and his famous rallying cry of "***Isapacka!***" had to give way to the exuberant young Swede who had the temerity to draw with Kyrylo in his favourite event.

The Wrestling was changed from the traditional back-hold to a more open style similar to sumo, demanding cunning as well as strength. The new style also resulted in more violent and long-lasting encounters. The first round pit local hero Neil Elliott against Sebastian Wenta and being a Glasgow man he was inclined to administer the ***Glasgow Kiss*** in a combat situation. However the possibility of a wounded monster chasing him around the field may have modified his strategy. Instead he rushed in flaying and slapping with his arms but merely bounced off his monolithic opponent. He then tried to turn Sebastian by grabbing his arm and managed to hurt the big man. The monster became enraged and Neil was bundled out of the ring, still fighting like a dervish. In the next round Wenta was unable to use his strength to maximum effect due to the injury inflicted by Neil. This allowed Kyrylo Chuprynin to take advantage and he managed to shove Sebastian out of the ring.

Neil's next opponent was the brooding, dark menace of Mark Felix. His Scottish mentality railed against the possibility of another defeat. Although Mark was a much stronger man Neil was a natural fighter and ferociously attacked before Mark could get his measure. Neil again tried an arm lock and managed to tear one of Mark's taut muscles. The latter then became easy prey and the injury was a precursor to the muscle coming off the bone during a later competition.

The final was a furious affair fought over the best of three rounds between Arsjo and Chuprynin. The latter tried to intimidate the young Viking and manage to use his body weight to push him out of the ring. Defeat in the first round merely aroused the ***Berserker*** and Arsjo became invigorated like a deranged Viking warrior. The fury could not be contained by the lumbering Cossack and the job was completed in the next two rounds. After receiving the accolade of victory, Arsjo proudly displayed a large bloodied gash on his shoulder which he regarded as a badge of honour.

Following the conclusion of the Wrestling those who qualified for the final were –

Kyrylo Chuprinin

Sebastian Wenta

Johannes Arsjo

Wout Zylstra

Scone Palace made a stunning backdrop with the river Tay flowing past at the foot of the field. At the other side of the river lay the field where the savage Battle of Perth had been fought at the King's pleasure. The vista served to imbue the athletes with a sense of history. Atmospherics were provided by the Clan Battle Society who displayed their ancient weapons of war and demonstrated how to use them. One was an ancient version of the Hammer called the Morning Star. It consisted of a long shaft with a steel ball at one end which bristled with sharp spikes, ideal for smashing through the helmet of an armour-clad knight. They added spice to the occasion by enacting the ***Highland Charge*** and the battle of Perth and their blood curling cries were enough to awake the ghosts of their ancient comrades. The Clan had also built a camp to show how the old Scots lived and prepared a bowl of black pudding by mixing fresh blood with oatmeal. To everybody's amazement the petite and extremely posh female commentator from national television, Natalie Pinkham, consumed it with gusto.

Sean Betz was aware that he had to excel in the traditional throws to have any chance of ultimate victory as he did not rate himself in the rugged highlander events. He rose to the occasion and easily won the Hammer Throw with a magnificent 141ft 7ins, beating Scott Rider who could only produce 136ft 9.5ins. Sean them proceeded to win the Mace by throwing the 28lb weight 91ft 7ins, a few inches short of the world record at the time. Many thought Kyrylo Chuprynin would have come to the fore, having made the final in the discus at the Sidney Olympics but although the technique is similar the implement was five times heavier and he languished in 5th place.

Sean's glory was short-lived as he was unable to toss the qualifying caber and along with Johannes Arsjo did not proceed to the giant Challenge Caber. The wooden log was 21ft long with a difficulty rating of 1140 on the ***Russ Murphy*** scale. Led by a piper, the six qualifiers ceremoniously carried the stick on their shoulders to the place of competition. They then issued their personal challenges and held a toasting with a quaich of ***Grouse Whisky.***

THE CHALLENGE CABER

Wout Zylstra was past his prime. During his career he had won many championships, held a world record and achieved third place in the World Strongest Man competition at Morocco in 1998. However a fierce pride still burned in his heart. The caber was his favourite event and after the first round nobody had produced the perfect toss. Wout steeled himself for his second and last effort and silenced his rivals with a great toss. He turned to the judge and gesticulated wildly. Grant Anderson was not the kind of man that could be intimidated and took his time to award the perfect 12 o'clock. Wout was ecstatic and ran around the field celebrating his victory. The sponsors presented him with a special trophy. It was one of the most important moments of his life, nothing else mattered, he had won the most prestigious event.

WOUT ZYLSTRA

The Pole Push was a brutal affair designed to emulate the Schiltron defence at Bannockburn.

Scott Rider bundled David Barron out of the ring while and the towering Wout Zylstra easily disposed of Sean Betz. When Johannes Arsjo set about Sebastian Wenta the giant Pole had no answer to the furious aggression. Once again Gregor Edmunds was matched against Chuprynin and when the tenacious Scot started to wear down his opponent the devious Cossack employed a different ruse. This time he lifted the pole over his head which had the effect if pulling rather than pushing the pole causing Gregor to fall on his face. The ruse was not in ther spirit of the game but the judges had not anticipated such an action and once again erroneously awarded the bout to Chuprynin, damaging Gregor's prospects in the overall standings.

Scott Rider faced Arsjo in the final and had learnt from previous encounters. Every time the Viking attacked with vigorous thrusts Scot moved to the side and effectively ran round the ring to counter his stronger opponent. In the end it was a stalemate with both men fighting to a standstill whereupon the Englishman obligingly collapsed and Arsjo was declared the winner.

POLE PUSH

The penultimate event was throwing the 56lb Weight for Height which suited the strongmen rather than the elegant hammer throwers. It is an event likely to have been introduced during the reintroduction of the games by the Highland Societies at the beginning of the nineteenth century. The implements used in the new era reflect the farmyard rather that the war like activities of an earlier age.

After two days of hard competition it was decided to expedite the Weight for Height by starting at the unusually high height of 14ft. Unfortunately Scott Rider was unable to recover from his valiant exertions in the Pole Push and despite being capable of achieving some two feet higher on another day he was unable to record a mark. Sebastian Wenta realised that his title was at risk after a poor showing in the Pole Push, roused himself and managed to share the honours with both the old Dutch war horse and the energetic young Viking. The all managed to throw over 16ft which was the world record in the days of Bill Kazmaier and Grant Anderson.

Throughout the games Gregor Edmunds lacked lustre and did not give of his best. He excused himself by citing that as one of the tournament organisers he had lost his power by having to set up the arena prior to the competition. However he was a proud man with fighting spirit and rallied himself for the last event, the grindingly painful Pictish Stone Carry. He was scheduled to compete in the first group of four and realised that the second group would have the advantage of following in his wake. Using his experience he resolved to follow Arsjo, his toughest opponent. As expected the exuberant Viking set a furious pace and pushed himself to exhaustion. Gregor hung on grimly and just managed to go a few inches further. The distances were too much for the others and as a result Gregor managed to propel himself on to the podium.

Results of the final – **Champion - Sebastian Wenta**

Second - Scott Rider

Third - Gregor Edmunds

Afterwards we were treated to a banquet by ***Grouse*** in their whisky distillery at Crieff. Before indulging, the Challenge Caber was presented for permanent display in the Banqueting Hall and then we were served with a remarkable meal which was a fitting ending to a great occasion.

FASAN UR DINNER MENU

Created by Robbie Gleave, Executive Development Chef, Heritage Portfolio for The Famous Grouse Experience

The Game Bird
The Famous Grouse Finest, elderflower cordial, apple sourz, freshly squeezed lemon, lengthened with ginger ale and garnished with a slice of apple

~~~~~

Still and Sparkling Water

~~~~~

The Black Grouse at 15.2% ABV
The peaty smoky notes of this Black Grouse is reduced to just 15.2% ABV by adding water, this gives the consistency of a fine burgundy wine perhaps.

~~~~~

Ginger Grouse
The Famous Grouse finest Scotch whisky served long with ginger beer on ice with a twist of lime

~~~~~

Naked Old Fashioned
The Naked Grouse whisky, gomme syrup and cocktail bitters stirred and garnished with the zest of orange

Macallan Gold
A new expression from Macallan using the colour of the liquid rather than an age statement.
This silky whisky has an abundance of vanilla and dark chocolate, with hints of ginger and cinnamon.

Hebridean and Shetland smoked salmon
With tomatoes, cucumbers, pickles and toast

~~~~~

Beetroot and Famous Grouse whisky water ice

~~~~~

Seared fillet of scotch beef
Chive and barley risotto, sauté of vegetables, creamed celeriac and herb infused Famous Grouse whisky jus

~~~~~

Lemon and lavender cheesecake
With saffron syrup

~~~~~

Hot savoury cheese taster
And home-made chutney

~~~~~

Organic & Fairtrade coffee
Velvet truffles
From the local Chocolatier.

THE BANQUET MENU
~~~~~

THE GAMES WE PLAY

Old memories were evoked on hearing that London Scottish Rugby Club was seeking funds. It was an obvious venue for staging a Highland Games having originally been set up as a gathering place for the London Scottish community which had grown to number about five hundred thousand in the Greater London area. Like Sir Tommy MacPherson I had tread the hallowed turf, not as a rugby player but as a Highland Games athlete. Many of the older members remembered the Richmond Games that had taken place during in 1969. The best amateur athletes of the day were assembled to do battle on the rain soaked rugby field but the ensuing quagmire resulted in the event being a one day wonder.

Among others athletes included -

Geoff Capes
Jeff Teale
Laurie Bryce
George McHugh
Ian McPherson
Doug Edmunds

After the games Laurie Bryce and I were the subject of an article in the Scotsman newspaper not for our athletic prowess but for our eating habits –

John Montgomery, the former London Scottish scrum half, speaks with awe of the time he went out to eat with Bryce and Edmunds and ordered the conventional Chinese meal – except that Bryce and Edmunds drank a pint of milk with it. The two athletes then ordered steak and chips – and a pint of milk. That finished, they returned to the menu, had another Chinese main course – and another pint of milk. This at one sitting. Montgomery and his wife, a demure French girl, sat astounded, unable to finish their own meal for watching the scene before them

Montgomery went on to say that he would sooner face the toughest of prop forwards than Laurie Bryce who was a menacing figure in his prime. Laurie himself recalls an invitation to a party later that same evening at the house of a committee member called Tommy Robertson. Our kindly host offered some snacks to quell the needs of the late revellers which included some slithers of beef. To the chagrin of his wife he was unaware of the passion such a feast would arouse and a whole side of beef was consumed. It was only after a frosty reception on the following morning that he realised that the entire family's Sunday roast had been consumed.

Seeing an opportunity I contacted Hamish Bryce the patriarch of the Bryce family and Laurie's elder brother. He was a man of substance, successful in business and a director of the club. His plaudits included winning a blue at Cambridge University, captaining the army rugby team and gaining an international cap for Scotland. He was also a great communicator, an ability that had percolated to his nephew, Colin who had become a popular sports commentator. On asking Hamish's advice as to the best course of action he made the comment that we would be –

*"**Pushing against an open door**."*

Gregor and I were invited to the London Scottish annual awards dinner held at the Chelsea football stadium and treated to plush accommodation at the stadium hotel. We found ourselves among a group of elite gentlemen who had been international players and virtually all bore the old scars of their rugged endeavours. Many had noses that had been broken, some had prominent scar tissue hooding their eyes and most of the big men had cauliflower ears. They were ***men of men*** and no doubt the warriors of their time. Also present were many prominent business men including the chairmen of Tesco PLC, affectionately known as Reidy, an ardent supporter of the club and the prime sponsor of our enterprise. The old adage came to mind that rugby was a ruffian's game played by gentlemen and football was a gentleman's game played by ruffians.

Guest speakers included Ian McGeechan who had managed the British Lions on their overseas tours against the likes of the Springboks, All Blacks and the Wallabies. He was a leader among arguably the greatest warriors of the age. Inevitably rugby tales abounded some referring to the old days when the backs were regarded as the handsome glory boys and the forwards their gnarled servants. The dichotomy stoked a simmering resentment and one story stuck in my mind. Something had been said or done in the heat of battle by a dilettante back which offended the sensitivity of a battle-scared prop. On seeing the latter running towards him with malevolent intent, the back kicked the ball out of play, thinking that would end the matter. However the prop continued relentlessly and both men disappeared out of the stadium, leaving the rest of the players perplexed and somewhat amused.

After receiving enthusiastic support for the project we were energised into bringing a stellar group of athletes to London in the hope of drawing attention to the magnificence of our games and breach the indifference of the English media barons. Gregor was also at the peak of his powers and wanted to leave a calling card.

Our plan was to stage two major competitions with the best highland athletes in the world competing in traditional throwing events and renowned strongmen contesting trials of strength which had emanated from rural traditions. On its part, London Scottish was to provide dancers, the services of pipers from the London Scottish regiment, a festival of rugby athletics and most importantly responsible for publicity.

The games were set for 5-6th of June 2010 and after all the arrangements had been irrevocably made, including hotel bookings, the purchase of air fares and the completion of contracts, disaster loomed. At the beginning of April an Icelandic volcano called Eyjafjallajokull erupted and a huge ash cloud enveloped Western Europe. The eruption did not subside until 21st of May causing the biggest disruption to air traffic since the Second World War. The Icelandic authorities also warned that an even bigger volcano also displayed signs of erupting. We were faced with the non-arrival of our overseas athletes. Furthermore we belatedly learned that the pitch was owned by the less than sympathetic Richmond Athletic Club. The rugby club merely leased the property and were susceptible to the demands of their landlords. With little regard for the consequences they expressed concerns about the pitch being damaged and withdrew their permission a fortnight before the games were due to take place.

We had big problems to solve.

Our first move was to employ Scott Rider to act as an emissary to negotiate a settlement about the use of the pitch. First and foremost he was an Englishman who might be able to overcome any animosity. Also being a handsome fellow with a charming, self-effacing character, we reckoned he might be able to ***tickle the fancy*** of the female official. The Richmond Athletic Club was finally mollified through the purchase of extensive layers of Astroturf. Naturally they chose the heavy duty material which had to be imported from France and was duly delivered on the morning of the day when the games were to begin

Progress on the other front was made when commercial concerns eventually forced the aviation authorities to establish safe corridors. With our previous plans in disarray, new tickets had to be purchased and the athletes had to be fetched from the airport on the eve of the games using expensive limousines.

The games got underway with the covers imparting an odd look to the field of play. It was an awesome sight when both sets of athletes lined up during the open ceremony which was carried out by a wee lassie who had won the Miss Scotland title.

The Highlanders were –

Sean Betz

Gregor Edmunds

Aaron Neighbour

Mike Zolkiewicz

Scott Rider

Sebastian Wenta

Lucasz Wenta

Hans Lolkema

Sinclair Patience

Neil Elliott

The Strongmen were an interesting group of characters -

Richard Skog, Norway - A giant of a man who as a young man had to take prescription medicine to inhibit his growth. He also served in special force in the Iraq War and tells of his escapades only to a private audience.

Arild Haugen, Norway - Styled as the ultimate warrior with his Viking tattoos and Mohican hairstyle. A winner of Norway's strongest man title and a professional cage fighter and boxer.

Stefan Petursson, Iceland - an exuberant Viking in the Jon Pal Sigmarsson mould. Always endearing himself with the audience and exhorting their support which always enhanced his efforts.

Mikhail Koklyaev, Russia - Affectionately known as Misha and the most charismatic strongman of his day. He was a formidable weightlifter having won six Russian Championships and holder of a national record with 212kgs in the Snatch Lift. He often entertained the audience with a talented performance on his melodeon and startled them with his outrageous singing voice.

Alex Curletto, Italy - An enormous fellow exhibiting great static strength but troubled with the mobile events due to his stature. His name prompted an association with vast amounts of Cornetto Ice cream.

Jimmy Marku, Hungry - One of the toughest looking men that I have ever met. Bred in Hungry he found favour in the mean streets of East London. Despite an early injury he challenged for first place in the Log lift.

Darren Saddler, England - Described as a pocket battle ship from Yorkshire and probably the best strongman in the world under 120kgs. He was an unusually handsome man in comparison with the monoliths that challenged him.

Mark Felix, Granada - With muscles that appeared to be hewn from obsidian rock, possessing a back strength that seemed to have no limit.

Laurence Shahlaei, England - A domesticated Iranian who had broken Jamie Reeve's longstanding British Record in the Log Lift.

Warrick Brant, Australia - Had the appearance of a giant Koala Bear.

Gregor Edmunds was once again confronted with his main rivals in the world of Highland Games namely Sebastian Wenta, Scott Rider and Sean Betz. Free from the shackles of having to provide the infrastructure, he was able to give of his best and dominated the field that included the best of the era.

At the end of the first day games both sets of athletes were brought together to provide a novel tussle for the title of World Champion in the Weight for Height. In the previous year Mikhail Koklyaev had established a world's best of 19ft 1ins and Mike Zolkiewicz had established an American Highland Games record with 18ft 9ins. Despite being tired, pride prevailed and honours were shared when Koklyaev and Zolkiewicz achieved the same height.

Mikhail Koklyaev was the outstanding competitor of the day and was pleased to avoid the rigours of the Pole Push which was won by the brutal efforts of Richard Skog who ably demonstrated his battle field experience. The audience could scarcely believe what they were seeing and clapped enthusiastically as they closed with the athletes who demanded their attention.

As is the custom the games provided the opportunity for a gathering of old friends. For the first time in about fifty years the entire Bryce Clan were present. They were a family that were woven through the pattern of my life. There was baby Laurie son of our commentator Colin Bryce who I had mentored as a young man. His father Laurie had been my sparring partner during the university years and his uncle Colin had been a companion in Zambia and Nigeria. I first encountered Hamish when I was a school boy on the day when he won the shot putt at the Scottish Schools Championship.

Old Ian McPherson felt compelled to point out to his lovely daughters that Gregor had only exceeded his hammer record of 123ft 3ins by a mere seven feet. He railed his audience about his victory some thirty one years before and reminded us all that the hammer had been two inches shorter and the earlier rules prohibited toe-spikes.

Scott Rider also brought along his family and his robust four-year-old son Jack, the product of two great shot-putters, looked as if he was going to be a future champion.

After the competition the athletes went back to their accommodation at the Twickenham Stadium Hotel. During the evening revelries the place to be was the room pompously labelled ***Champion's Bedroom*** where Misha and Gregor could be found with a copious amount of Russian Vodka.

However, despite our efforts we were let down by our partners. There was no back-up rugby events and very few of the half million Scots who lived in London knew about the games. None of the various Scottish clubs, including the Highland Society, had been informed and even the denizens of Richmond were unaware. Together with the unforeseen expenses the games were a financial disaster.

The open door that had initially welcomed us was slammed shut.

A few weeks later took us to Northern Ireland for the next ***Highlander Challenge***. My interest in the MacDonald legacy was inflamed some years before following an introduction to the estate manager of Glenarm Castle in County Antrim. His name was Adrian Morrow who had come to the Oban Games in search of ideas for staging an event at the estate which belonged to the Earl of Antrim. He first spoke to Stephen King of the McGregor Clan who then introduced him to me as the most likely source of help. I am now in debt to Stephen for the subsequent enlightenment about the significance of the MacDonalds in Gaelic history. There could be no more appropriate place to have Highland Games.

Hitherto my only awareness of the Irish tradition was the games held in Munster. In my youth I had encountered Tadgh Twomey at the old White City athletic ground in London. He was a ***broth*** of a man whose red hair and massively freckled skin suggested that he had been raised on a diet of porridge. He won throwing of the 56lb Weight for Height using the peculiar Irish style of lifting the weight directly from the ground instead of swinging the implement between his legs. The technique came from the old Irish sport of throwing for distance from behind a line without a follow through.

The first games were held in 1999 with the Earl of Antrim participating as chieftain. He was a direct descendant of Sorley Boy and the blood kin of Alasdair MacColla MacDonald. During the course of my involvement with the games up until 2011 Adrian took my wife and I on a tour of the Antrim coast. From the high headland it was easy to see the beckoning finger of Kintyre and to imagine the bonfires warning of imminent invasion. The treacherous waters surrounding Rathlin Island that once foiled an English landing were evident due to the coursing currents caused by the constriction of the Atlantic tides. The Earl's brother, the Rt Honourable Hector MacDonald told us about the time when a great ball was held at Dunluce Castle and the floor gave way and many of the revellers plunged to their deaths in the subterranean cave below. In its hey-day it must have been a forbidding place – high on a promontory above the sea over a huge cave giving direct access to the sea where many a ***Redshank*** landed. This was the place where the young MacColla nearly lost his life when he was wounded while besieging the castle during an English occupation and then a few years later faced a conspiracy to murder him at the hands of the Campbells.

On the way back to Glenarm we visited the Bushmills distillery to find the next best thing to Scottish Whisky.

On our way to Glenarm in 2011, which turned out to be my last visit, we were met with a severe weather warning then experienced the conditions that so frustrated the attempts by the English to subject the Irish in the fastness of the Ulster wilderness in the days of MacColla and Sorley Boy. Considering the disruption caused by the volcano and the ongoing extreme weather events throughout the world it seemed that mother earth was reacting to the human race who were hell bent in turning her world into a desert

By the year 2011 Gregor's back problems were beginning to signal the end of his career was not long in coming. He had acquitted himself well in the strongman challenges by achieving a creditable eighth place out of forty competitors in the World's Strongest Man. At the Highland Games he was particularly proud of winning the Scottish Championship at Crieff on six occasions. He had also been victorious at Braemar and won both versions of the World Championship.

It was time to lay down his legacy.

He established field records at the Fair Hill Games in Delaware, USA with the following performances –

22lb Hammer Throw – 119ft 7 ½ins (2012)

17lb Light Stone Putt – 60ft 0ins (2011)

Throwing the 56lb Weight for Distance – 46ft 3ins (2011)

Throwing the 28lb Weight for Distance – 89ft 5ins (2011)

At the beginning of June 2011 he presented himself at the Markinch Games in Fife and proceeded to break the World Record for throwing the 28lb Weight for Distance with a phenomenal 95ft 10ins, using a standard weight that was subsequently taken away and measured before ratification by the Scottish Highland Games Association. Of more relative importance to his father was that Gregor had gone to Gourock and beaten George McHugh's thirty year old record – rivalries never die.

When he arrived at Glenarm Castle he was determined to take the title that had long eluded him – ***The Highlander Challenge***. With no set-up demons to sap his energy he was in full flight and able to set about his old protagonists with gusto. The posted results show how he devastated the challengers and his swansong remembered forever in the land of the MacDonalds.

Champion – Gregor Edmunds 47pts

Second – Sebastian Wenta 38pts

Third – Scott Rider 36.5pts

The games went ahead in the presence of the Earl of Antrim accompanied by Gregor's South African wife with nobody else in sight. It was a financial disaster due to the severe weather warning and the continuation of the games reverted to a local level.

The 2013 ***Highlander Challenge*** was held at the appropriate setting of Glasgow Green during the World Pipe band Championships, involving the participation of eight thousand bagpipe players from all over the world. The atmosphere aroused the passion of the competitors in the same way as the battle tunes aroused the warriors of old. This was the place where St Mungo had baptised his converts in the Molendinar burn during the six century which eventually led to the birth of a great city. In 1450 King James the 2nd granted the Green to the people of Glasgow for use as common grazing ground. Later it became associated with fairs and political rallies when the people struggled for reforms and justice.

It was a priority to have my lifelong friend David Webster as guest of honour. Over a period of fifty two years we had been involved in more Highland Games and Strongman competitions than anyone else in history. David had recently been appointed the honorary life president of the Commonwealth Games Council and was an appropriate person to conduct the opening ceremony.

We had gathered a formidable group of athletes and uniquely there was also a woman's championship for the first time. The elite group buzzed with excitement in anticipation of the challenges that lay before them.

Some of my old friends arrived to cast a critical eye and blether, as old men do, about past glories and to exchange stories about Geordie Clark. They included Ian McPherson, Laurie Bryce, Hamish Davidson and Alec McKenzie from Garve.

The occasion was of such importance that Burger Lambrechts from South Africa had turned down an invitation to compete in the IAAF World Championships in Moscow in favour of coming to Glasgow. Burger had won a gold medal at the Commonwealth Games and had won the All Africa Championship on several occasions. His correspondence read -
.

"Hi Doug,
The more I thought last night about the option of me coming to your highland event the more excited I got about it. I'm now almost one hundred percent convinced that I would rather come to your event than the World's Athletic Championship.
Thanks,
Burger Lambrechts."

Burger arrived at Glasgow Airport emblazoned with his South African colours. Standing six feet seven inches and wearing a leather bush hat he looked like a colossus. Inevitably he was stopped at immigration and asked why he had come to Scotland. His response startled the wee man.

"I have come to learn to be a Tosser!" he replied.

As a result we had to wait a long time before they released him.

BURGER LAMBRECHTS

Burger's elder brother and his wife telephoned to say they had also arrived in Scotland for a holiday and to lend support. Arno was even bigger than Burger, standing just short of six foot eight inches and weighing more than four hundred pounds. Built in proportion with lean muscles he was indeed a giant of a man. Arno held the continental record for the Squat with 460kilos, performed under strict IPF rules and had a penchant for trekking into the bush with his brother where no man had ever set foot. Small wonder they were left well alone. Accompanied by his Afrikaner wife they spent more than a week camping in the Highlands with the smallest tent that I have ever seen. They welcomed the rain after living in the Karoo Desert where water was a precious commodity and found only in deep boreholes.

We sent them up to the Inveranon Inn, situated at the northern tip of Loch Lomond to experience an ancient environment. Here he enjoyed the delights of a good quality haggis and his wife reported that for the rest of their holiday he asked to be served haggis at every restaurant he came to. Before they left Arno's wife asked us if we could find a kilt that would fit the big man. Apparently, back in South Africa my old friend, Claude Parnell from Durban was planning to organise a National Highlander Championship.

Adriane Blewitt from America, the most decorated exponent of the woman's Highland Games, having won the world title six times, could not resist the lure. Despite harbouring a niggling injury she wrote –

"Aaaaaahhh – You make it so hard to decline this amazing offer."

Also on his first trip to Scotland was the remarkable Matt Vincent who had surpassed the legendary Brian Oldfield's stone putt record but was subsequently denied ratification due to the implement being marginally underweight. Not a big man but seemed to be made of reinforced rubber, both flexible and strong. He had the look of a tough, Cajun Frenchman hailing from Louisiana and was the undisputed Highland Games World Heavy Event Champion. He was an ebullient fellow and relished the brutality of the Highlander Challenge. He had already been to Iceland and managed to carry the Husafell Stone around the historic sheep pen. The winsome side of his character was revealed by his signature pink stockings and his passion for painting his toe nails. When we invited him out for dinner he expressed a desire for an Indian curry which he believed to be similar to the savoury Cajun food that he enjoyed. So we took him to our favourite restaurant called the Turban. The proprietor was so impressed and compared Matt to Clark Kent when he put on his glasses to examine the menu. This elicited favourable treatment should he return at a later date.

On meeting his opponents Matt said -

"The Games in Glasgow this year is the strongest gathering of stone throwers ever assembled. The pedigree of the group has never happened before on a games field. I can't wait to have the chance to test myself against such a strong group of stone throwers."

Adriane showed her true ability in the woman's events during the early stages by easily winning the 14lb Weight for Distance and narrowly winning the Log Toss over Nina Geria from the Ukraine. We all expected the competition to be dominated by the clash between the class athlete and the holder of the World's Strongest Women title. Unfortunately after struggling with the Barbell Lift her old injuries flared up but she doggedly continued despite being severely handicapped. The challenge was taken up by her compatriot Kristy Scott, the game was on and the rivalry between the superpowers continued apace.

Nina Geria was expected to dominate the strength events and Kristy the throws but it was the other way about. Surprisingly Donna Moore from the Highlands of Scotland beat Nina in the Barbell Lift where the contestants had to lift a circus barbell weighing 160kgs for repetitions within ninety seconds. Kirsty Scott astounded everyone by steadily lifting the weight almost twice as often as her nearest rivals.

Adriane managed to suppress her pain and duly won the Short 28lb Hammer but the Atlas Stones finished her challenge. The event was narrowly won by Nina with Kristy less than two seconds behind.

ADRIANE BLEWITT WILSON

With Adriane unable to give of her best, the Stone Putt was keenly contested between two old enemies, both of whom had qualified for the coming Commonwealth Games. The feisty Kirsty Yates representing Scotland took on Shaunagh Brown from England who had won a British Championship in all three of the international heavy throws. Both girls screamed with effort and ended up with exactly the same distance.

With a heavily strapped leg Adriane gamely drew with Nina in the Weight for Height but the event was dominated by the astounding efforts of Kristy Scott. Inspired by the rhythmic clapping of the audience she amazed everyone by achieving a world record of 21ft. The weight of 28lbs 2ozs was verified by Gregor Edmunds and the measurement verified by David Webster.

Only three of the girls managed to toss the long Challenge Caber which was won with a powerful effort by Nina with Kristy a close second. Kristy responded with blistering speed in the Weight Carry over forty metres. In contrast, two of the athletes were unable to lift the cylinders that had a combined weight of 140kgs.

Kristy's magnificent challenge foundered during the last event when she had to face up to Nina's effort of six laps with the Shield Walk which amounted to a distance of 240 metres. She managed only 39 metres before slumping to the ground. Afterwards she showed me her badly grazed arm which still trembled with the exertion of going to the limit of her endurance.

After a pregnant pause while the scores were counted Kristy was declared the winner by the margin of a mere half point. She appeared in a state of rapture when she received the prize of a ***Quaich*** emblazoned with the Glasgow coat of arms and engraved with the words

"Highlander World Champion"

In the wake of Gregor Edmunds's retirement and the demise of Sebastian Wenta due to an injury, Scott Rider had dominated the Scottish circuit. In the course of the season he had established twenty one field records and was perceived as the favourite to win his first Highlander title. Gregor had even fashioned a new challenge caber that he thought only ***Scotty*** would be able to toss. He had not reckoned on Sebastian's attachment to the title that he regarded as his personal property. In preparation he had gone through a series of injections to subdue the pain in his knees and as a result looked as formidable as ever, parading about like a Polish aristocrat. His fierce-looking brother was also up for the challenge. We also heard that Lucasz had decided to become a Scotsman and had made arrangements to settle in Scotland with his family on a permanent basis. This would make him eligible to compete for Scotland after a two year residency.

Matt Vincent's ambition of breaking records was stymied by the pouring rain at the start of the competition. His turning style was hampered by the slippery surface and he was a disappointing fifth in the Heavy Stone Putt.

Burger Lambrechts was utterly determined to become the inaugural World Stone Putting Champion which would be decided by the aggregate distance of both heavy and light stones. His initial efforts also suffered from the ground conditions and he resorted to a standing style and produced an amazing standing putt with the 22lb stone of 48ft 11ins, exceeding Scott Rider's effort by nine inches despite the latter being able to execute a perfect turning style due to his experience on the Scottish circuit. However during the course of 16lb competition, he found himself behind Sebastian Wenta and Matt Vincent, with less than twelve inches separating the first five contenders. With one throw remaining Burger retired to the trees and was heard growling as he gathered his strength. Regardless of a leg strain he produced the big one and was ecstatic, swaggering about in his kilt as he waved to the enthralled audience. He then approached my wife and asked if he could buy the kilt that we had procured for him. We were pleased to give it to him as a present in anticipation of his breaking the record at Braemar the following year.

The Weight for Height was an unremarkable affair with the continuing rain but the Caber was keenly contested. Seven men qualified to take on the Challenge Caber and on his first throw the reinvigorated Sebastian achieved a perfect 12 o'clock throw which was unbeatable. Scott tried to equal him and came close with 12. 02. With Neil Elliott and Matt Vincent also succeeding it was no longer a mystical caber, requiring Gregor to fashion a new challenge for the future. The Log lift was a grinding experience with the competitors trying to lift the same giant log that had been used by the legendary Zydrunas Savickas when he established his world record. Sebastian easily won reminding us that he had once been a runner up in the World's Strongest Man contest

The Barrel Carry proved to be an exciting affair where two ***Grouse*** whisky barrels were mounted on a frame and carried in a two man race over eighty metres. The first piece of drama occurred when Jonathan Kelly fell on his face and his opponent raced ahead gaining about thirty metres. He quickly recovered and raced in pursuit. It was like an episode of the tortoise and the hare with Jonathan steadily regaining lost ground. Heidar Geirmundson just managed to beat him to the finish line with his last gasp. If the course had been five metres longer Jonathan would have won. Scott Rider was pitted against Matt Vincent. They were like two pocket battle ships both eager to win bragging rights. They set off at a furious pace each keeping pace with the other then on the return lap Matt fell. Scott took advantage and struggled on and collapsed with exhaustion a few metres short of the finish. Matt caught up while Scott struggled to relift the barrels. Both collapsed simultaneously with about two metres left. With no power left they had to resort to a desperate struggle and only managed to push the weights over the line.

Despite being a farmer from the Karoo desert Burger Lambrechts had never heard of pitching the sheaf. On the other hand Matt had brought his fork with him. It looked more like a trident and we wondered how he managed to get such a lethal weapon on the plane. He had graciously taught Burger the fundamentals in my back yard and was rewarded by having to share the points as the big man was a fast learner.

The final event was brutal, requiring the 180 kilo Pictish Stone to be carried as far as possible. Only Lucasz Wenta was able to complete the forty metre course in a heroic effort to overcome his floundering rivals. The triumphant Lucasz had a crazed look on his face, with mad staring eyes, indicating that he really had gone beyond the pain barrier. Conversely, Matt Vincent was bitterly disappointed after he passed out during his attempt. The incident cost him a place on the winner's podium but he endeared himself with everybody with his sanguine attitude.

The final placings were – **Champion Sebastian Wenta**

Second Scott Rider

Third Lucasz Wenta

The girls led by Annett von der Weppen warm up for the games

After the presentations Craig Sinclair arrived, fresh from winning the Crieff Championship. Unfortunately it had been held on the same day as the ***Highlander Challenge*** and for the first time in many years had only been contested by Scottish athletes. He had arranged to take Matt to Royal Deeside to visit Braemar and with little regard for his battle scars Matt wanted to try and lift the Inver Stone and test his mettle with the Dinnie Stones. When Adriane and the newly crowned champion, Kristy Scott requested to join them, our man in Deeside, the trusty Murray Brown, arranged free accommodation at the historic Huntly Arms Hotel in Aboyne.

There are few more beautiful drives and our American friends were able to enjoy the quirky pleasures of the Highlands. On reaching Braemar they entered the games arena and lay on their backs breathing the sweet aroma of the heather clad hills and imagined the ghosts of past champions drifting over them. They could only gaze at the magnificent Balmoral Castle as the Queen was in residence prior to her visit to the Braemar Games. Next they came to the village of Crathay where the Inver Stone rests in the garden of the official guardian who is a little old lady. After signing the mandatory register Matt proceeded to join the select few that had lifted the stone above their head. On reaching Ballater they visited the famous candy shop and loaded up with presents to take back home. Finally they arrived at the Inn of Potarch where the scarred remains of the Dinnie Stones lie. Matt lifted them with relative ease but used straps which were not in keeping with tradition. His main intention was merely to enjoy the experience. After a long day he returned to Glasgow and made straight for the Turban where he enjoyed a hot ***Biryani*** and received a discounted bill as previously promised.

After returning home Matt wrote –

"After finishing in fourth place I am a bit disappointed in my own performance. I know that if there was a small adjustment or improvement made that would have allowed me to earn a better placing. However I cannot go back in time and change any of it. I came to Scotland and accepted the challenge, not to earn a sure victory and stroke my own ego, but to challenge myself against the best in the world. A challenge is exactly what I found. Throwers and athletes were all of the top calibre and performed as champions. I am honoured to be part of an amazing competition and gain another perspective on my training. I am in awe of the power and ability of my fellow athletes. This provides the necessary motivation needed to make progress in my own skills. Nothing like a proper challenge against the world's best to make you want to become the best. I will return to Scotland a better thrower and a stronger athlete. This was an amazing challenge to be part of."

At the end of the competition Burger Lambrechts turned to Matt and said –

"I wish somebody had told me about this ten years ago!"

Regardless of her disappointment, Adriane wrote –

"I was so impressed with the competition and pleased with my performance despite a knee injury. I could not help notice the level of the athletes' display by both men and women. The Highlander really shows what it means to be a strong athlete."

MATT VINCENT WITH INVER STONE

FOR WHOM THE BELL TOLLS

Most of us look forward to a retirement consisting of champagne for breakfast, relaxing in the sun with cherished grandchildren frolicking nearby and reminiscing about the triumphs of youth. Reality is cruelly different. Pervious health problems were brought into insignificance just after my seventieth birthday. My old colleagues had maintained a remarkable camaraderie across the years and expressed concern about the welfare of our iconic friend – Bill Anderson. This seemingly indestructible man had succumbed to prostate cancer and heart problems. My son Gregor, Grant Anderson and I resolved to travel up to Aberdeen to visit him and cheer him up with some of the old banter.

Bill's predicament had heightened our awareness of the problem that often blights the golden years. Grant already had malfunctions and I was prompted to have a PSA (prostate specific antigen) examination. The unexpected high reading set off alarm bells and I was subsequently sent for a MRI. The later erupted in considerable controversy due to the fact they were unable to fit me into the machine. The possibility loomed of being sent down to the Vet College where a scanner existed for the purpose of examining horses. The hospital administrator was called which resulted in a Cat Scan and I was found to have a similar problems.

The realisation that I had a terminal condition led to a revaluation of life. My religious convictions strengthened immeasurably. Simple observations had more meaning and my attitude to others transformed. There were no more enemies, the old macho image was irrelevant and I sought a spiritual connection with my fellow travellers. My affection seemed boundless. To my surprise my feelings were reciprocated in spades. The tough competitive guys of my youth opened their long guarded hearts with a flow of tender sympathy. ***Men of Men*** now expressed a love for an old friend and a remarkable awareness of the meaning of life permeated the conversations. It was as if a cork had come out of a bottle containing shared anxieties.

I was incarcerated in the medieval bowels of the Southern General Hospital following an emergency summons due to a kidney infection caused by back pressure from my swollen prostate. Little did I realise that one of ther most memorable experiences of my life was imminent. In the depths of the night a young nurse approached offering to administer the insertion of a catheter, necessary to relieve my condition. In all my experience as a young man such a desired prostration was the subject of erotic dreams. Permission was also granted for a young student nurse to assist in the process. During the mandatory washing of the appendage and the application of a soothing lubricant my thoughts turned to my old pal McPherson who would have no doubt been an interested observer. I was brought back to reality by the insertion of the implement which caused a searing pain during the upward passage crowned with an explosion of agony as it plopped into the bladder. I was left to pass blood throughout the night, only made tolerable with a dose of morphine.

Among my first visitors was no less than Magnus Ver Magnusson the proud winner of Four World's Strongest Man titles. He was a man that I had a love – hate relationship for many years but mutual respect had won through over time. He was accompanied by Bruno who was a fearsome character and like others of a similar nature served as a lunatic asylum nurse back in Iceland. Next was a threesome that breeched the two visitor rule – Darren Saddler, Collin Bryce and Benedict Magnusson, the latter fresh from exceeding the world dead lift record when he hoisted 560 kilos. Benedict was a lovable character just like a giant teddy bear but I feared for his safety as he looked as though he might burst such was his astounding girth. The visitors included my three old university pals all of them national athletic champions in their day. From a' the airts came Ian McPherson, David Birkmyre and Gordon Muir who had been an international sprinter and long jumper. The latter I had not seen for several years and he was still damnably handsome which had caused some grief to my youthful ambitions with regard to the fair sex. Gordon had also survived the ravages of age and was still able to score better than his age on the golf course. Another surprise was young fire officer Ross Pollock who arrived after parking his fire engine with crew on full alert in the hospital car park

The most awe inspiring of my visitors was Misha Koklyaev. He had now amassed eight Russian weightlifting titles and possessed a deep intellect which included mastery of a grand piano. I had discovered him during a visit to Lutnitski Stadium in Moscow after persuading officials to bring him from Celjabinsk for a strongman competition after seeing his performance stats. We became firm friends and I used my influence to have him invited to every strongman show for which he was eligible. The world opened up for him and he became an international star. After years of shared experience throughout the world he seemed depressed to witness my demise. He presented me with his personal icon which he had kept close throughout his successful career. It had brought him good luck and he wished to pass its power to me. We then engaged in an extraordinary ritual of spiritual bonding, almost like a touching of souls and he referred to me as his Scottish father. Although not a member of any formal faith he spoke of witnessing the death of his father during communist times when the old people were denied the comfort of religion and they died badly. We resolved to attend Mass together but I was unable to leave hospital before he was scheduled to return back to Russia.

The icon was a thoughtful and appropriate gift. It was a copy of the Kursk Root icon of the Mother of God dating from the 13th century, depicting the mother of God holding the Christ Child with the Lord of Hosts above her, surrounded by the nine prophets that predicted the birth. A hunter found the icon lying on a root and when he lifted it a spring of pure water surged from the place. The location became a grotto where many came to pray for their sorrows and needs and the mother of God healed all who came to her icon.

Included in the pantheon of remarkable friends was Aaron Collins the Maori All Black rugby player who was sweet enough to bring me a small box of chocolates.

The year 2014 was one of the most important periods in Scottish History. It was the year of the "***Homecoming***", the Glasgow Commonwealth Games, the Ryder Cup at Gleneagles and the year of the Scottish Independence Referendum. It seemed to me that regardless of political arguments every red-blooded Scotsman had to vote to regain our long lost sovereignty which had been lost to English blackmail after the Darien Fiasco. My father would have turned in his grave if his progeny did not seize the opportunity.

Early in the year I gained the cooperation of Fife Council to support a World Highland Games Heavy Event Championship to be held at Pittencrieff Park in Dunfermline as part of the national Homecoming Programme. There could not be a more appropriate venue. The ancient cathedral is the burial place of King Malcolm Canmore who allegedly started the concept of Highland Games in the twelfth century when he sought to entertain his Norman Guests. His wife Margaret was also a Norman who did much to gentrify Scotland and became our first canonised saint. Within the Abbey rests the body of King Robert the Bruce. It could be said the athletes were indeed coming home to the land of their heroes.

Due to my illness I had left the organisation of our games to my wife Linda and Gregor. During my absence they had organised an event in Perth to act as a focal point for the culmination of the Perth marathon which was restricted to kilted athletes and about fifteen hundred participated. As the Perth Highland Games were due to take place our hosts asked us to do something a little different which set the scene for the Highlander approach which incorporated the gladiatorial warrior element. One of our participants was Jonathan Kelly the Irish Strongman and highland games champion. He became the subject of much discussion particularly among the Americans who alleged that he was the son of the mighty Bill Kazmaier. It occurred to me that I might have participated by inviting Bill to come to Scotland during the eighties when the Callander Games were at their zenith. Certainly Jonathon had more than a passing resemblance to the great man. Our heavy athletes were backed up by Vadim's warriors who were in the vanguard of warrior games that were growing in popularity in places such as China and Russia. They delighted the audience with their combat skills which often drew blood from the vanquished as the contests were real and often ended with a brutal conclusion.

I also missed the Glasgow Games held during the World Pipe band Championship. Once again Linda with her flaming red hair took charge, very much in the role of the feisty Barbara Stanwick when she took control of unruly cowboys during her movie role as a tough rancher.

David Webster had registered the concept of World Highland Games Heavy Event Championship and staged the first event of the modern era in Melbourne during 1981 with the speaker of the Australian House of Parliament as chieftain. Later the same year I organised my version of the Championship in Lagos Nigeria with Sunday Dankaro, the Chairman of the National Sports Commission as chieftain. David and I then combined to run the championships up until the event in Finland in 1998. Over the years we established a genuine championship recognised by the main organisers across the world. As the proposed games in Dunfermline were likely to be my swansong I decided to cooperate with David to maintain credibility with the Scottish Government.

The following athletes were invited –

Matt Doherty
Burger Lambrechts
Scott Rider
Lorne Colthart
Dan McKim
Heidar Geirmundson
Sinclair Patience
Matt Vincent
Jimmy van de Walle
Sebastian Wenta

The international referees were Bill Crawford from Loon Mountain games in New Hampshire and Steve Conway from the Pleasanton games in California.

We welcomed back the flamboyant Matt Vincent with his pink stockings and painted nails and I thought it appropriate to call him the ***"Cajun Cowboy***". Since last year Matt had lost his title to fellow American Daniel McKim from Kansas City who had broken the American version of the world hammer throwing records with throws of 132ft 2.75ins with the heavy and 157ft 7.25ins with the light. Both were achieved at Lehi Utah but in contrast to the rough farm yard weights used in Scotland the Americans had taken to hammers with small alloy heads and swivelling handles. Crucially Matt had arrived a week earlier to compete in the Highlander in Glasgow and the Scottish open championship at Crieff. Although he finished second to Scott Rider in both competitions he was able to acclimatise for the Championship set for the following week. During the intervening days he went to London with Scott and spent time taking in the sights between refreshments at various historic public houses – what a splendid thing to do.

In contrast Daniel arrived on the eve of the Games. He was a splendid looking fellow, standing about 6ft 5ins with that typical all American boy image from the 1950s. He reminded me of Dan Dare the heroic spaceman from the popular Eagle comic of the era. I had also been told that he was a religious man who openly thanked God for his prowess. I was moved to ask Daniel for his blessing which he duly administered in the middle of the field with great passion. Much to the astonishment of the other athletes.

Scott Rider had established himself as the best European having finally vanquished the Wenta Brothers. He was confident after winning at Crieff. Scotland's main hope lay with Lorne Colthart who had blossomed into a giant of a man but had still to reach his full potential and the future glory of the homeland rested with him. His lack of experience showed when he failed to score in the Weight for Distance due to his inability to remain within the throwing area but his performance in the Putts and Hammer were a harbinger of things to come. Being a nephew of Stephen King, one of Scotland's greatest hammer throwers, suggested that the fierce McGregor blood ran in his veins.

The Vikings were represented by Heidar Geirmundson who was a wild looking character displaying tattoos depicting Viking folklore from head to foot. His gentle nature was in contrast to his appearance and his intellect had enabled him to assimilate the skills of an aircraft engineer. Short and dynamic he had exceeded Magnus Ver Magnusson's Icelandic record in the Log Lift.

Sinclair Patience was a burly rugby player who had won selection by winning the Scottish Native Championship the year before. He had also won the World Amateur Championship in Minnesota in 2010. Typical of the "***Warrior Breed***" his father George, had won the accolade of World Champion in 1994.

We were also pleased to welcome Matt Doherty on his first visit to Scotland. He had qualified by winning the Canadian Championship at Antigonish, the oldest continuous games outside Scotland, celebrating their 151st anniversary in 2014. The games that had emerged following the Highland Clearances after mass migrations to Nova Scotia in the wake of Culloden. Compared to the others he was slightly built but in sport parlance "tightly wrapped" and looked in fine physical condition. He reminded me of a Hollywood version of Colin Bryce and was equally garrulous. He had proved himself in the wider world of Track and Field by winning the Canadian national championship in the hammer throw.

Jimmy Van de Walle the Belgian Champion had won his place by beating the best of the Netherlands and Germany where a surprising number of Highland Games had taken root since we had invited the likes of Huub van Eck and Siem Wulfse to Callander back in the Eighties.. The Games were also established in Poland and the Wenta Brothers had more than embraced the call since my invitation ten years before. Sebastian had endeared himself to the public with his prowess and good humour and his record as a Highlander was second to none. Lucasz his younger brother had found the games so endearing that he had brought his family and settled as a permanent resident.

Having been smitten by the games Burger Lambrechts had gone home and cut himself a caber and could be seen running around the veldt trying to master the ancient art. His attempt to fashion a durable Scots hammer ended with a steel shafted implement which all too easily slipped from his grasp during practice. He was not familiar with the ***tacky*** employed by the more experienced athletes. Shortly after his arrival in Scotland we tried a quick fix by organising sessions with two of Scotland's most promising young athletes namely Danny Carlin and Kyle Randalls while Gregor bequeathed an old pair of Grant Anderson's spikes.

In the shadow of the Cathedral with the ethereal presence of Malcolm Canmore as chieftain, the games began. The occasion seemed to inspire the athletes and three new championship records were established in the first three events, each by different athletes, indicating the ferocity of the competition. Lambrechts would have set a new world record for the Light Stone Putt but for a narrow foul when he threw over 67ft. The final result was in the balance until the last event after which Matt Vincent emerged as the winner. He was ecstatic about regaining the title from Dan McKim who had won at Pleasanton the year before.

THE DUNFERMLINE LINE-UP

The renaissance of my group of university friends was complete when George McHugh came to visit. With the exception of a brief encounter I had not seen him for forty three years. He brought memories of our youth and once again we wallowed in self-aggrandisement and mutual wicked humour. His wife Janet sent me an image of a guardian angel which glowed in the dark. Together with the Russian Icon, McKim's blessing and a deluge if holy water from Lourdes, powerful forces had been evoked.

The intervention of God became apparent when I unexpectedly received information that Fr Neal Carlin was scheduled to launch a book describing his journey through life and the spirituality that has sustained him through difficult times. This was the prop I needed to cope with my situation. Long ago I was introduced to Fr Carlin by my friend Harry Doyle to help deal with the moral difficulties of celebrating a mixed marriage with Moira (Gregor's Mother). In the days when bigotry prevailed he had an uplifting spiritual view of the situation which led to conciliation. Throughout my life Harry Doyle's intrinsic decency had provided a counterweight to the wilder side of my life - always there when needed.

In his youth Fr. Carlin was an international class runner and feared Gaelic Football player which helped to mould the strength of character needed to leave the security of a parish to spend the better part of his life trying to reconcile the bitter factions in the sectarian war that blighted Ireland. He had the courage and conviction to confront the hard men on both sides and was very much a warrior in the spiritual sense. Much of his time was spent in the Maze Prison bringing peace to many a troubled soul.

The last time I encountered him was seemingly an amazing coincidence, while trawl fishing in the wilderness of the Solwezie River in darkest Africa, sailing down the other side was none other than Fr. Carlin. On receiving his book, titled ***"They that wait on the Lord"*** I received a powerful blessing. I also discovered that he had been responsible for building the Columbia Centre where a new form of Catholicism was emerging which encouraged the empowerment of lay communities to form Charismatic Societies, spreading the word of God through mutual support and reconciliation. Out of this had emerged a centre for the rehabilitation of addicts, a Reconciliation Centre and of particular interest to me, a Healing Centre where events strongly suggested that God was in attendance.

Colin Bryce boosted my personal Salvation Army when he interviewed George Foreman, the former World Heavy Weight Boxing Champion. George sent a personal message in his own hand writing which read:-

"Yours George Foreman to Douglas – Fighting is all we know. I'm pulling for you – God loves you. So do I."

With the great tide of moral support it was no wonder that my health indicators vastly improved and I began to believe I would be able to fight another day.

THE CHIEFTAIN'S CHAMPION

I have often been asked who I consider to be the best Highland Games athlete of all time. The answer may lie in the following considerations:-

During 1989 Hamish increased the 28lb weight record at Oban and broke the 22lb putt record at Inverkeithing. This was his vintage year breaking records and winning at Crieff and Braemar. I believe he might have won the inaugural world championship in Los Angeles in 1980 and two years later in Melbourne had he been invited. Not surprisingly promoters were a bit wary of inviting Hamish. He is remembered for his arrival at Montréal when a splendidly attired pipe-band played in his honour as he stepped down from the plane. When our dishevelled hero appeared he was plainly ***steaming drunk***.

Although Hamish competed for many years he was unable to consolidate his initial greatness due to injury. He fell down a rabbit-hole while on a training run, carrying a railway sleeper on his back and damaged his leg. This frustrated his caber tossing and affected his ability to throw the hammer.

Geoff dominated the circuit during his era and many of his records still stand. He won the World Championship a record six times, won Crieff twice and shared first place with Grant Anderson on two occasions. He also made Braemar his happy hunting ground by winning the championship five times.

If there was no hammer throwing he could have claimed to be the best ever heavy event athlete. It was in 1983 that Geoff's Achilles heel became obvious. He appeared to have an unassailable lead until coming fifth in both the light and heavy hammer throws. Grant was also a superior Caber tosser and remember him being the only athlete to toss the ***untossable*** caber at Kilbirnie International Highland Games. Capes managed about thirty degrees and I was an exalted third having been one of three that had managed to toss the heavy qualifying caber. Capes tried to neutralise the adverse hammer effect by travelling with Bob Dale an English international shot-putter but this was neutralised when Grant occasionally won the 56lb weight over the bar to add to his exploits with the hammer.

After Alistair Gunn famously beat Capes in the Stone putt at Inveraray in 1989 he established himself as the top Scottish athlete. Comparatively diminutive he was deceptively strong and athletic and an irritatingly ***cheeky chappie*** as Capes and McGoldrick found out. I witnessed him lift four McGlashen Stones embarrassing some of the strongman of the time. He also was the first to win the World Hammer Throwing championship based on combined distances with the 16lb and 22lb hammers. His performances with big heavy cabers were beyond belief and he won the caber at Braemar an amazing eight times.

Alistair's record includes the Scottish Championship at Crieff seven times, Braemar three times, the North American Championship five times and an authentic world championship at Kilmarnock in 1995. Most of Alistair's success was at the expense of Francis Brebner who was an excellent caber tosser and weight for distance thrower but Alistair was better over all the events and it was not surprising that they were not the best of friends.

MAGNUS VER MAGNUSSON, PETUR GUDMUNDSSON, HJALTI ARNASON, CHARLIE VAN DEN BOSCH, O. D. WILSON, JIM McGOLDRICK, DOUGLAS EDMUNDS, ILKKA NUMMISTO

Jim McGoldrick became champion when the games moved to Aviemore and held the title until 1993. There was no championship in 1992 in Callander because the games were to be televised by BBC television for their ***Record Breakers*** programme. Matt Sandford duly obliged and then sent the programme into oblivion by failing a drugs test. Jim only came to Scotland at our invitation and therefore did not feature at Crieff or Braemar. He preferred his home games in Santa Rosa which was often held on the same day as Braemar. He won at Santa Rosa six times and won the Challenge Caber eleven times.

When David took the games out of Scotland in 1996 Ryan Vierra from America became champion. Although his record shows him to be a worthy champion, the absence of Sandford cast a controversial shadow. Although he had served his banishment for failing a drug test in 1992 the Americans objected to his presence and it took considerable pressure from the likes of David Webster and Shannon Hartnett to enable his eventual return to the top table. This was at the expense of Ryan Vierra who was arguably the best ever

American. Ryan won the title from 1996-98 and then had to be content with second place over the next four years when the awesome Australian returned to the fray.

RYAN VIERRA

Matt was able to regain the form that had astonished everyone in his earlier years and established a seemingly unassailable world record with the heavy hammer when he threw 129ft 10 ½ ins at Halkirk in 1998. However, Bruce Aitken, from Auchenblae, took back the light hammer record to Scotland when he threw 156ft 8 ½ ins at Aboyne in 2000.

I continued to work with David organising the World Championship up until 1994 when the competitions took place in Aviemore (1988-89) and then at Callander (1990-94). We also jointly promoted the championship at Kilmarnock in 1995 and Oulu, Finland, in 1998. During the intervening years and beyond David assumed full control while I became involved in the World's Strongest Man Series.

It was not until 1991 that the SGA decided to organise a world championship at Balloch. It had the advantage of being an open competition but was not rated by the leading athletes because there were no invitation funds available. On the other hand the VL championship was by invitation and guaranteed the presence of invited elite. The problem with a purely invitational competition is the emergence of favouritism and unpopular champions may be passed over. To ensure against this the victors at major championships such as Crieff and Braemar should have a right of entry.

MATT SANDFORD

In an attempt to establish a Champion of Champions I have constructed a score sheet featuring the athletes who were the giants of the modern era. Each athlete has his best verifiable performance with the six standard events included in a fantasy score sheet in an attempt to stage a grand shoot out.

CHAMPIONS SCORE SHEET

	16LB PUTT	22LB PUTT	16LB HAMMER	22LB HAMMER	28LB WEIGHT	56LB WEIGHT
GRANT ANDERSON	53FT 6INS BURNTISLAND 1982	46FT ½ IN PERTH 1980	151FT 11INS BURNTISLAND 1985	123FT 8½INS SANTA ROSA 1983	81FT 11INS ABERFELDY 1983	16FT 7½INS OBAN 1981
BILL ANDERSON	52FT 4INS STRATHPEFFER 1968	44FT 11INS TOBERMORY 1989	151FT 2INS LOCHEARN 1969	123FT 5INS CRIEFF 1969	87FT 2INS CRIEFF 1966	16FT ABERDEEN 1977
HAMISH DAVIDSON	59FT 10INS OLD MELDRUM 1979	51FT 1IN INVERKEITHING 1989	149FT BUCKIE 1979	109FT 3INS OLD MELDRUM 1980	89FT 1IN OBAN 1979	15FT 3INS FORFAR 1985
GEOFF CAPES	65FT 3INS OXTON 1982	53FT 4INS CRIEFF 1982	128FT 9INS AIRTH 1986	108FT 1IN BIRNAM 1986	95FT ½IN KILBIRNIE 1985	17FT 2INS LAGOS 1981
ALASDAIR GUNN	55FT 1IN DUNBEATH 1999	44FT SKYE 1996	150FT 2INS HALKIRK 1996	122FT 5INS HALKIRK 1996	87FT 2INS DUNBEATH 1997	15FT 9INS FREDRICKSBURG 1998
JIM MCGOLDRICK	55FT 6INS SACRAMENTO 1993	46FT 8IN UNKNOWN	132FT 11INS SACRAMENTO 1985	110FT SACRAMENTO 1985	88FT 11INS ALEXANDRIA	17FT 3INS SAN DIEGO 1985
MATT SANDFORD	57FT 7INS BRAEMAR 1992	46FT 6INS TOMINTOUL 2002	156FT 2¾INS ESTES 1999	129FT 10½INS HALKIRK 1998	94FT 6½INS ESTES 1999	18FT PLEASANTON 1999
RYAN VIERRA	59FT 5INS PINEWOOD 1995	49FT 2INS LAS VEGAS 2005	150FT 9INS FREDRICKSBURG 1997	121FT 7INS OULU 1998	93FT ½INS BETHLEHEM 2002	16FT WAIPU 1996
GREGOR EDMUNDS	60FT FAIRHILL 2010	49FT 4INS TAIN 2007	140FT 6½INS LUSS 2010	119FT ½IN FAIRHILL 2009	95FT 10INS MARKINCH 2011	17FT CORK 2003
MATT VINCENT	63FT 2INS CELTIC CLASSIC 2012	46FT TEXAS CELTIC 2012	142FT PLEASANTON 2014	117FT CELTIC CLASSIC 2012	94FT 2INS ALBUQUERQUE 2012	17FT 6INS DETROIT 2014

A problem arises with trying to rank each athlete's prowess with the caber. In my opinion the order would be:

Grant Anderson
Jim McGoldrick
Bill Anderson
Geoff Capes
Gregor Edmunds
Alistair Gunn
Matt Vincent
Matt Sandford
Ryan Vierra
Hamish Davidson

The score sheet although not a perfect comparison does indicate that Matt Sandford was probably the best and therefore the Chieftain's Champion and worthy of our adulation.

Grant remarked that the only way to settle the argument is to have games in heaven, with God as the referee. However Hamish reminded us that staging such games might be a problem because we might not all be there, and he quoted the Book of Zechariah 13.8

"And it will come to pass, that in all the land saith the Lord, two parts therein will be cut off and die…"

And Hamish added that he does not intend to be one of them.

Whatever the outcome of that ultimate contest, it would surely provoke further debate, in Heaven and in Hell.

ROLL OF HONOUR

AUSTRALIA
Derek Boyer
David Huxley
Nathan Jones
Bill Lyndon
Joe Quigley : Commonwealth Games Silver Medallist
Matt Sandford : World Highland Games Champion and World Record Holder

BULGARIA
Eugeny Popov : Olympic Silver Medallist

CANADA
George Chiappa
Geoff Dollan
Hugo Gerrard
Greg Hadley
Harry MacDonald
Dan Markovic

CZECH REPUBLIC
Jiri Zaloundec : Olympian

DENMARK
Henning Thorsen

ENGLAND
Lee Bowers
Russ Bradley
Geoff Capes : World Strongest Man, Olympian
Eddie Ellwood : Mr Universe
Mark Felix
R Fullerton
Mark Higgins
Graham Mullins
Bill Pittuck
Mike Proctor : Olympian
Jamie Reeves : World Strongest Man
Scott Rider : Commonwealth Games Competitor
Ade Rollinson
Darren Sadler
Dean Slater
Olli Thompson
Fraser Tranter
Emeka Udechuku Olympian

FINLAND
Jouka Ahola : Worlds Strongest Man
Ilkka Kinnunen
Riku Kiri
Tommi Lotta
Pavi Pavisto
Petronnen

GERMANY
Manfred Hoebrel
Heinz Ollesch
Omar Orloff

HAWAII
Joe Onosai

HOLLAND
Peter Baltus
Peter Bouma
Hans Lokema
Charlie Van Der Bosch
Huub Van Eck
Wout Zilstra : World Record Holder

ICELAND
Hyalti Arnason
Andres Gudmundsson
Pertur Gudmundsson : Olympian
Audunn Jonsson : World Championship Silver Medal
Benni Magnusson : World Record Holder
Torfi Olafsson
Stefan Solvi Petursson
Saemi Saemundsson
Jon Pall Sigmarsson : World Strongest Man
Magnus Ver Magnusson : World Strongest Man

IRELAND
Glen Ross

LATVIA
Raimonds Bergmanis : European Championship Silver Medal, Olympian
Oscar Brugemanis
Kaselniks

LEBANON
Michael Abdulla

SCOTLAND

Bruce Aitken : World Record Holder
Steven Aitken
Bill Anderson : World Record Holder
Grant Anderson : World Highland Games Champion, World Record Holder
Stuart Anderson
Jamie Barr
Brian Bell
Chris Black : Olympian
Francis Brebner : World Record Holder
David Carney
Lorne Colthard
Forbes Cowan
Hamish Davidson : World Record Holder
Doug Edmunds
Gregor Edmunds : World Highland Games Champion, World Record Holder
Neil Elliot
Alistair Gunn
Gary Hagan
Eric Irvine
Steven King
Lee Maxwell
Ian Murray
Stuart Murray
George Patience : Commonwealth Games Competitor
Sinclair Patience
Bruce Robb
David Sharp
Kevin Thom
Brian Turner
Steve White : Commonwealth Games Competitor

SOUTH AFRICA

Gerrit Badenhorst : World Record Holder
Wayne Price

SWEDEN

Johannes Arsjo
Magnus Samuelsson : Worlds Strongest Man

UKRAINE

Kyrylo Chupyrin : Olympian
Igor Pekanof
Mikail Starov
Vasyl Virastyuk : Worlds Strongest Man

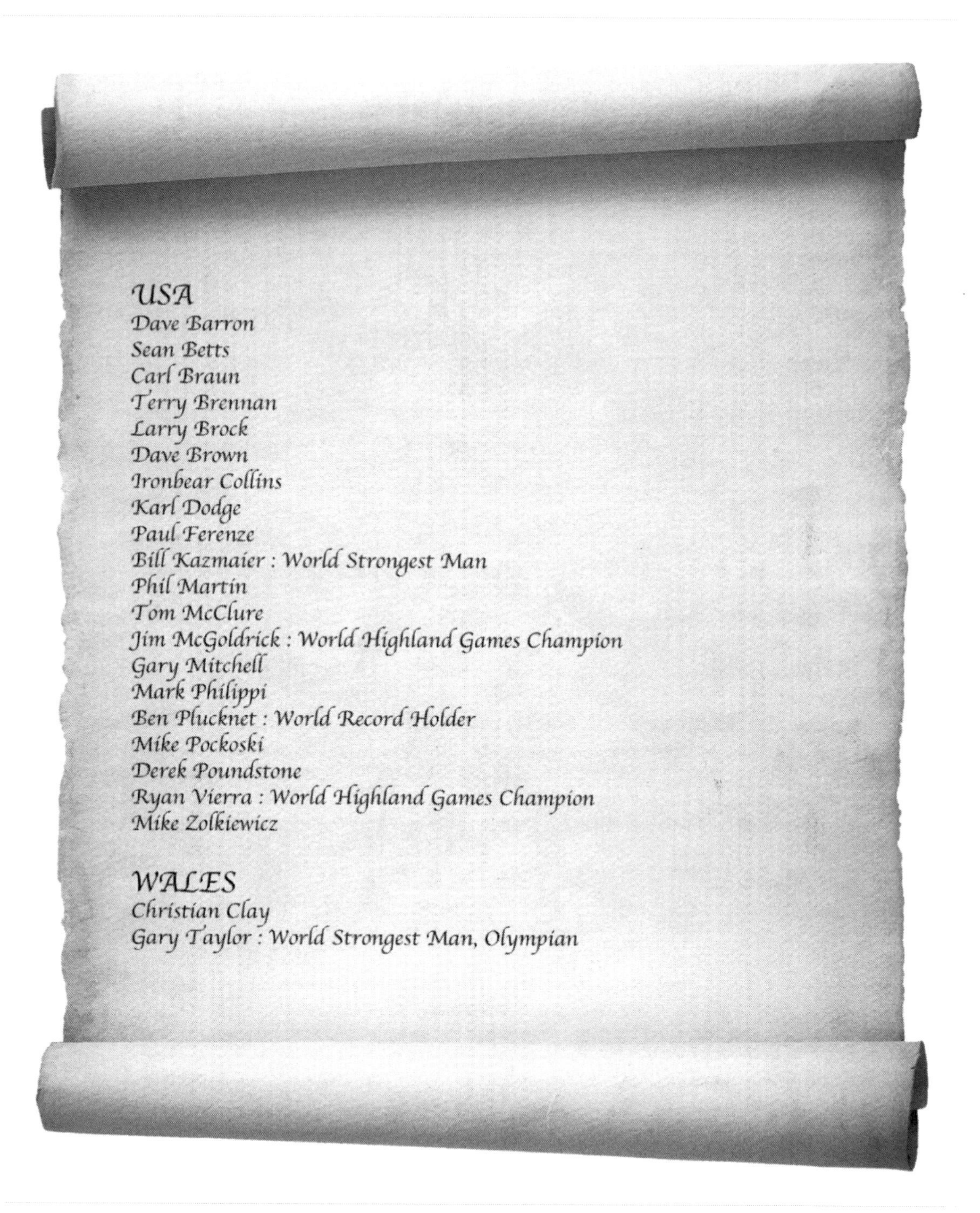

USA

Dave Barron
Sean Betts
Carl Braun
Terry Brennan
Larry Brock
Dave Brown
Ironbear Collins
Karl Dodge
Paul Ferenze
Bill Kazmaier : World Strongest Man
Phil Martin
Tom McClure
Jim McGoldrick : World Highland Games Champion
Gary Mitchell
Mark Philippi
Ben Plucknet : World Record Holder
Mike Pockoski
Derek Poundstone
Ryan Vierra : World Highland Games Champion
Mike Zolkiewicz

WALES

Christian Clay
Gary Taylor : World Strongest Man, Olympian

	LIGHT HAMMER	28LB FOR DISTANCE	CABER TOSS	22LB STONE PUTT	HEAVY HAMMER	16LB STONE PUTT	CABER FOR DISTANCE	SHEAF PITCH	56LB FOR HEIGHT
SEAN BETZ	127ft 4ins	88ft 1/2ins	50deg	40ft 8 3/4in	104ft 1in	52ft	37ft 8in	24ft	16ft
GREGOR EDMUNDS	130ft	81ft 8in	2mins	49ft 2in	105ft 5 1/2in	58ft 3 1/2in	41ft 2in	28ft	16ft
AARON NEIGHBOUR	115ft 11in	79ft 11in	9th	38ft 1in	92ft 8in	52ft 9 1/2in	38ft 3in	0	15ft
MIKE ZOLKIEWICZ	110ft 9in	78ft 6in	1 min	40ft 8in	91ft 11 1/2in	50ft	38ft	26ft	17ft
SCOTT RIDER	121ft 7 1/2in	86ft 5in	3 mins	50ft 7in	92ft 10in	59ft 4in	39ft 4in	0	15ft
SEBASTIAN WENTA	116ft 4in	82ft 7in	12 o'clock	49ft 6 1/2in	100ft 5 1/2in	58ft 9in	39ft 9in	24ft	15ft
LUCASZ WENTA	119ft 7 1/2in	72ft 6in	8th	46ft 5in	96ft 9in	56ft 1 3/4in	38ft 1in	0	16ft
HANS LOLKEMA	116ft	77ft 1in	7th	43ft 3in	90ft 4 1/2in	50ft 11in	40ft 6in	0	15ft
SINCLAIR PATIENCE	113ft 3 1/2in	69ft 5in	10th	38ft 5in	93ft 9in	47ft 4 3/4in	34ft 2in	0	0
NEIL ELLIOTT	106ft 3in	71ft 6 1/2in	13 mins	0	85ft 2in	44ft 3in	39ft 9in	0	13ft

LONDON GAMES 2010

	LIGHT HAMMER	16LB STONE PUTT	56LB FOR HEIGHT	CABER	POLEPUSH	28LB FOR DISTANCE	ROCK LIFT	CABER FOR DISTANCE	SHEAF PITCH
GREGOR EDMUNDS	128ft 3in	56ft 3 1/2in	15ft 6in	1st	1st	86ft 1 1/2in	4 stones 34.83secs	43ft 2in	27ft
SCOTT RIDER	124ft 10in	57ft 9in	15ft	3rd	7=	80ft 5 1/2in	3 stones 59.26secs	44ft 1in	25ft
VYTAUTAS LALAS	95ft 10 1/2in	44ft 3 1/2in	15ft	9=	5=	62ft 4in	4 stones 24.35secs	0	20ft
SEBASTIAN WENTA	124ft 5 1/2in	55ft 3in	15ft 6in	5th	2nd	75ft 11 1/2in	4 stones 43.19secs	39ft 8in	27ft
MIKE ZOLKIEWICZ	113ft	50ft 4 1/2in	15ft 6in	2nd	4th	76ft 8 1/2in	2 stones 28.90secs	42ft 5 1/2in	29ft
HANS LOLKEMA	117ft 6 1/2in	47ft 11in	14ft	7th	5=	75ft 7in	3 stones 54.36secs	42ft 1in	23ft
NEIL ELLIOTT	116ft 5in	42ft 5in	14ft	4th	3rd	70ft 1in	3 stones 37.25secs	41ft 7in	25ft
JONATHAN KELLY	110ft 7in	43ft 5in	13ft	9=	7=	57ft 8in	4 stones 120.48secs	0	23ft
OSKAR BRUGEMANIS	104ft	44ft 3 1/2in	14ft	6th	9=	65ft	4 stones 35.14secs	40ft 10in	23ft
GARY HAGEN	116ft 7in	44ft 7in	13ft	8th	9=	68ft 4in	1 stone 15.37secs	0	20ft

GLENARM GAMES 2011

	16LB SHOT PUTT	56LB FOR HEIGHT	CABER	LOG LIFT	BARREL CARRY	28LB FOR DISTANCE	22LB SHOT PUTT	PICTISH STONES	SHEAF PITCH
MATT VINCENT	57ft 6in	15ft	11.00 challenge	140kg	39.64secs	87ft 7in	45ft 2in	7.10mtr	26ft
SEBASTIAN WENTA	57ft 10in	15ft	12.00 1st	160kg	34.01secs	79ft 6in	47ft 5in	31.22mtr	26ft
SINCLAIR PATIENCE	50ft 2in	15ft	75deg qual	no lift	42.54secs	79ft 1in	41ft 4in	29.90mtr	0
BURGER LAMBRECHTS	60ft 4in	14ft	55deg qual	150kg	41.75secs	77ft 10in	48ft 11in	26.50mtr	26ft
SCOTT RIDER	57ft	15ft	12.02 2nd	130kg	34.43secs	88ft 2in	48ft 2in	29.65mtr	26ft
LUCASZ WENTA	56ft	16ft	85deg challenge	no lift	33.24secs	76ft 7in	46ft 6in	29.30mtr	24ft
NEIL ELLIOTT	39ft 10in	0	12.14 3rd	no lift	37.77secs	71ft 7in	30ft 4in	16mtres	24ft
JONATHAN KELLY	44ft 11in	14ft	40deg challenge	160kg	51.02secs	61ft	36ft	7.80mtr	26ft
HEISI GEIRMUNDSSON	52ft 11in	14ft	40deg challenge	150kg	49.26secs	67ft 5in	41ft 2in	11.35mtr	0

HIGHLANDER GLASGOW 2013

LADIES HIGHLANDER GLASGOW 2013

	14LB FOR DISTANCE	LOG TOSS	BARBELL LIFT (160kg)	16LB HAMMER	ATLAS STONES	STONE PUTT	28LB FOR HEIGHT	CABER	WEIGHT CARRY	SHIELD WALK
ADRIANE WILSON USA	79ft 2in	32ft 7in	2 reps	51ft 4in	no lift	38ft 4in	16ft	12.15 3rd	6.70m	no lift
SHAUNAGH BROWN ENGLAND	69ft 11in	27ft 4in	6 reps	45ft 1in	2 stones 1.03.62	46ft 10in	15ft	70deg challenge	17.89sec	5 laps 8.27m
SYLVANA BOMHOLT GERMANY	60ft 7in	30ft	10 reps	36ft 9in	1 stone 21.29sec	32ft 2in	13ft	30deg qualifying	18.84sec	4 laps 7m
NINA GERIA UKRAINE	66ft 3in	31ft 8in	12 reps	34ft 6in	3 stones 19.01sec	40ft 8in	16ft	12.03 1st	14.58sec	6 laps
DONNA MOORE SCOTLAND	47ft 10.5in	no throw	13 reps	30ft 2in	2 stones 21.96sec	27ft 4in	13ft	40deg qualifying	15.93sec	4 laps 2.30m
PORA PORSTEINS DOTTIR - ICELAND	59ft 5in	no throw	7 reps	31ft 8in	1 stone 18.25sec	32ft 9in	13ft	60deg qualifying	19.31sec	2 laps
PATRICIA WENTA POLAND	44ft 7in	no throw	no lift	24ft 1in	no lift	26ft 5in	no throw	no throw	no lift	1 lap
KIRSTY YATES SCOTLAND	38ft 9in	no throw	no lift	37ft 4in	no lift	46ft 10in	no throw	50deg qualifying	20.70sec	4 laps
STACEY WILSON SCOTLAND	50ft 5in	no throw	no lift	29ft 6in	no lift	30ft 10in	11ft	30deg qualifying	no lift	1 lap 4.40m
KIRSTY SCOTT USA	70ft 5in	27ft 10in	20 reps	47ft 2in	3 stones 20.86sec	40ft 1in	21ft WORLD RECORD	12.14 2nd	13.81sec	3 laps 39m

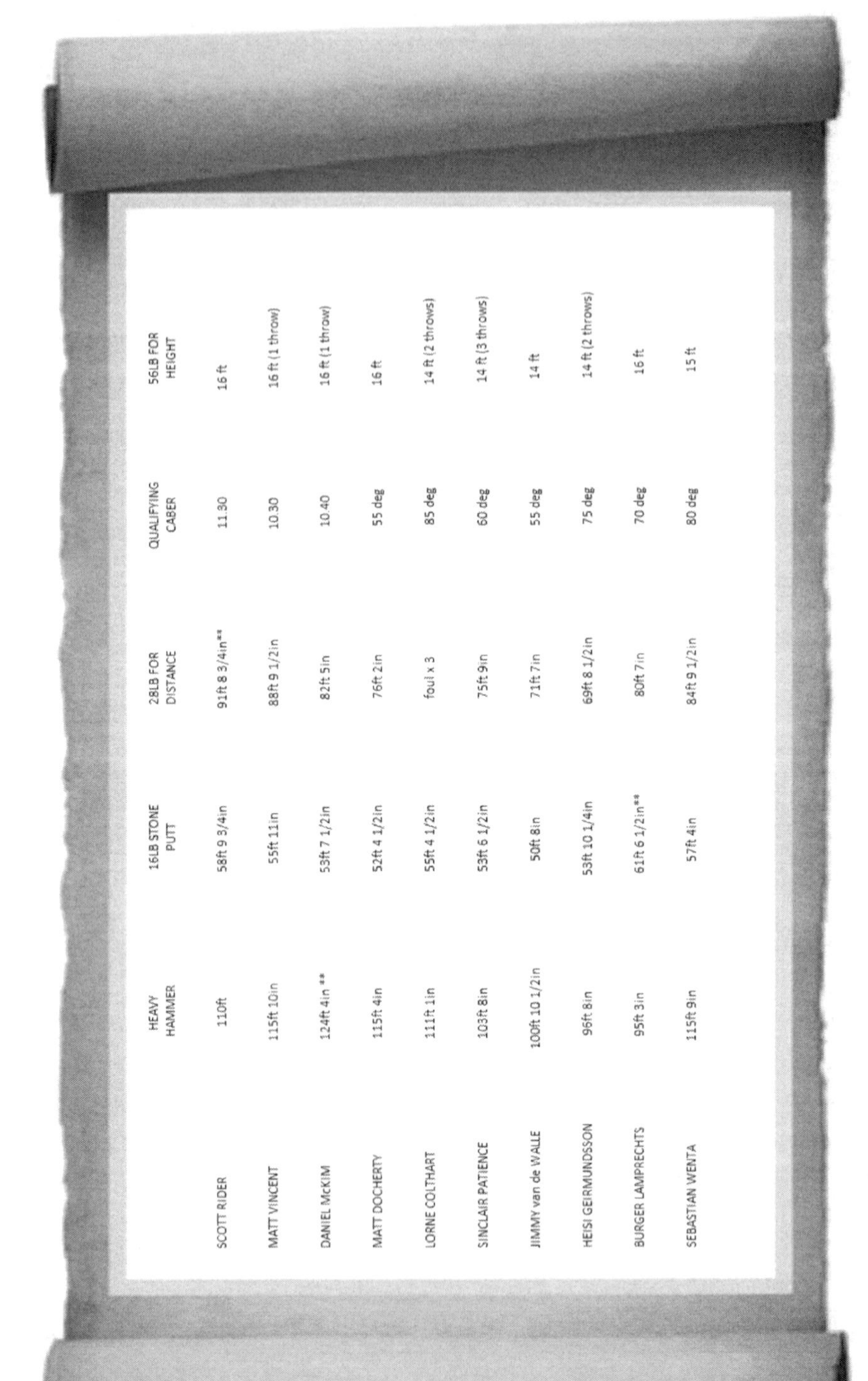

	HEAVY HAMMER	16LB STONE PUTT	28LB FOR DISTANCE	QUALIFYING CABER	56LB FOR HEIGHT
SCOTT RIDER	110ft	58ft 9 3/4in	91ft 8 3/4in**	11.30	16 ft
MATT VINCENT	115ft 10in	55ft 11in	88ft 9 1/2in	10.30	16 ft (1 throw)
DANIEL McKIM	124ft 4in **	53ft 7 1/2in	82ft 5in	10.40	16 ft (1 throw)
MATT DOCHERTY	115ft 4in	52ft 4 1/2in	76ft 2in	55 deg	16 ft
LORNE COLTHART	111ft 1in	55ft 4 1/2in	foul x 3	85 deg	14 ft (2 throws)
SINCLAIR PATIENCE	103ft 8in	53ft 6 1/2in	75ft 9in	60 deg	14 ft (3 throws)
JIMMY van de WALLE	100ft 10 1/2in	50ft 8in	71ft 7in	55 deg	14 ft
HEISI GEIRMUNDSSON	96ft 8in	53ft 10 1/4in	69ft 8 1/2in	75 deg	14 ft (2 throws)
BURGER LAMPRECHTS	95ft 3in	61ft 6 1/2in**	80ft 7in	70 deg	16 ft
SEBASTIAN WENTA	115ft 9in	57ft 4in	84ft 9 1/2in	80 deg	15 ft

DAY 1 DUNFERMLINE 2014

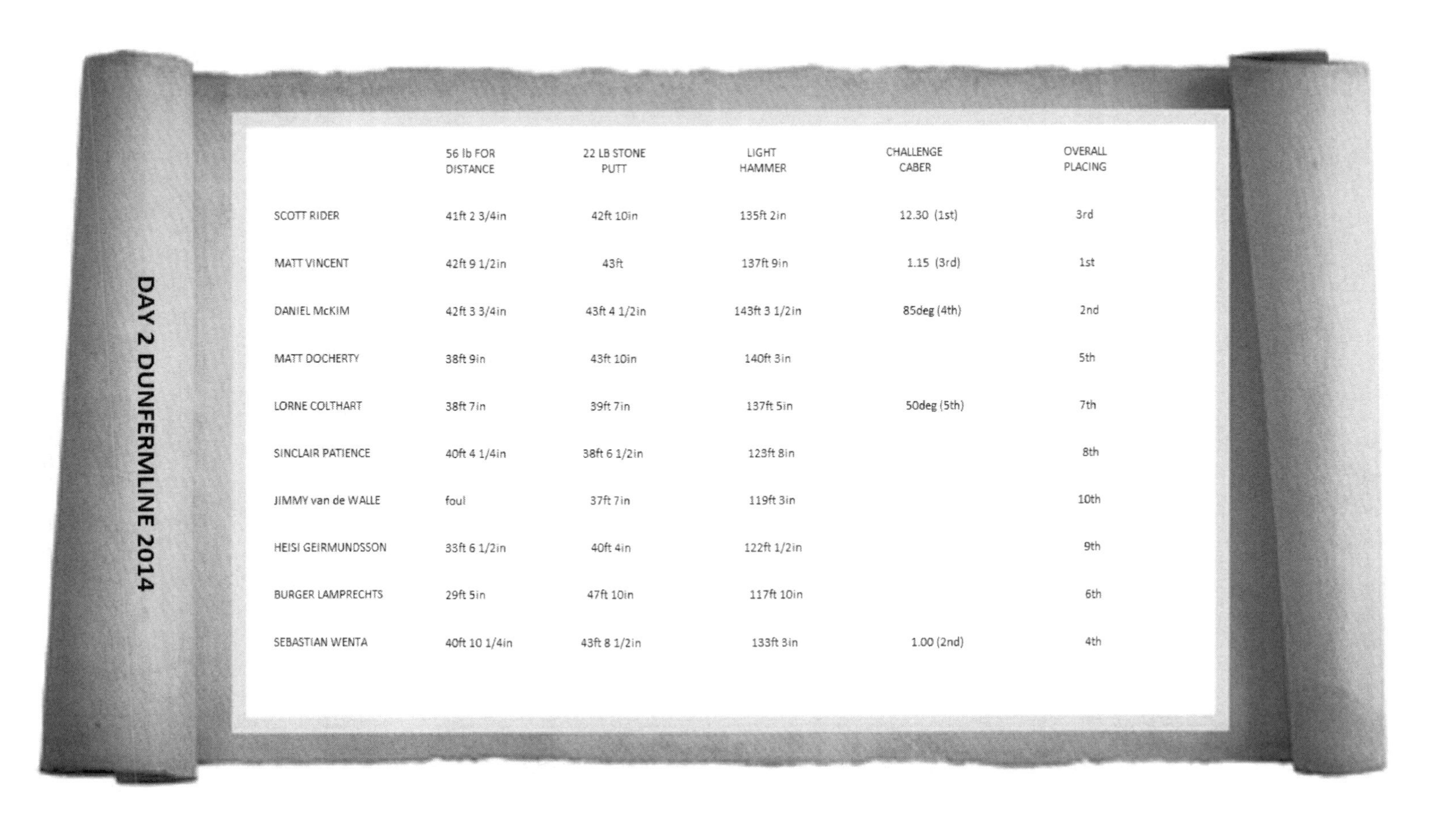

	56 lb FOR DISTANCE	22 LB STONE PUTT	LIGHT HAMMER	CHALLENGE CABER	OVERALL PLACING
SCOTT RIDER	41ft 2 3/4in	42ft 10in	135ft 2in	12.30 (1st)	3rd
MATT VINCENT	42ft 9 1/2in	43ft	137ft 9in	1.15 (3rd)	1st
DANIEL McKIM	42ft 3 3/4in	43ft 4 1/2in	143ft 3 1/2in	85deg (4th)	2nd
MATT DOCHERTY	38ft 9in	43ft 10in	140ft 3in		5th
LORNE COLTHART	38ft 7in	39ft 7in	137ft 5in	50deg (5th)	7th
SINCLAIR PATIENCE	40ft 4 1/4in	38ft 6 1/2in	123ft 8in		8th
JIMMY van de WALLE	foul	37ft 7in	119ft 3in		10th
HEISI GEIRMUNDSSON	33ft 6 1/2in	40ft 4in	122ft 1/2in		9th
BURGER LAMPRECHTS	29ft 5in	47ft 10in	117ft 10in		6th
SEBASTIAN WENTA	40ft 10 1/4in	43ft 8 1/2in	133ft 3in	1.00 (2nd)	4th

DAY 2 DUNFERMLINE 2014

ALSO AVAILABLE

GIANTS AND LEGENDS

by
Dr Douglas Edmunds

Printed in Great Britain
by Amazon